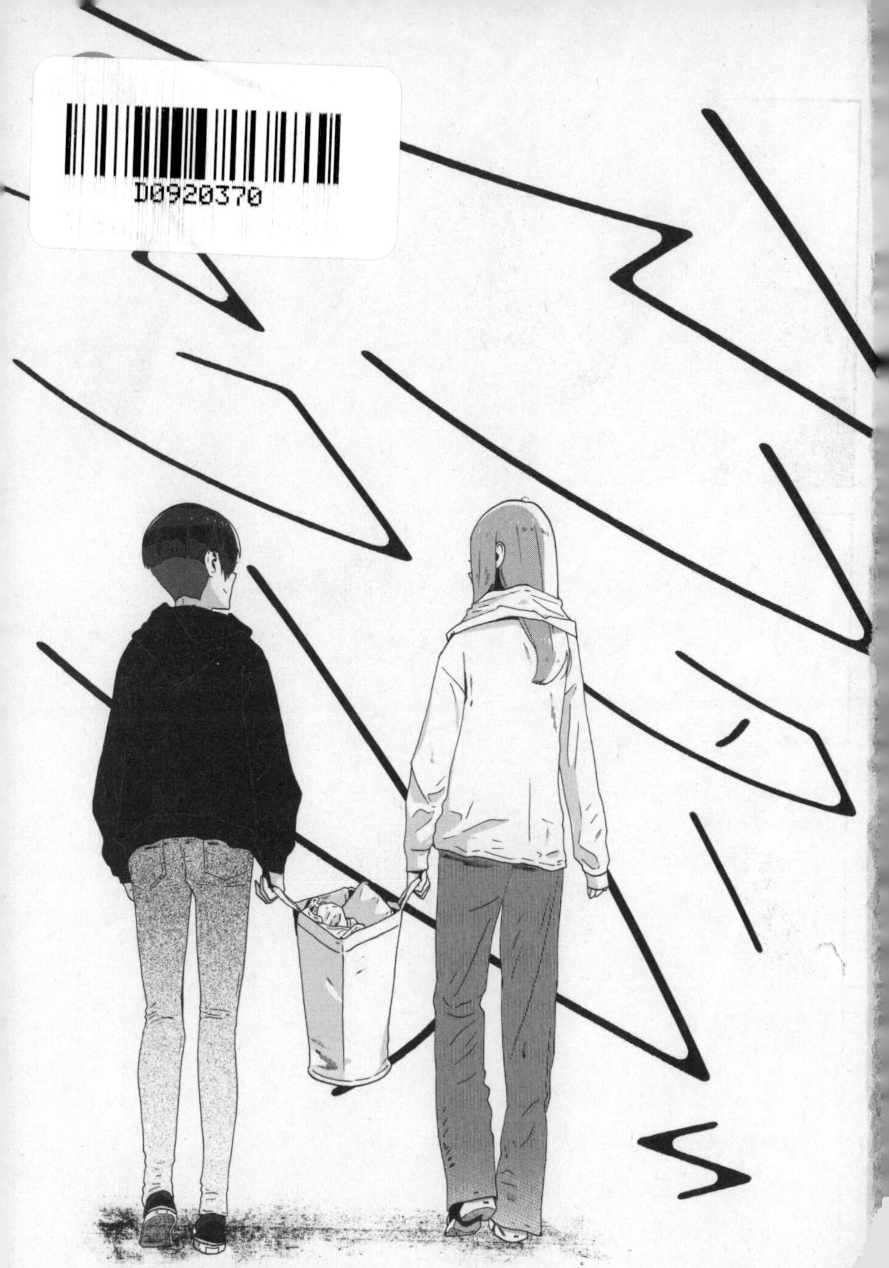

AFTER HOURS

STORY AND ART BY
YUHTA NISHIO

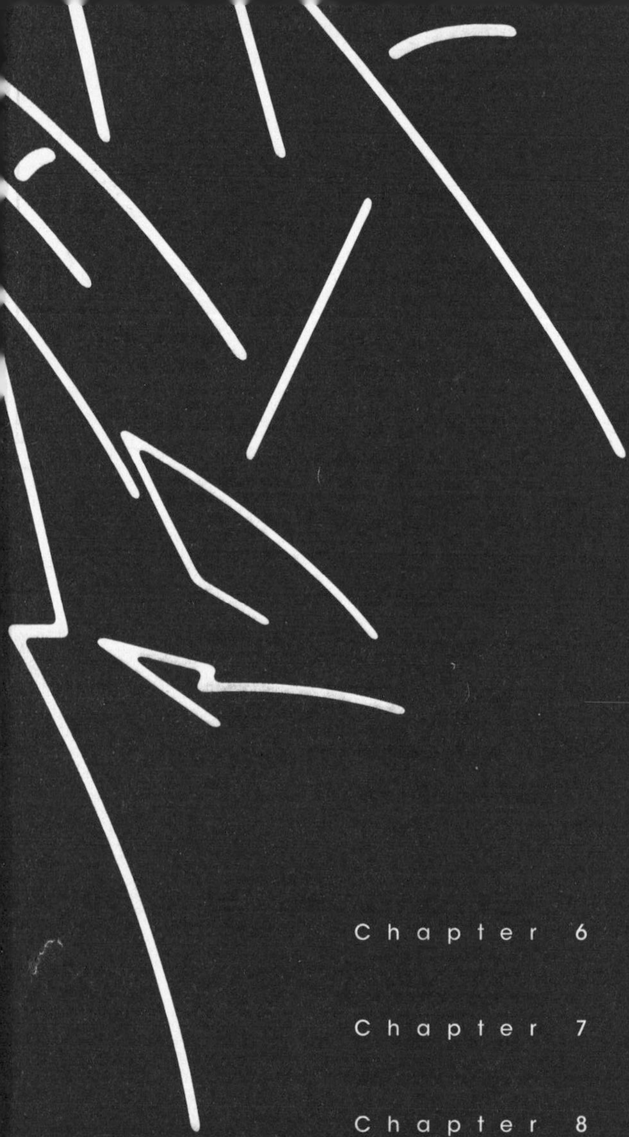

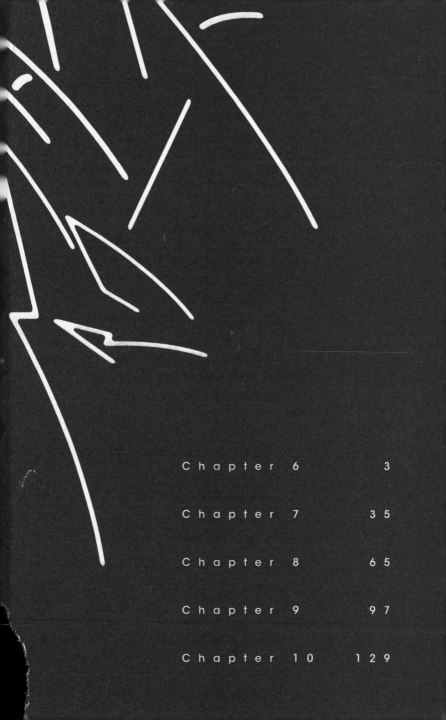

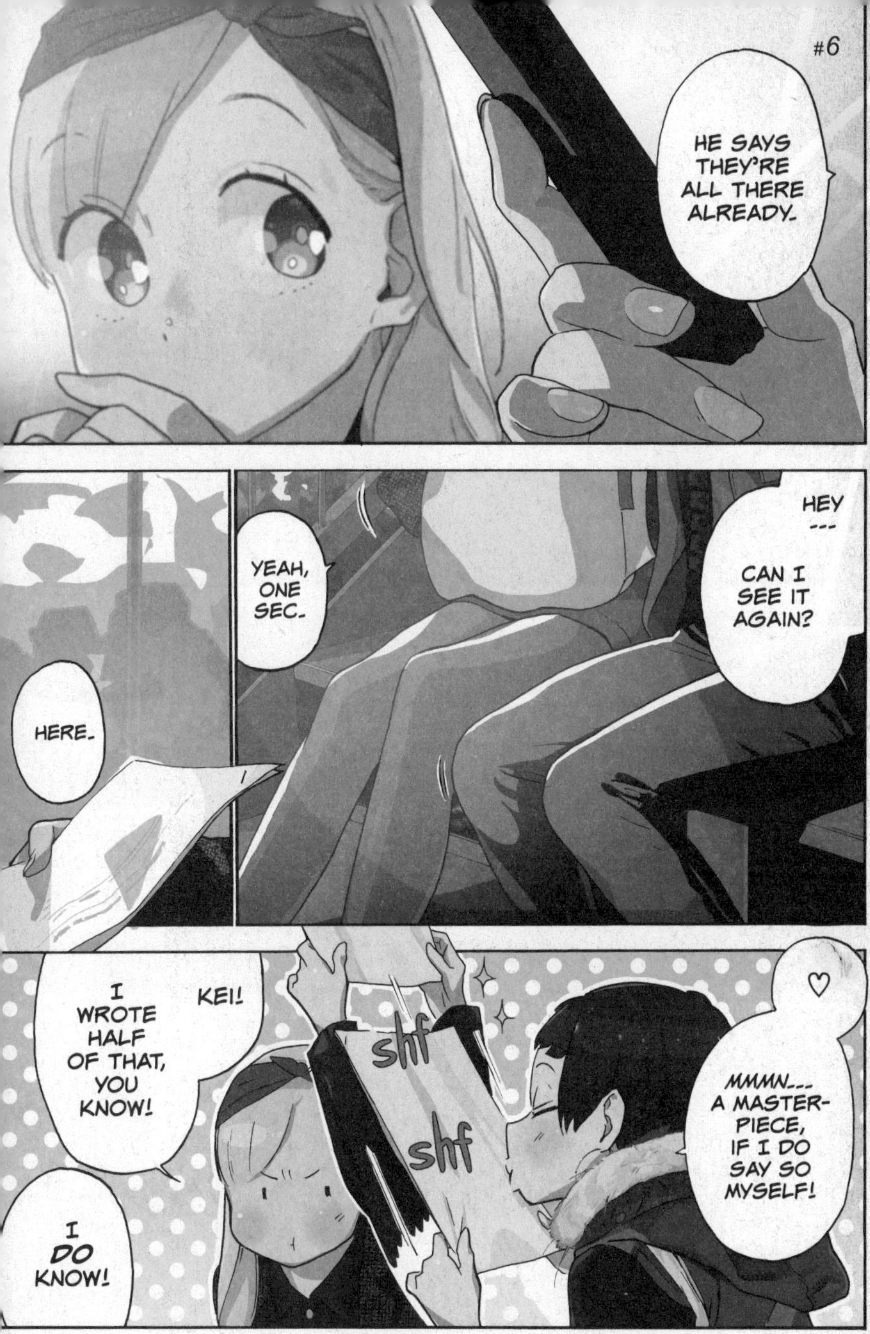
#6
HE SAYS THEY'RE ALL THERE ALREADY.
HEY --- CAN I SEE IT AGAIN?
YEAH, ONE SEC.
HERE.
♡
MMMN... A MASTERPIECE, IF I DO SAY SO MYSELF!
shf
shf
KEI! I WROTE HALF OF THAT, YOU KNOW!
I *DO* KNOW!

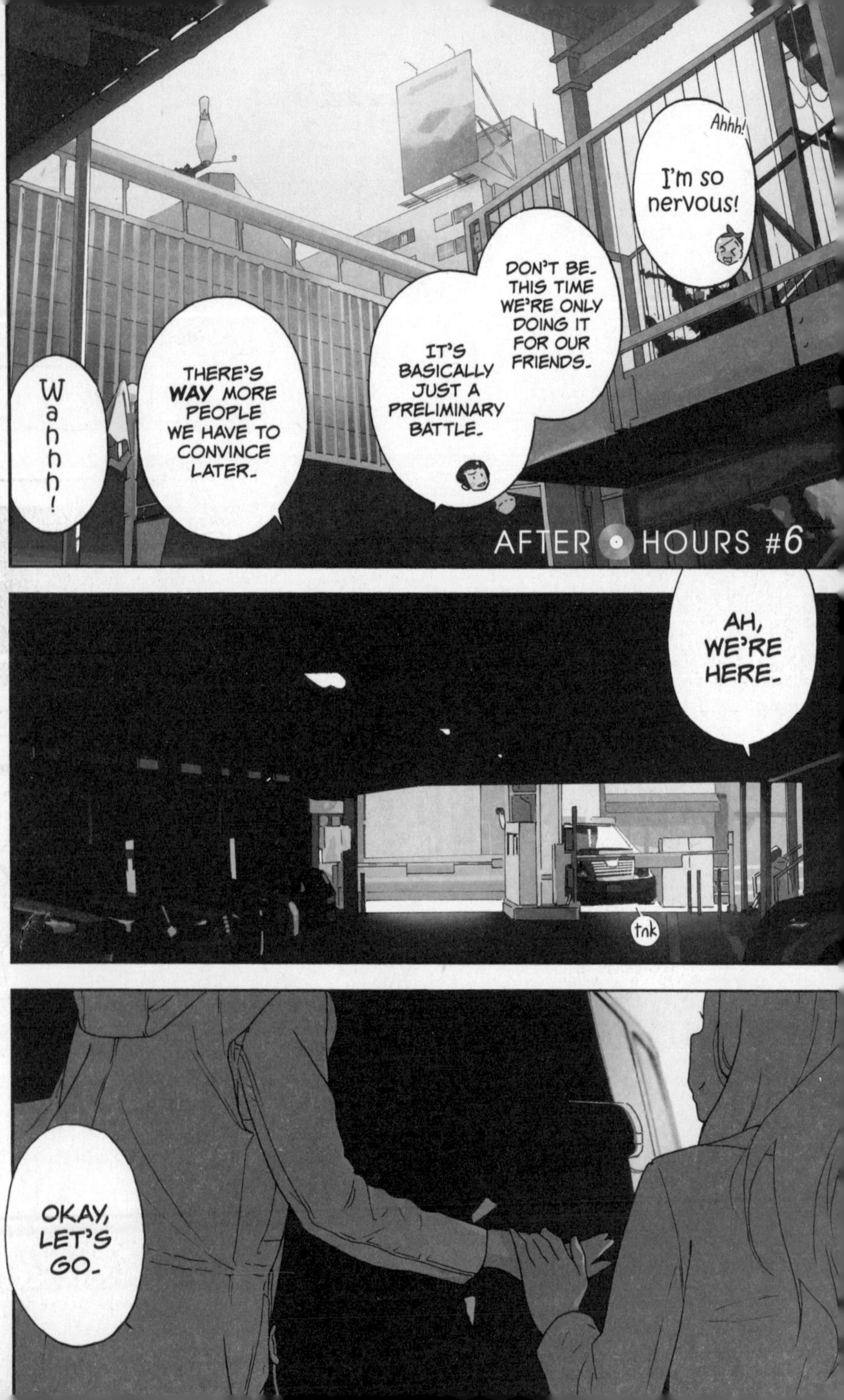
Ahhh!
I'm so nervous!
DON'T BE. THIS TIME WE'RE ONLY DOING IT FOR OUR FRIENDS.
IT'S BASICALLY JUST A PRELIMINARY BATTLE.
THERE'S WAY MORE PEOPLE WE HAVE TO CONVINCE LATER.
Wahhh!
AFTER HOURS #6
AH, WE'RE HERE.
tnk
OKAY, LET'S GO.

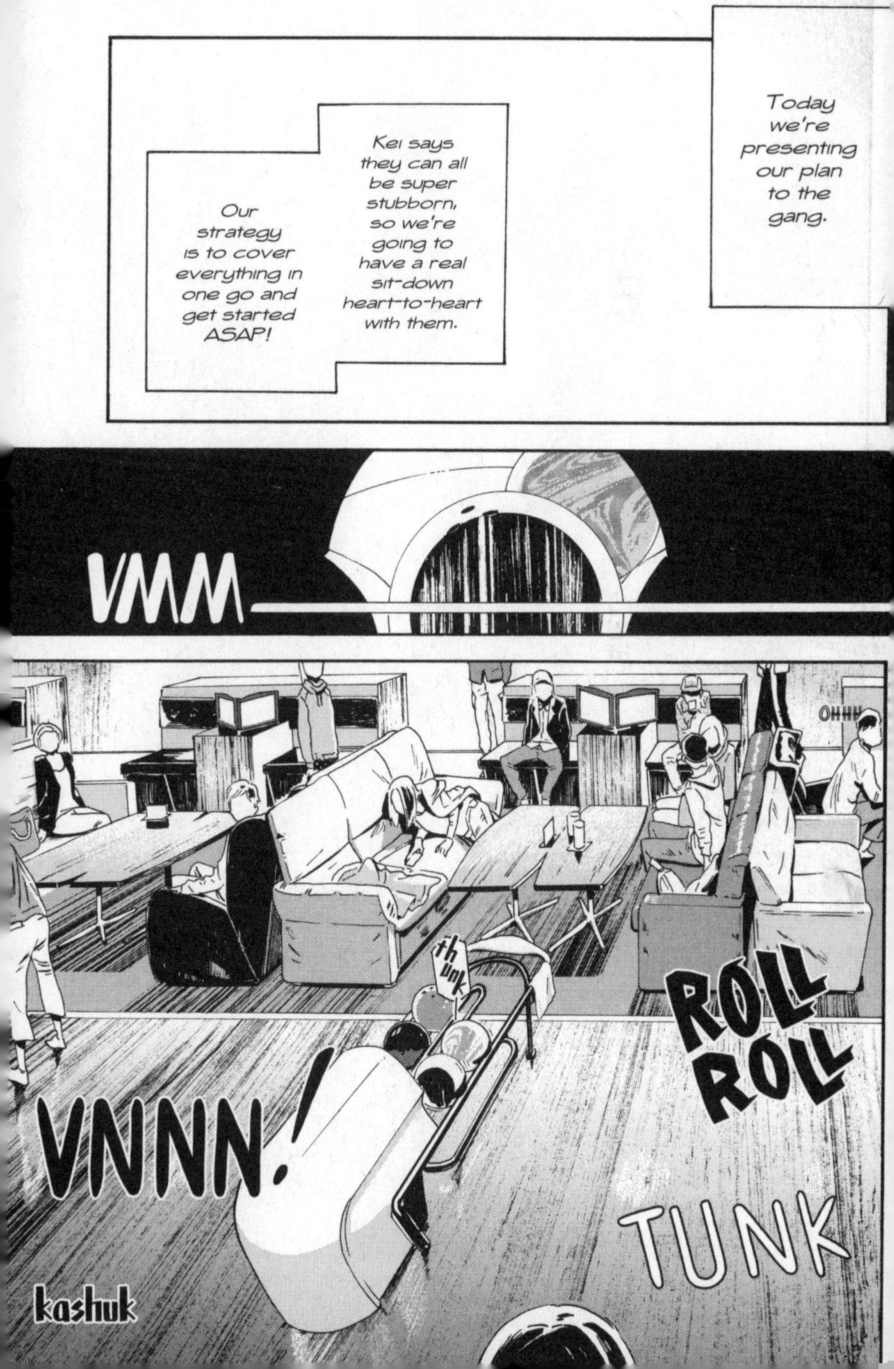
Today we're presenting our plan to the gang.
Kei says they can all be super stubborn, so we're going to have a real sit-down heart-to-heart with them.
Our strategy is to cover everything in one go and get started ASAP!
VMMM
OHHH
ROLL ROLL
thunk
TUNK
VNNN!
kashuk

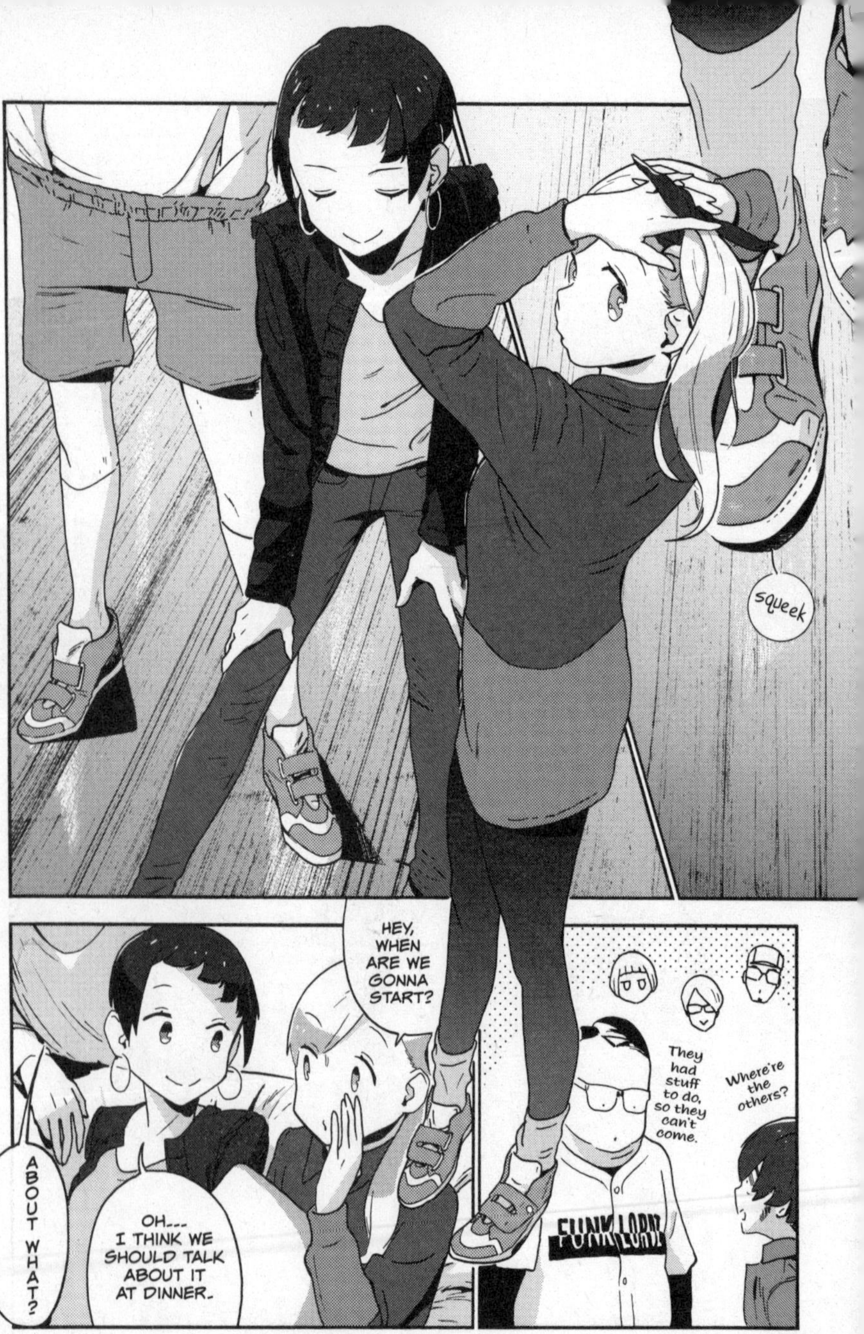
squeek
Where're the others?
They had stuff to do, so they can't come.
HEY, WHEN ARE WE GONNA START?
OH... I THINK WE SHOULD TALK ABOUT IT AT DINNER.
ABOUT WHAT?
FUNK LORD

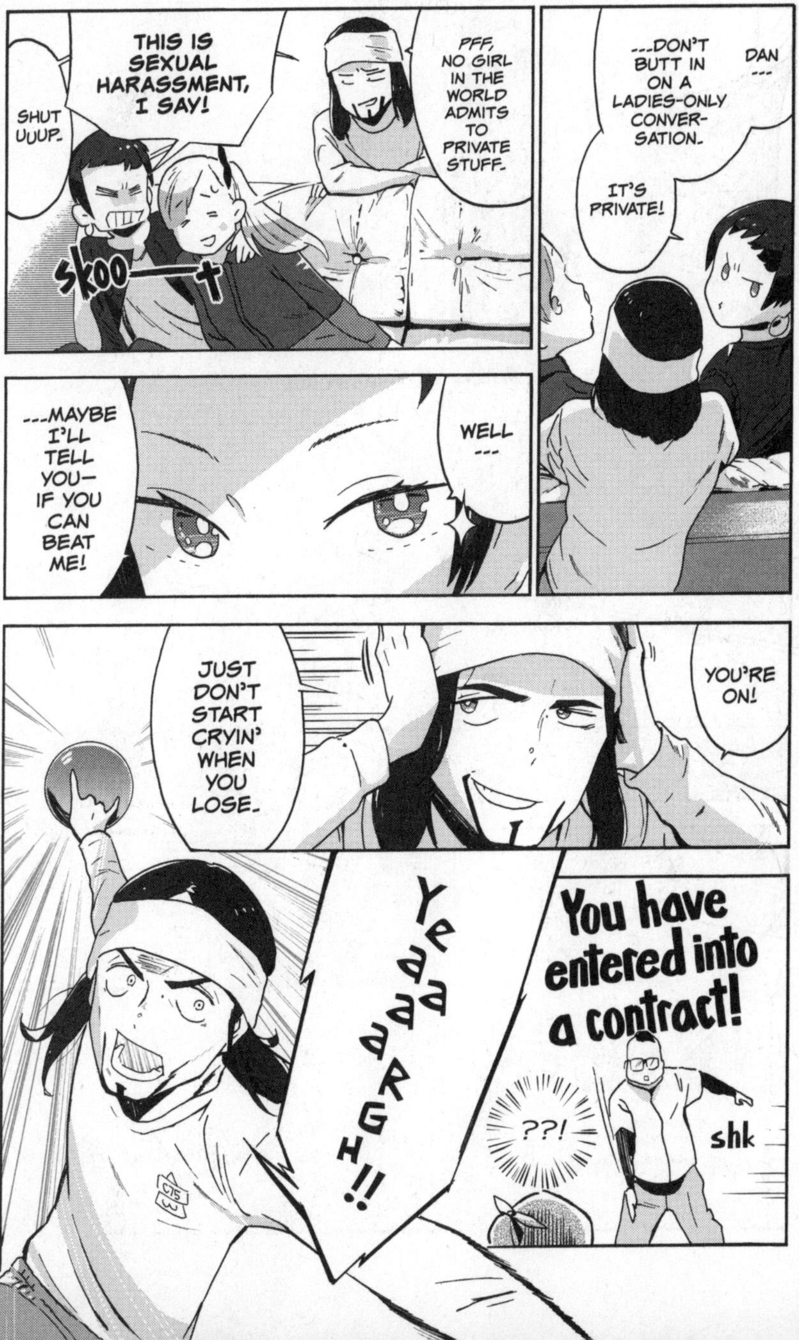
DAN---
---DON'T BUTT IN ON A LADIES-ONLY CONVERSATION.
IT'S PRIVATE!
PFF, NO GIRL IN THE WORLD ADMITS TO PRIVATE STUFF.
THIS IS SEXUAL HARASSMENT, I SAY!
SHUT UUUP.
skoo
WELL---
---MAYBE I'LL TELL YOU— IF YOU CAN BEAT ME!
YOU'RE ON!
JUST DON'T START CRYIN' WHEN YOU LOSE.
You have entered into a contract!
shk
??!
YeaaaaARGH!!

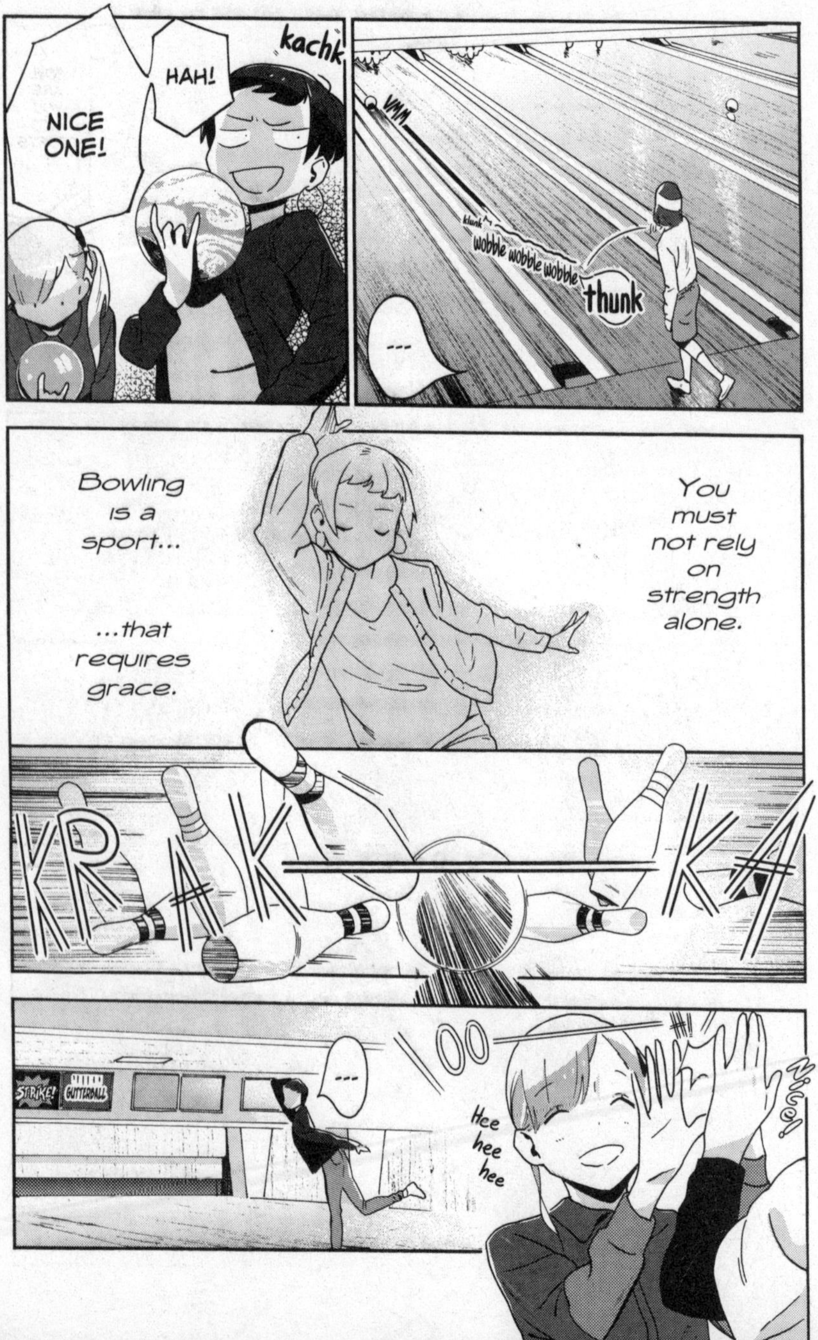
VMM
klunk
wobble wobble wobble
thunk
...
kachk
HAH!
NICE ONE!
You must not rely on strength alone.
Bowling is a sport...
...that requires grace.
KRAK—KA
Nice!
Hee hee hee
...

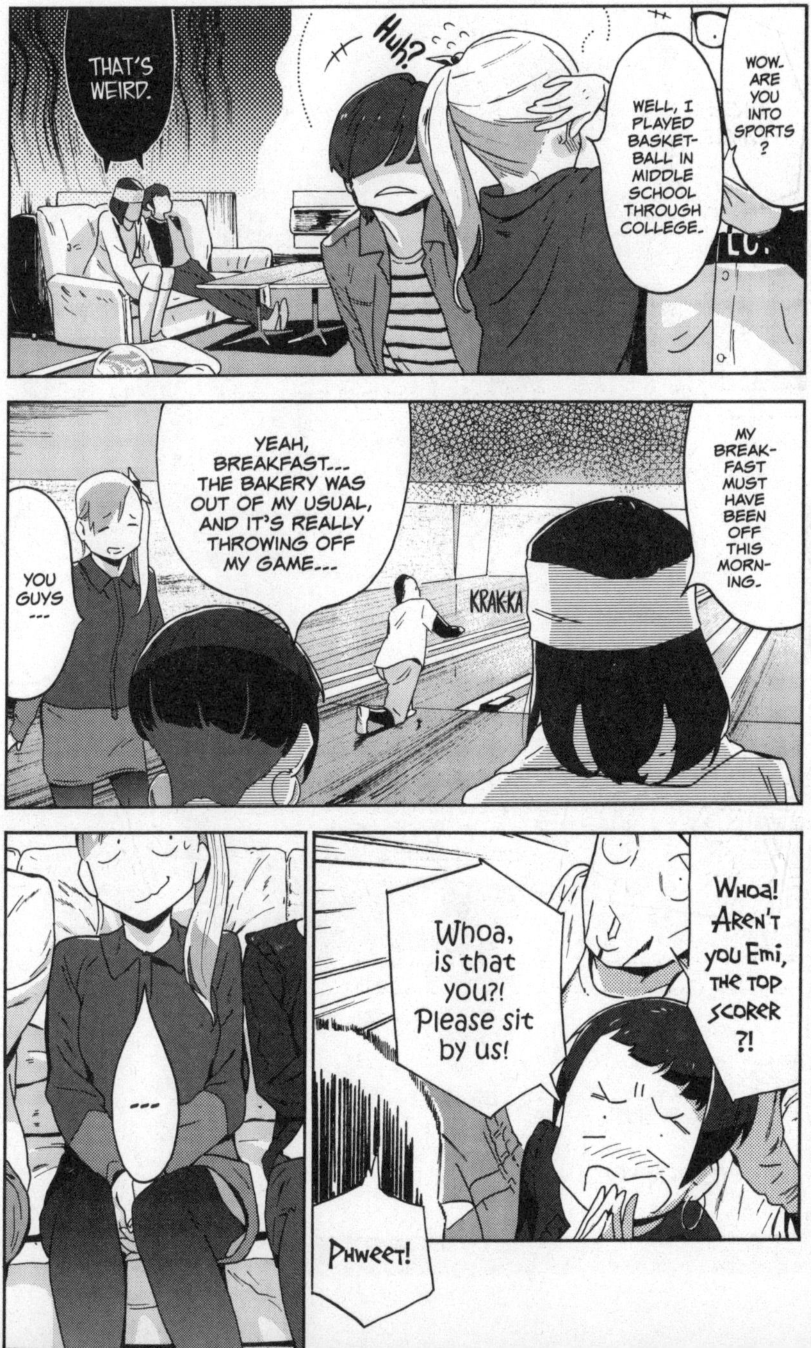
WOW. ARE YOU INTO SPORTS?
WELL, I PLAYED BASKET-BALL IN MIDDLE SCHOOL THROUGH COLLEGE.
Huh?
THAT'S WEIRD.
MY BREAK-FAST MUST HAVE BEEN OFF THIS MORN-ING.
YEAH, BREAKFAST... THE BAKERY WAS OUT OF MY USUAL, AND IT'S REALLY THROWING OFF MY GAME...
KRAKKA
YOU GUYS...
Whoa! Aren't you Emi, the top scorer?!
Whoa, is that you?! Please sit by us!
Phweet!
...

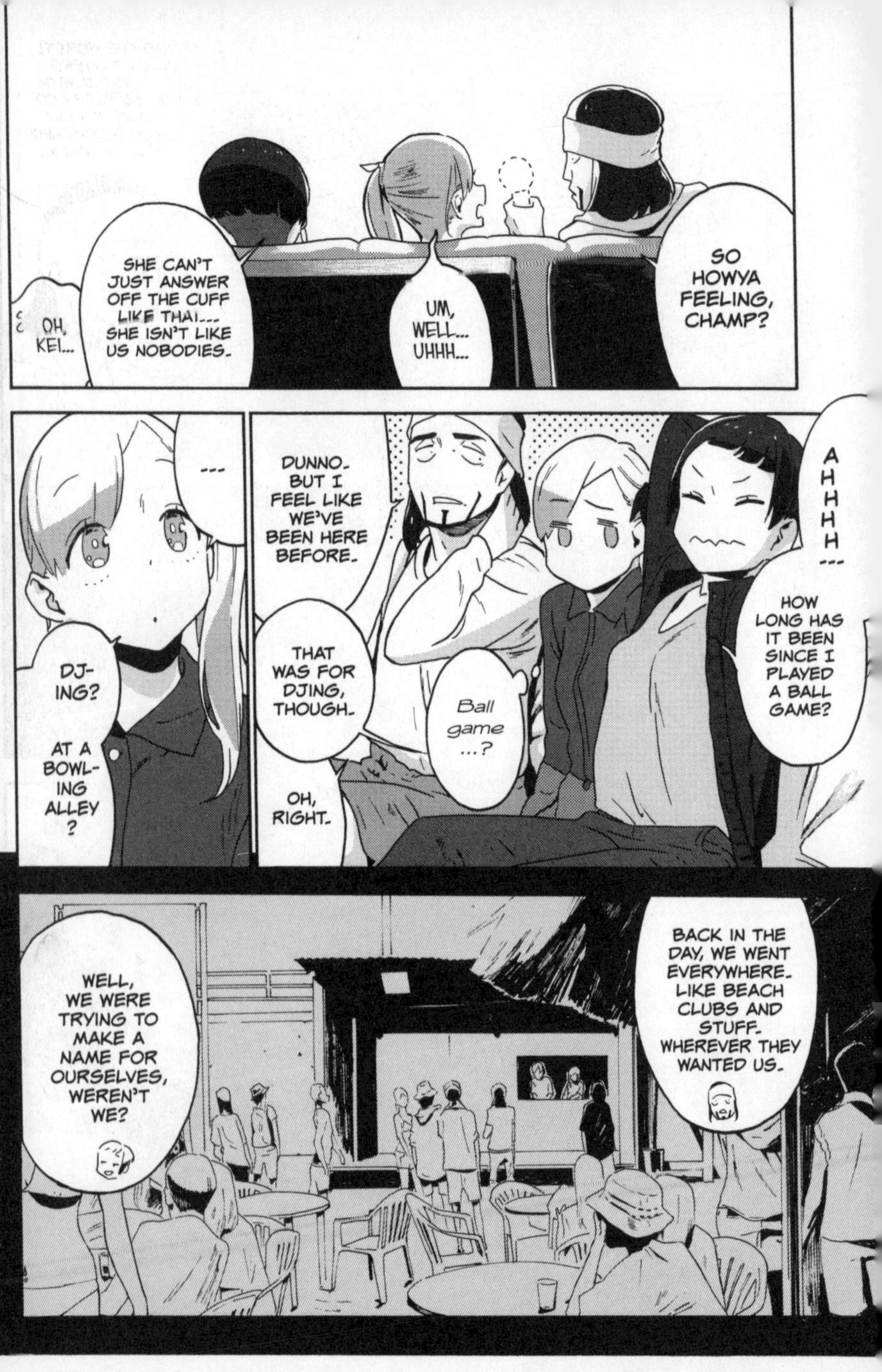
SO HOWYA FEELING, CHAMP?
UM, WELL... UHHH...
SHE CAN'T JUST ANSWER OFF THE CUFF LIKE THAT... SHE ISN'T LIKE US NOBODIES.
OH, KEI...
AHHHH...
HOW LONG HAS IT BEEN SINCE I PLAYED A BALL GAME?
DUNNO. BUT I FEEL LIKE WE'VE BEEN HERE BEFORE.
Ball game ...?
THAT WAS FOR DJING, THOUGH.
OH, RIGHT.
...
DJ-ING?
AT A BOWLING ALLEY?
BACK IN THE DAY, WE WENT EVERYWHERE. LIKE BEACH CLUBS AND STUFF. WHEREVER THEY WANTED US.
WELL, WE WERE TRYING TO MAKE A NAME FOR OURSELVES, WEREN'T WE?

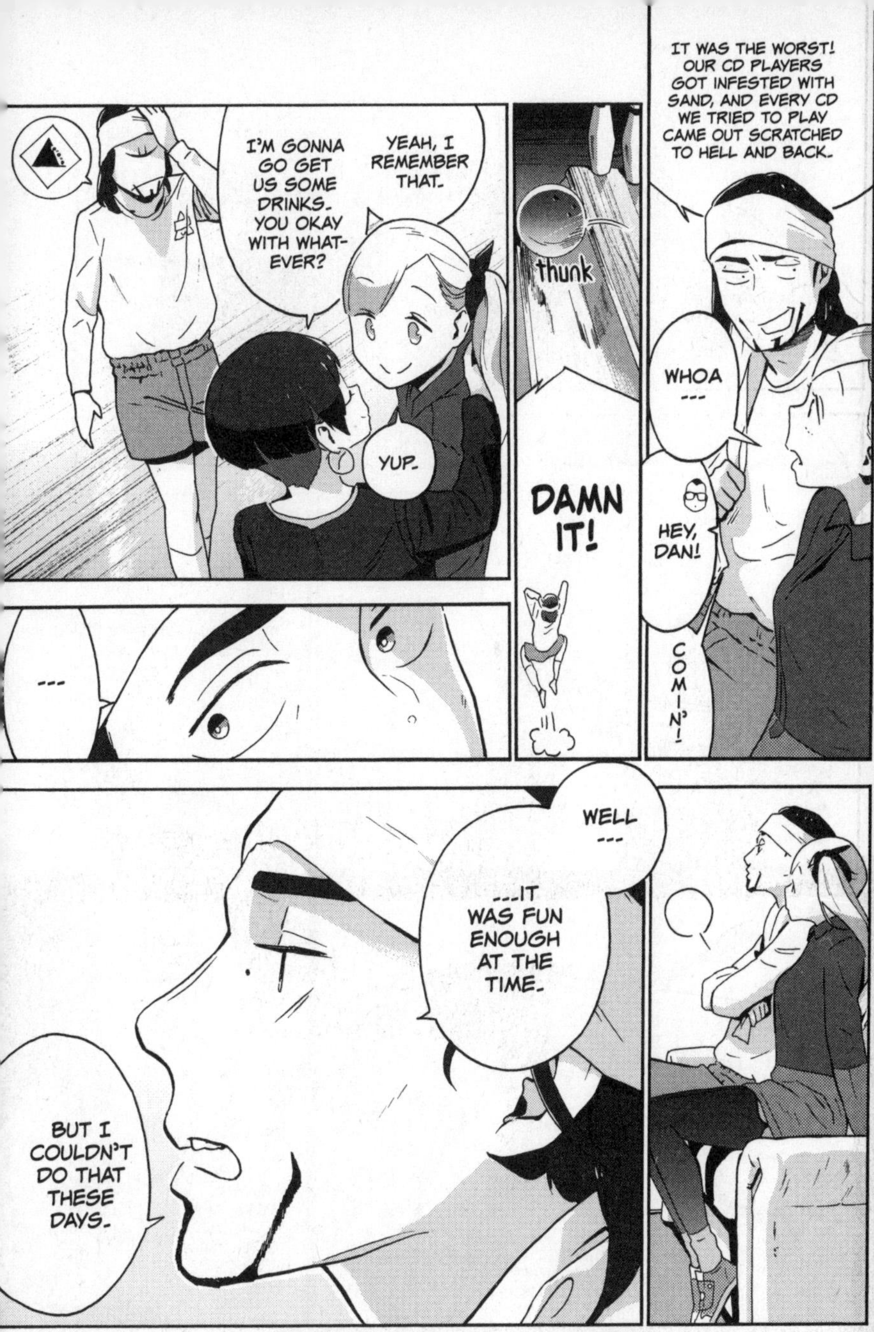
IT WAS THE WORST! OUR CD PLAYERS GOT INFESTED WITH SAND, AND EVERY CD WE TRIED TO PLAY CAME OUT SCRATCHED TO HELL AND BACK.
WHOA...
HEY, DAN!
COMIN'!
thunk
DAMN IT!
YEAH, I REMEMBER THAT.
I'M GONNA GO GET US SOME DRINKS. YOU OKAY WITH WHATEVER?
YUP.
...
WELL...
...IT WAS FUN ENOUGH AT THE TIME.
BUT I COULDN'T DO THAT THESE DAYS.

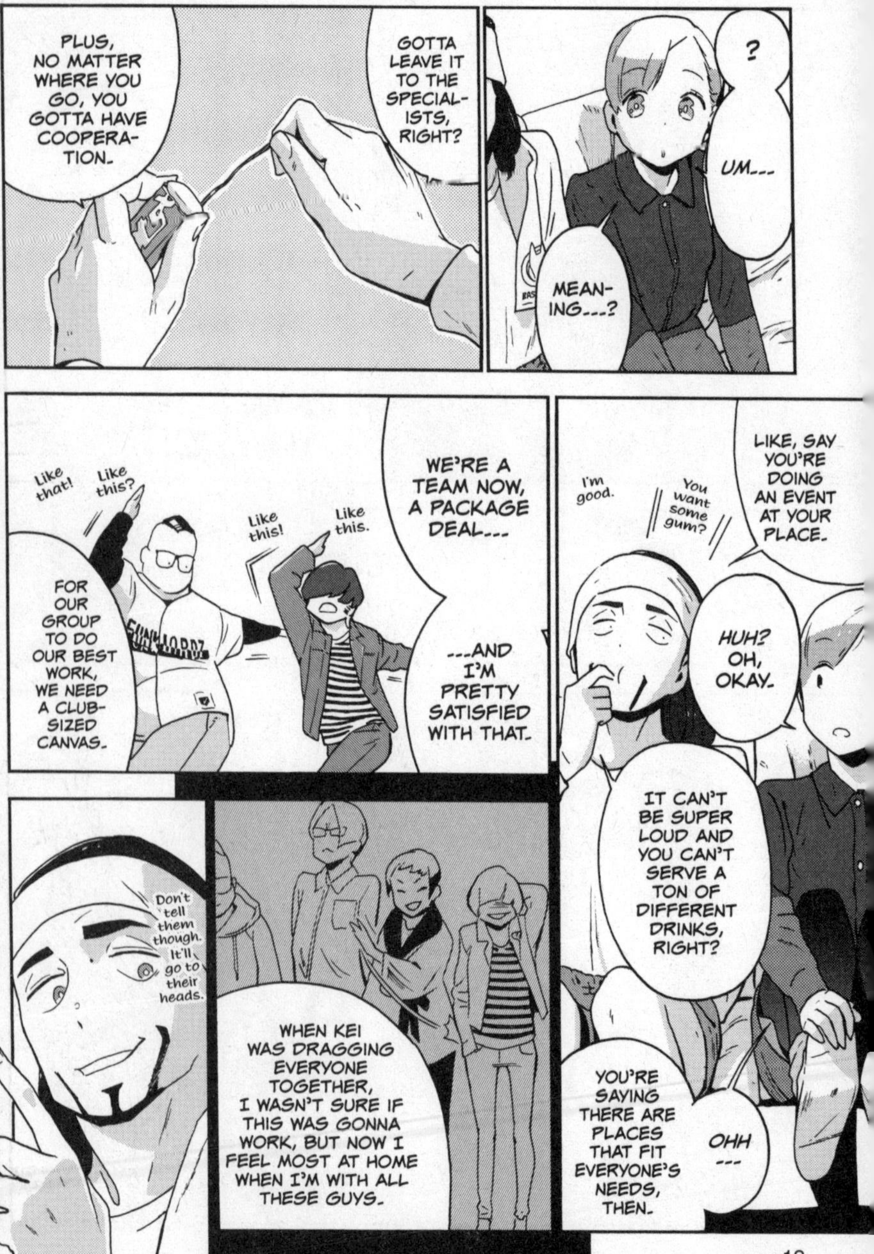
?
UM...
MEANING...?
GOTTA LEAVE IT TO THE SPECIAL-ISTS, RIGHT?
PLUS, NO MATTER WHERE YOU GO, YOU GOTTA HAVE COOPERA-TION.
LIKE, SAY YOU'RE DOING AN EVENT AT YOUR PLACE.
You want some gum?
I'm good.
HUH? OH, OKAY.
IT CAN'T BE SUPER LOUD AND YOU CAN'T SERVE A TON OF DIFFERENT DRINKS, RIGHT?
OHH...
YOU'RE SAYING THERE ARE PLACES THAT FIT EVERYONE'S NEEDS, THEN.
WE'RE A TEAM NOW, A PACKAGE DEAL...
Like this.
Like this!
Like this?
Like that!
...AND I'M PRETTY SATISFIED WITH THAT.
FOR OUR GROUP TO DO OUR BEST WORK, WE NEED A CLUB-SIZED CANVAS.
WHEN KEI WAS DRAGGING EVERYONE TOGETHER, I WASN'T SURE IF THIS WAS GONNA WORK, BUT NOW I FEEL MOST AT HOME WHEN I'M WITH ALL THESE GUYS.
Don't tell them though. It'll go to their heads.

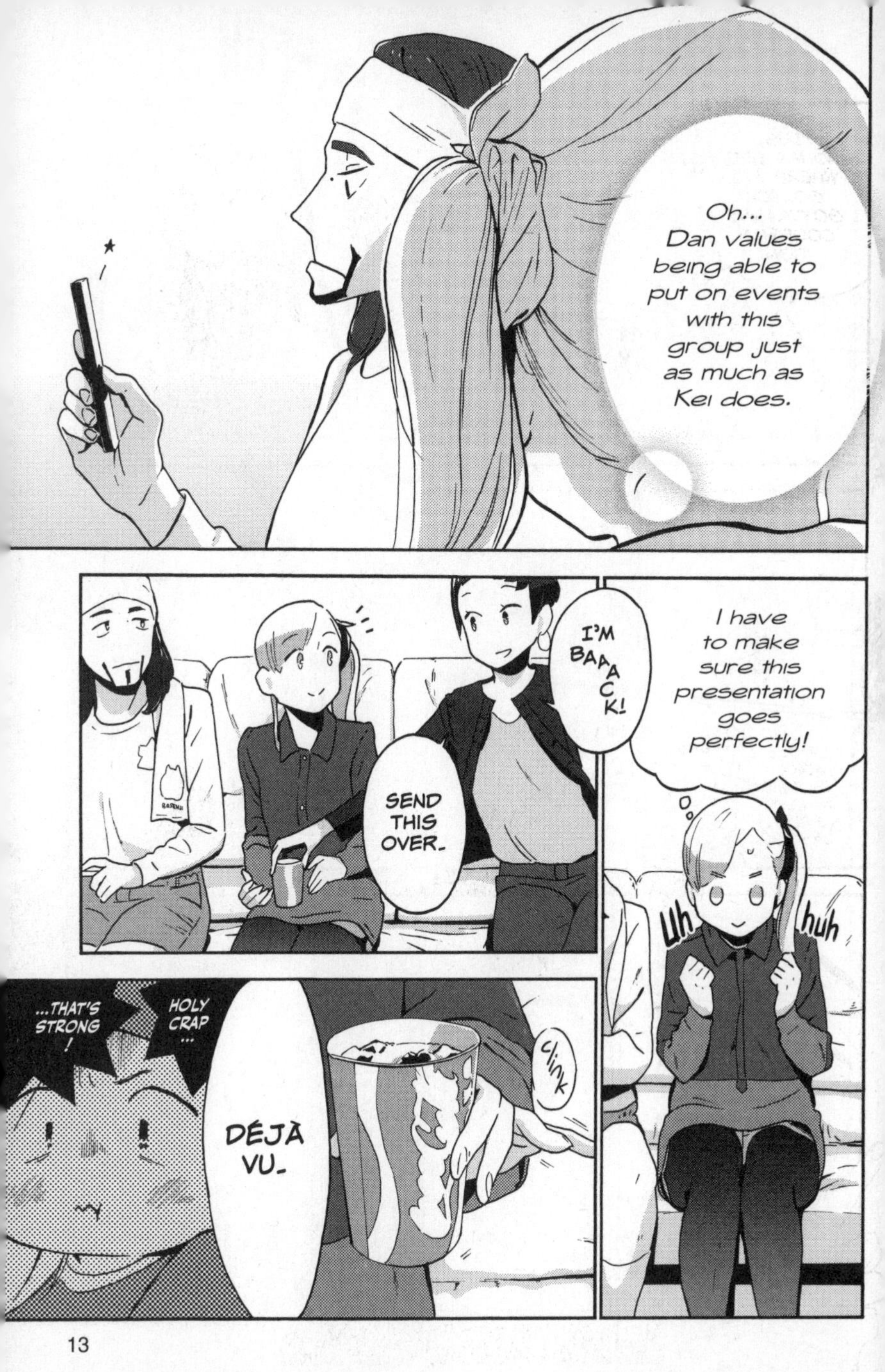
Oh... Dan values being able to put on events with this group just as much as Kei does.
I have to make sure this presentation goes perfectly!
Uh huh
I'M BAAAACK!
SEND THIS OVER.
clink
DÉJÀ VU.
HOLY CRAP...
...THAT'S STRONG!

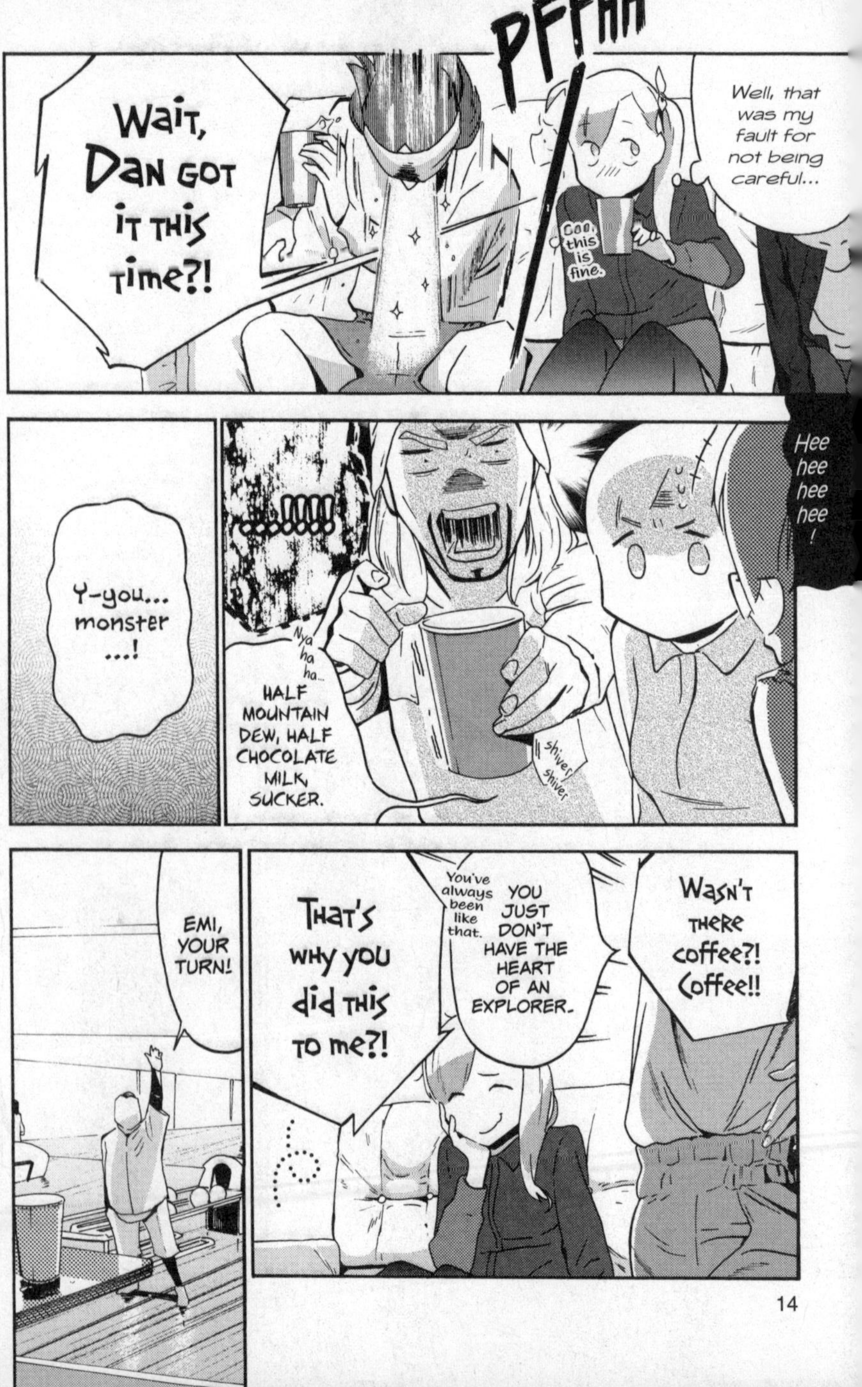
Well, that was my fault for not being careful...
PFFHH
Ooo, this is fine.
Wait, Dan got it this time?!
Hee hee hee hee!
!!!!!!
Nya ha ha...
HALF MOUNTAIN DEW, HALF CHOCOLATE MILK, SUCKER.
shiver shiver
Y-you... monster ...!
Wasn't there coffee?! Coffee!!
YOU JUST DON'T HAVE THE HEART OF AN EXPLORER.
You've always been like that.
That's why you did this to me?!
EMI, YOUR TURN!

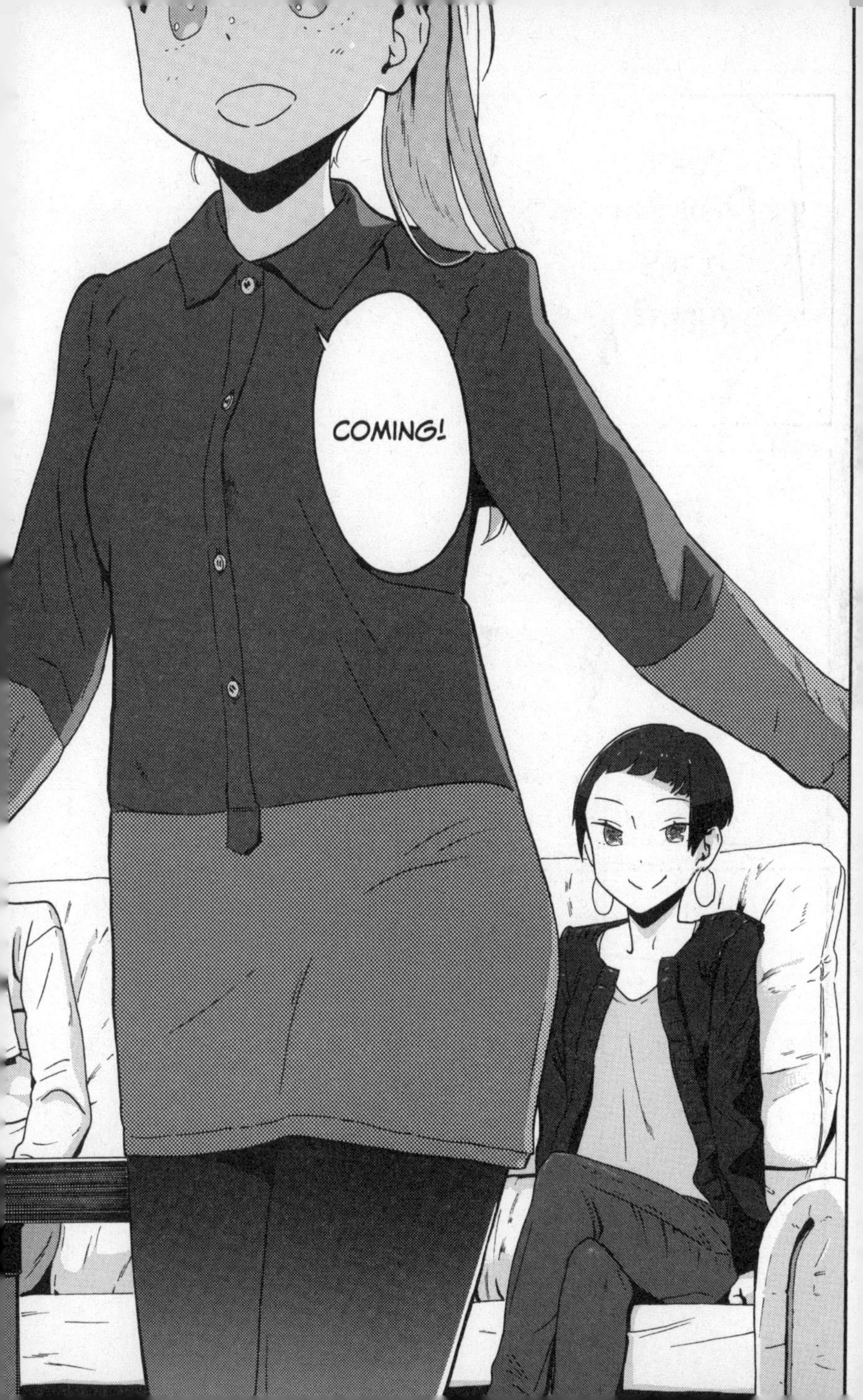
COMING!

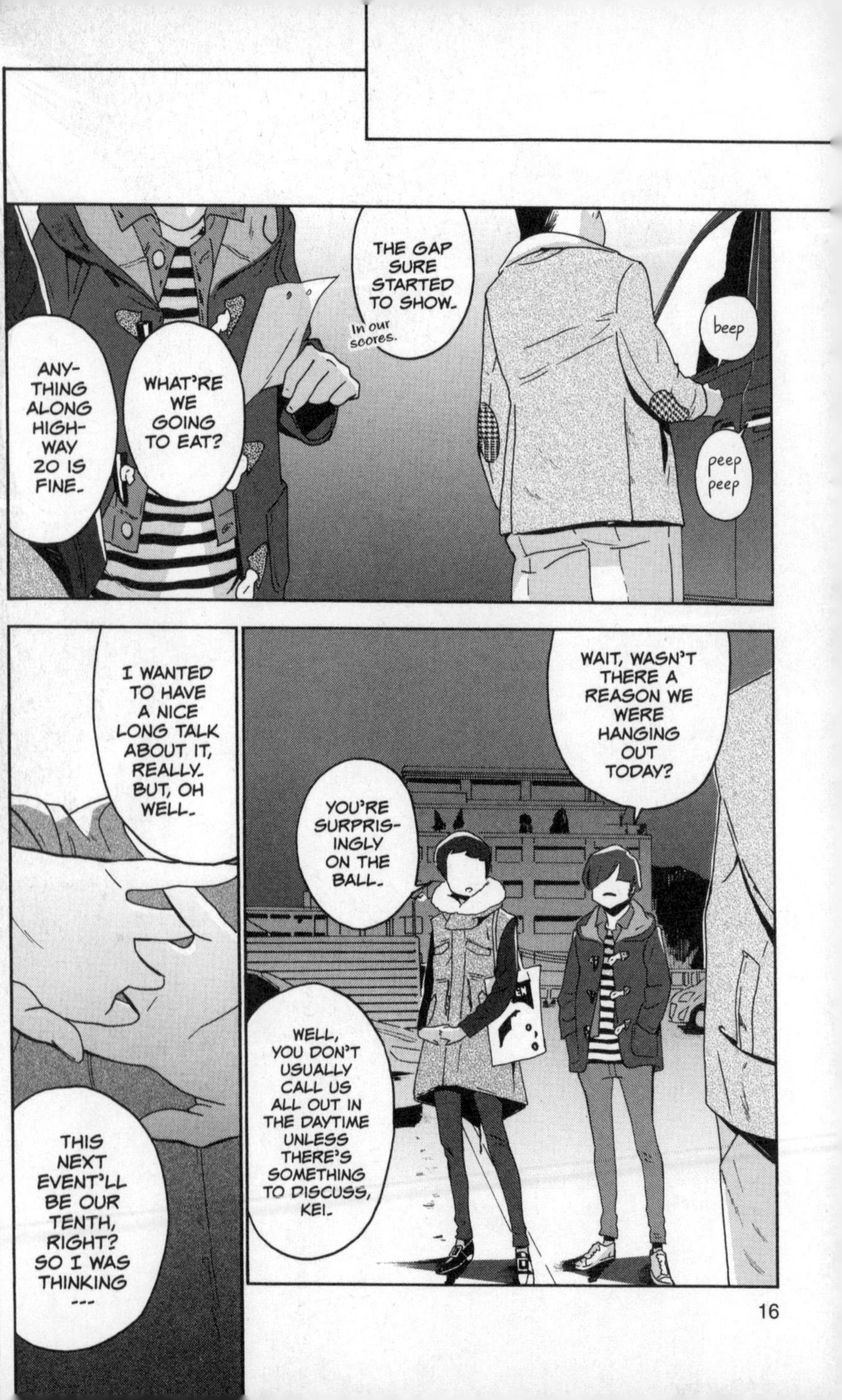
beep
peep peep
THE GAP SURE STARTED TO SHOW...
In our scores.
WHAT'RE WE GOING TO EAT?
ANYTHING ALONG HIGHWAY 20 IS FINE...
WAIT, WASN'T THERE A REASON WE WERE HANGING OUT TODAY?
YOU'RE SURPRISINGLY ON THE BALL...
WELL, YOU DON'T USUALLY CALL US ALL OUT IN THE DAYTIME UNLESS THERE'S SOMETHING TO DISCUSS, KEI...
I WANTED TO HAVE A NICE LONG TALK ABOUT IT, REALLY... BUT, OH WELL...
THIS NEXT EVENT'LL BE OUR TENTH, RIGHT? SO I WAS THINKING---

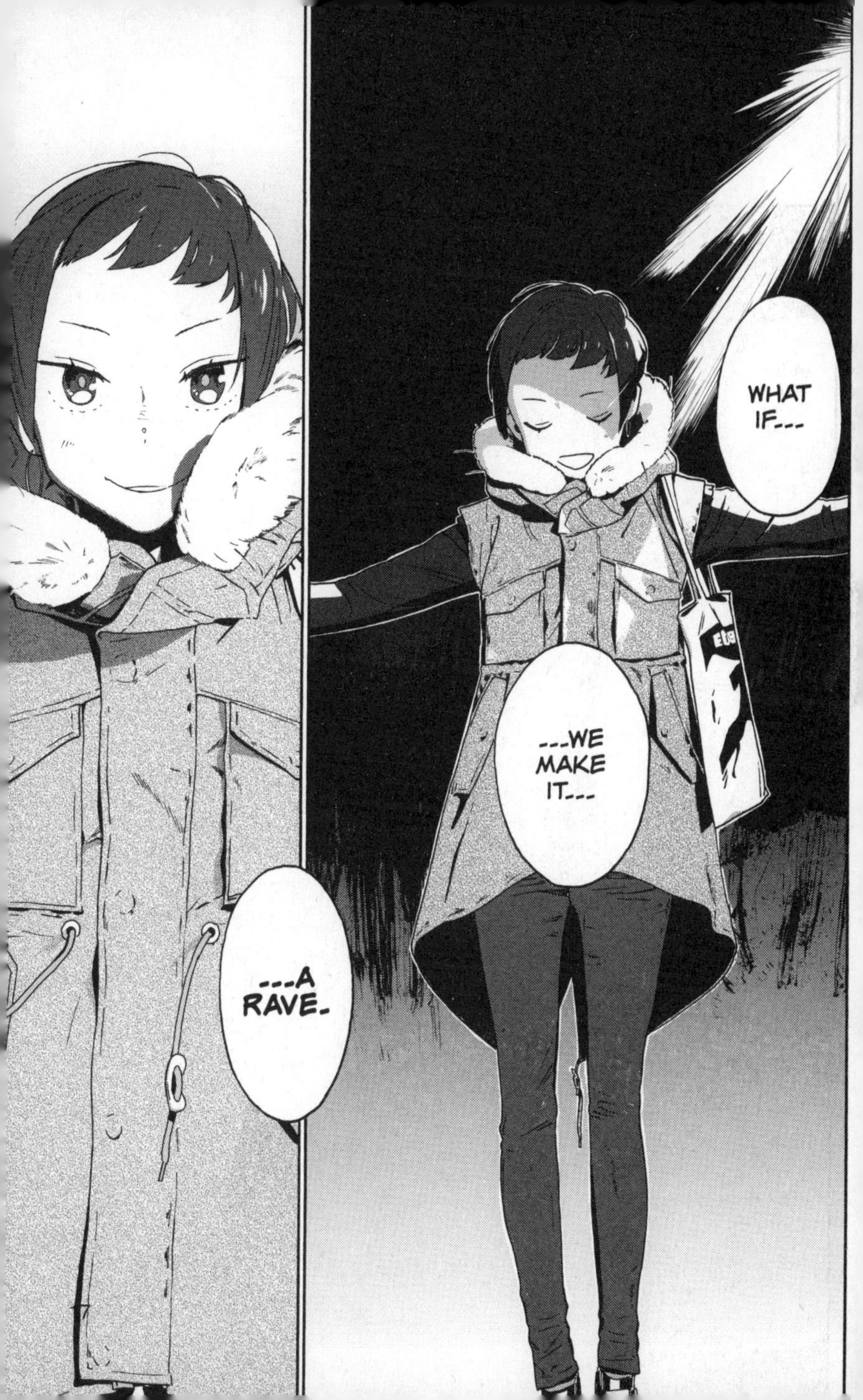
WHAT IF...
...WE MAKE IT...
...A RAVE.

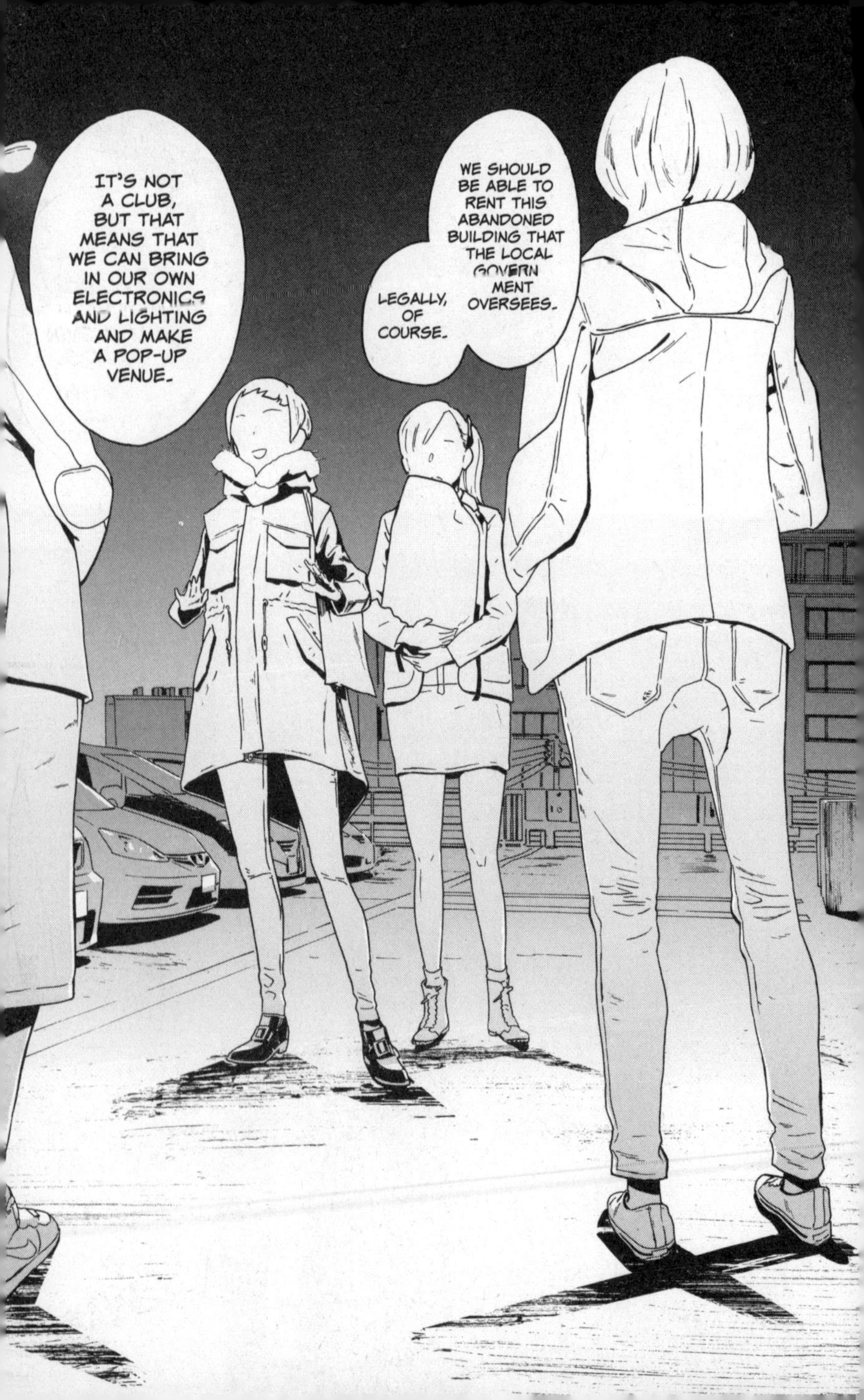
WE SHOULD BE ABLE TO RENT THIS ABANDONED BUILDING THAT THE LOCAL GOVERNMENT OVERSEES.
LEGALLY, OF COURSE.
IT'S NOT A CLUB, BUT THAT MEANS THAT WE CAN BRING IN OUR OWN ELECTRONICS AND LIGHTING AND MAKE A POP-UP VENUE.

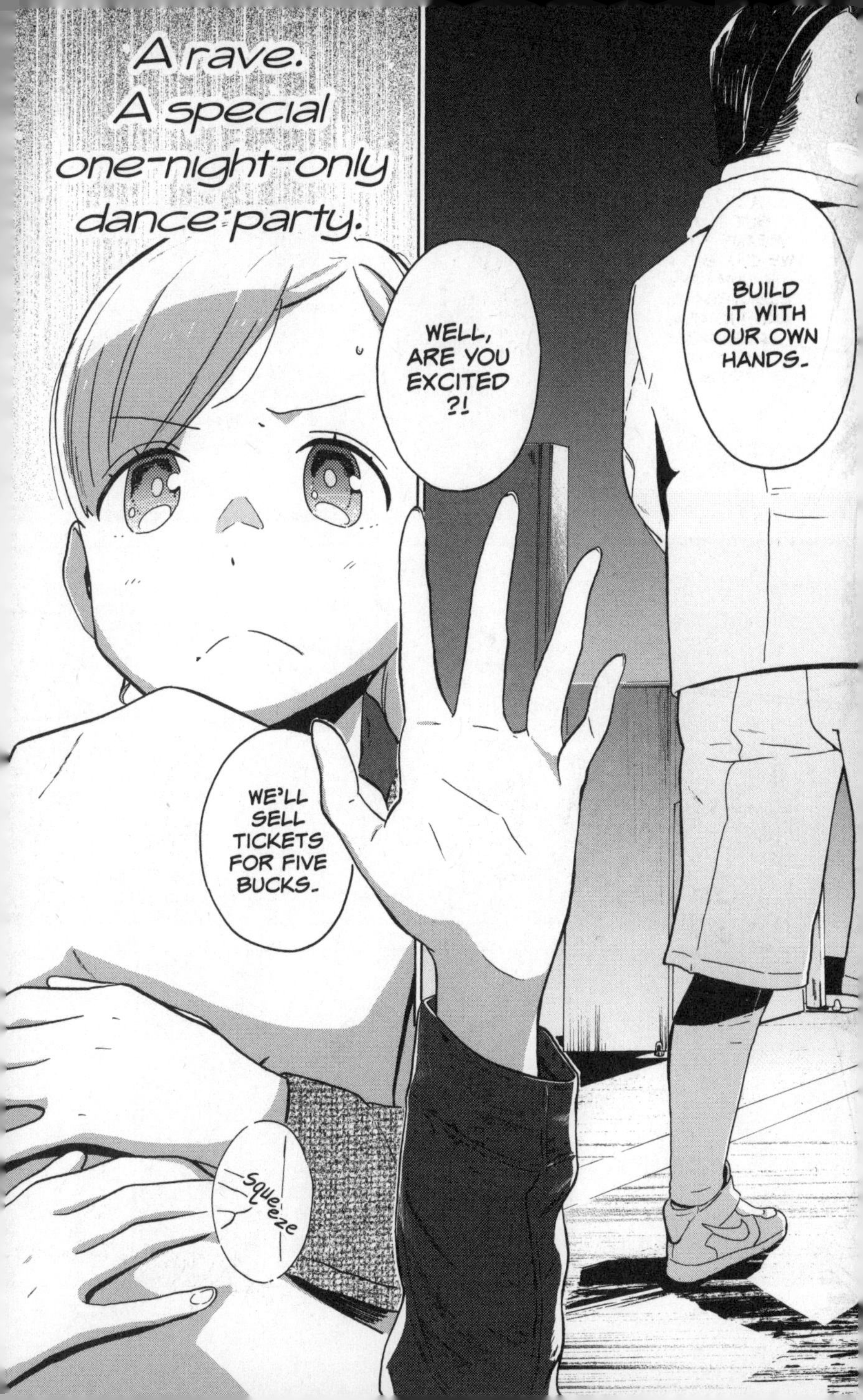
BUILD IT WITH OUR OWN HANDS.
A rave. A special one-night-only dance party.
WELL, ARE YOU EXCITED?!
WE'LL SELL TICKETS FOR FIVE BUCKS.
squeeze

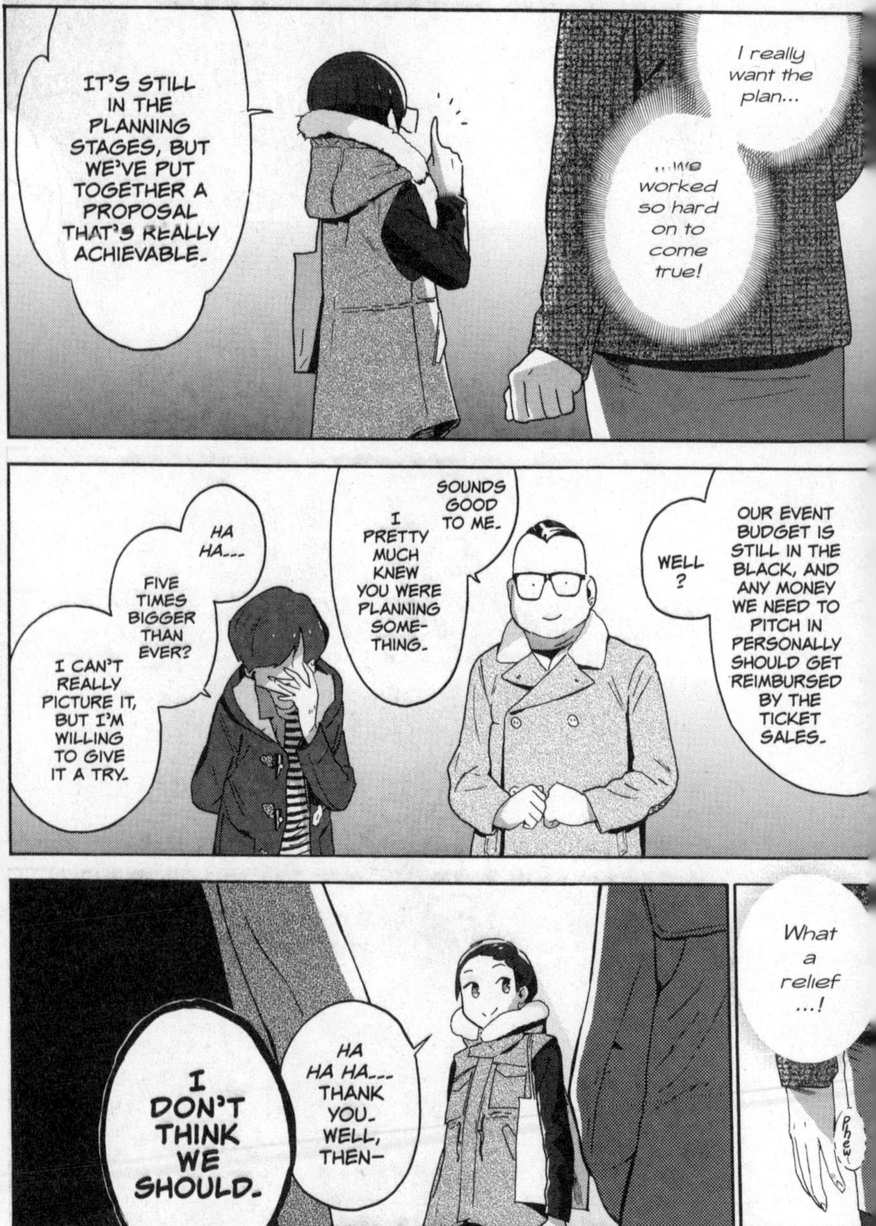
I really want the plan...
...we worked so hard on to come true!
IT'S STILL IN THE PLANNING STAGES, BUT WE'VE PUT TOGETHER A PROPOSAL THAT'S REALLY ACHIEVABLE.
OUR EVENT BUDGET IS STILL IN THE BLACK, AND ANY MONEY WE NEED TO PITCH IN PERSONALLY SHOULD GET REIMBURSED BY THE TICKET SALES.
WELL?
SOUNDS GOOD TO ME.
I PRETTY MUCH KNEW YOU WERE PLANNING SOME-THING.
HA HA...
FIVE TIMES BIGGER THAN EVER?
I CAN'T REALLY PICTURE IT, BUT I'M WILLING TO GIVE IT A TRY.
What a relief...!
Phew...
HA HA HA... THANK YOU. WELL, THEN-
I DON'T THINK WE SHOULD.

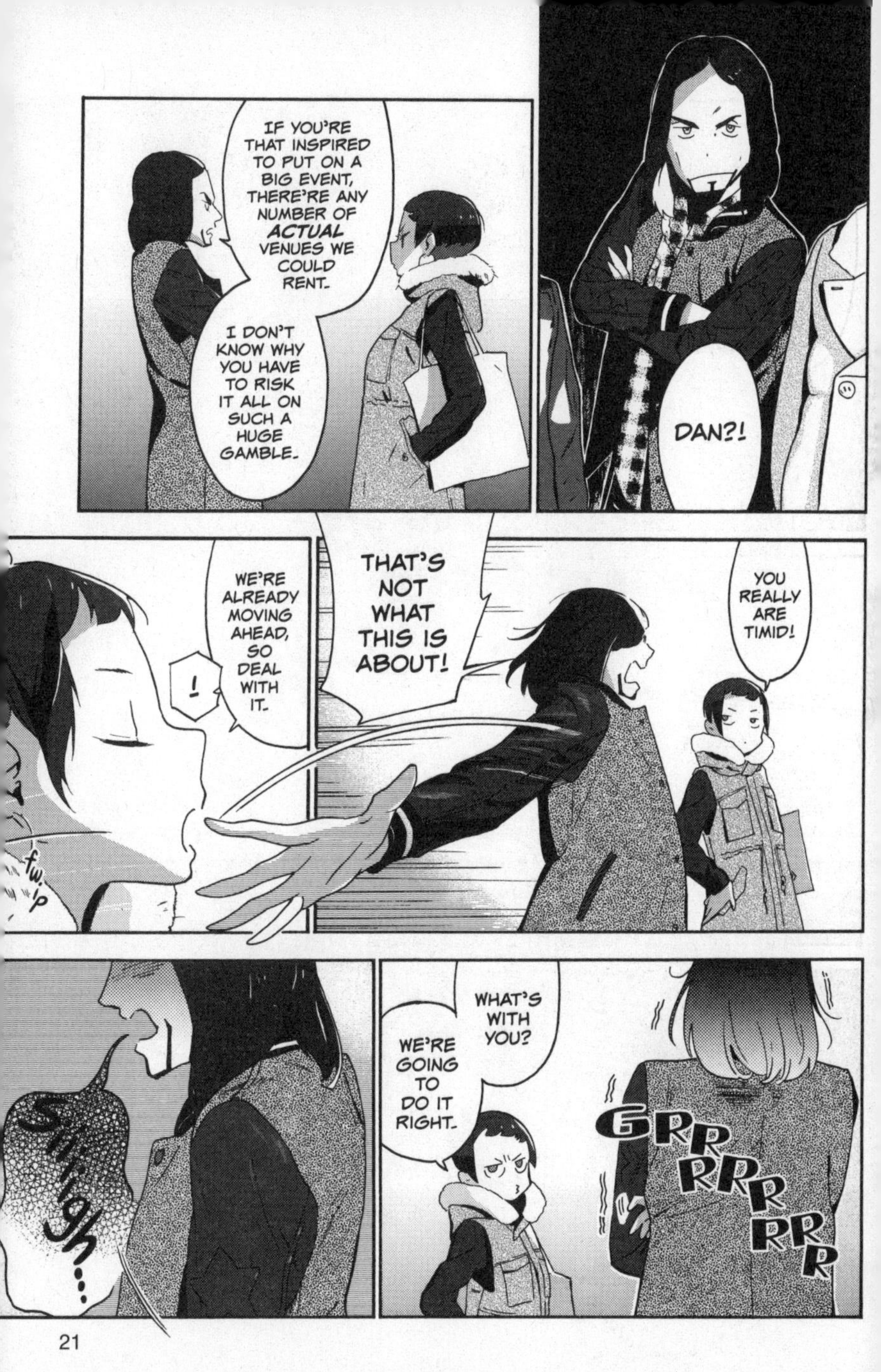
DAN?!
IF YOU'RE THAT INSPIRED TO PUT ON A BIG EVENT, THERE'RE ANY NUMBER OF *ACTUAL* VENUES WE COULD RENT.
I DON'T KNOW WHY YOU HAVE TO RISK IT ALL ON SUCH A HUGE GAMBLE.
YOU REALLY ARE TIMID!
THAT'S NOT WHAT THIS IS ABOUT!
WE'RE ALREADY MOVING AHEAD, SO DEAL WITH IT.
!
fwip
WHAT'S WITH YOU?
WE'RE GOING TO DO IT RIGHT.
GRRRRRRRRR
Sigh...

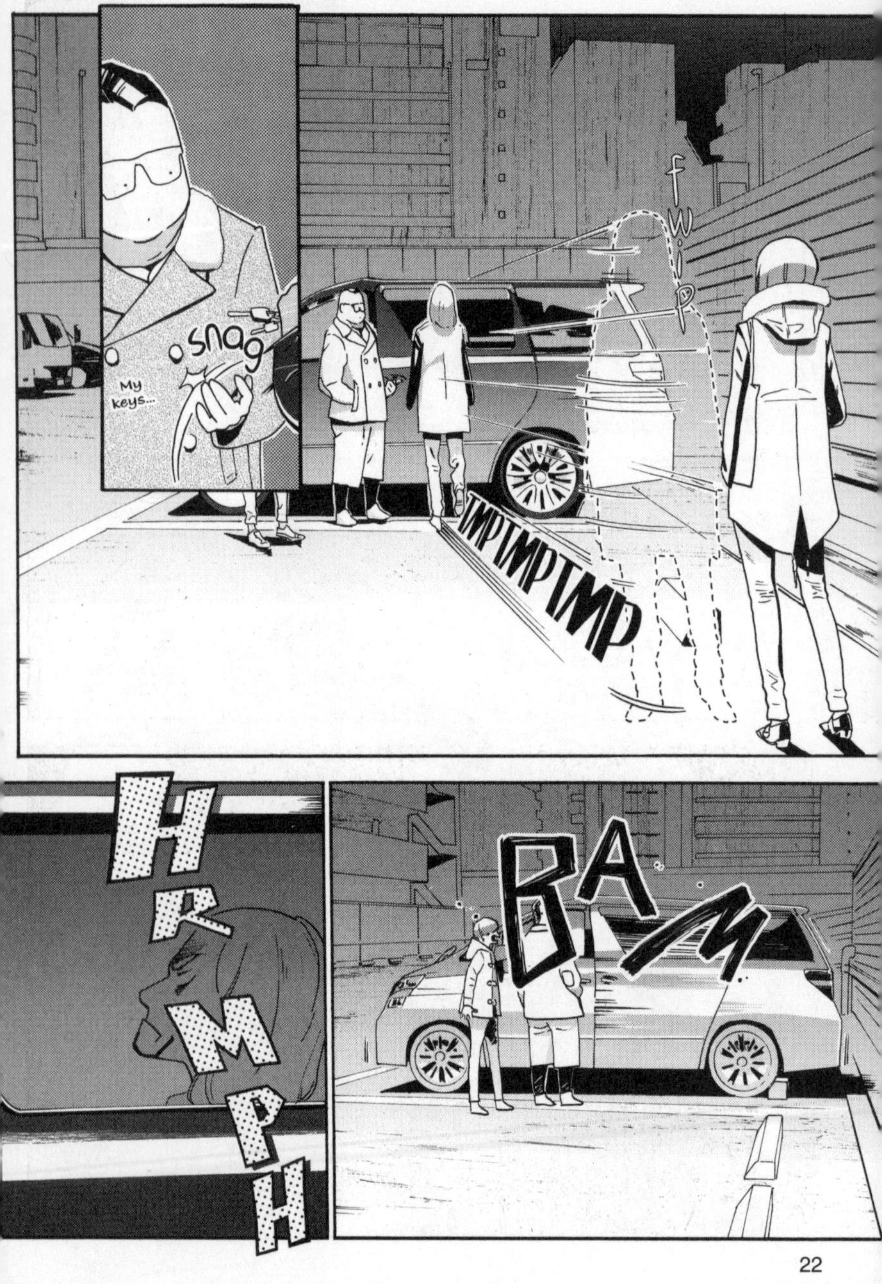
fwip
TMPTMPTMP
snag
My keys...
BAM
HRMPH

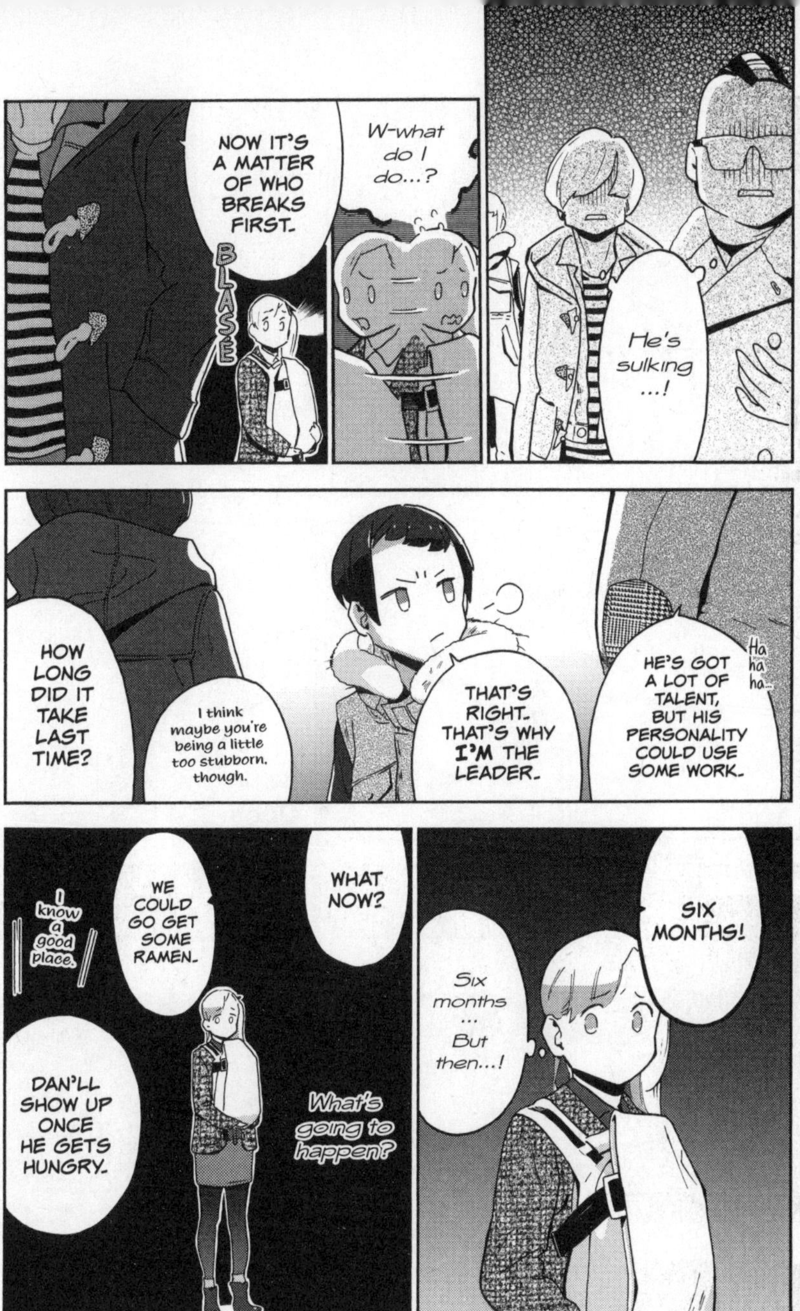
He's sulking ...!
W-what do I do...?
NOW IT'S A MATTER OF WHO BREAKS FIRST.
BLASÉ
Ha ha ha...
HE'S GOT A LOT OF TALENT, BUT HIS PERSONALITY COULD USE SOME WORK.
THAT'S RIGHT. THAT'S WHY I'M THE LEADER.
I think maybe you're being a little too stubborn, though.
HOW LONG DID IT TAKE LAST TIME?
SIX MONTHS!
Six months ... But then...!
WHAT NOW?
WE COULD GO GET SOME RAMEN.
I know a good place.
DAN'LL SHOW UP ONCE HE GETS HUNGRY.
What's going to happen?

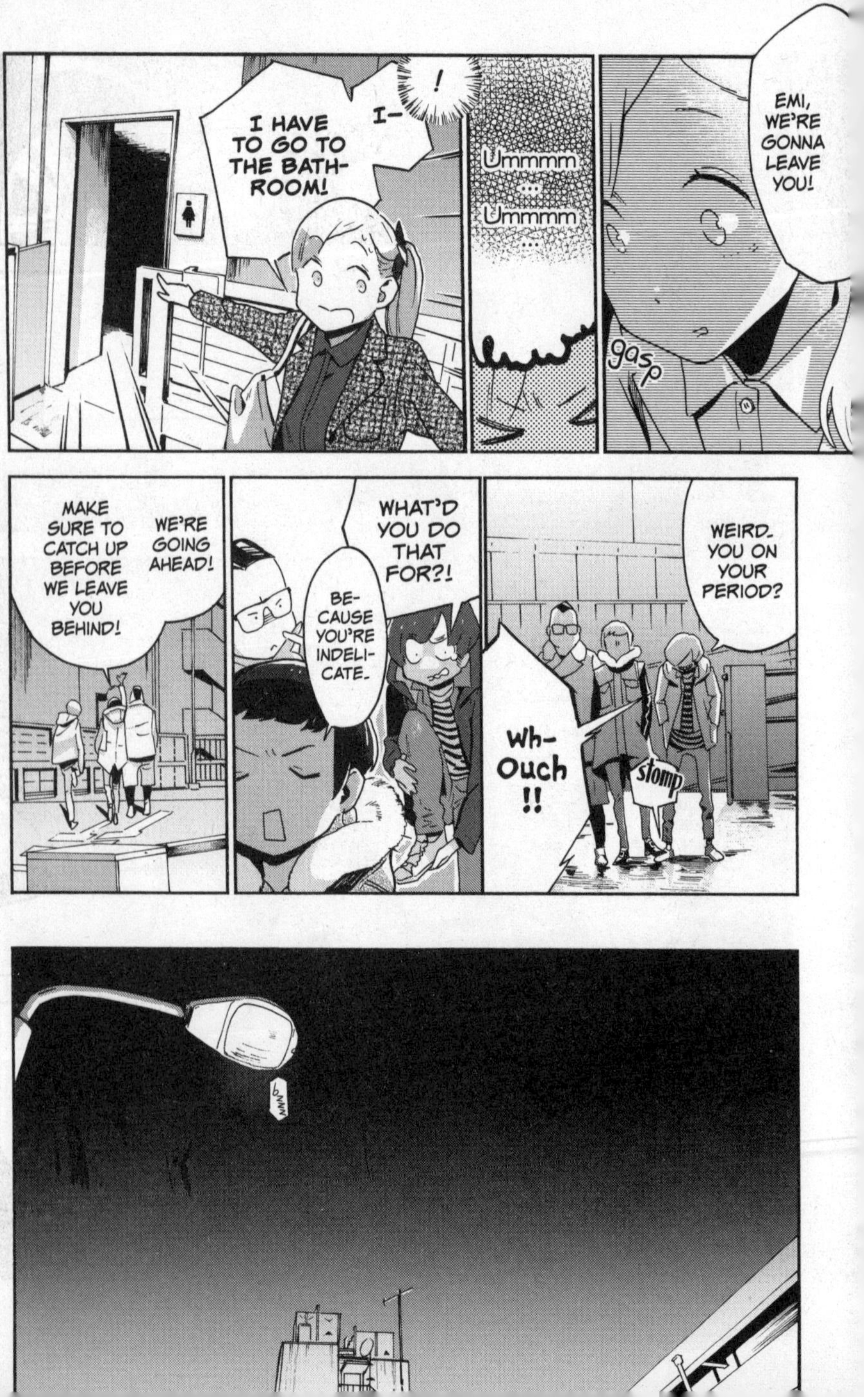
EMI, WE'RE GONNA LEAVE YOU!
gasp
Ummmm ... Ummmm ...
!
I—
I HAVE TO GO TO THE BATH-ROOM!
WEIRD. YOU ON YOUR PERIOD?
Wh- Ouch!!
stomp
WHAT'D YOU DO THAT FOR?!
BE-CAUSE YOU'RE INDELI-CATE.
WE'RE GOING AHEAD!
MAKE SURE TO CATCH UP BEFORE WE LEAVE YOU BEHIND!

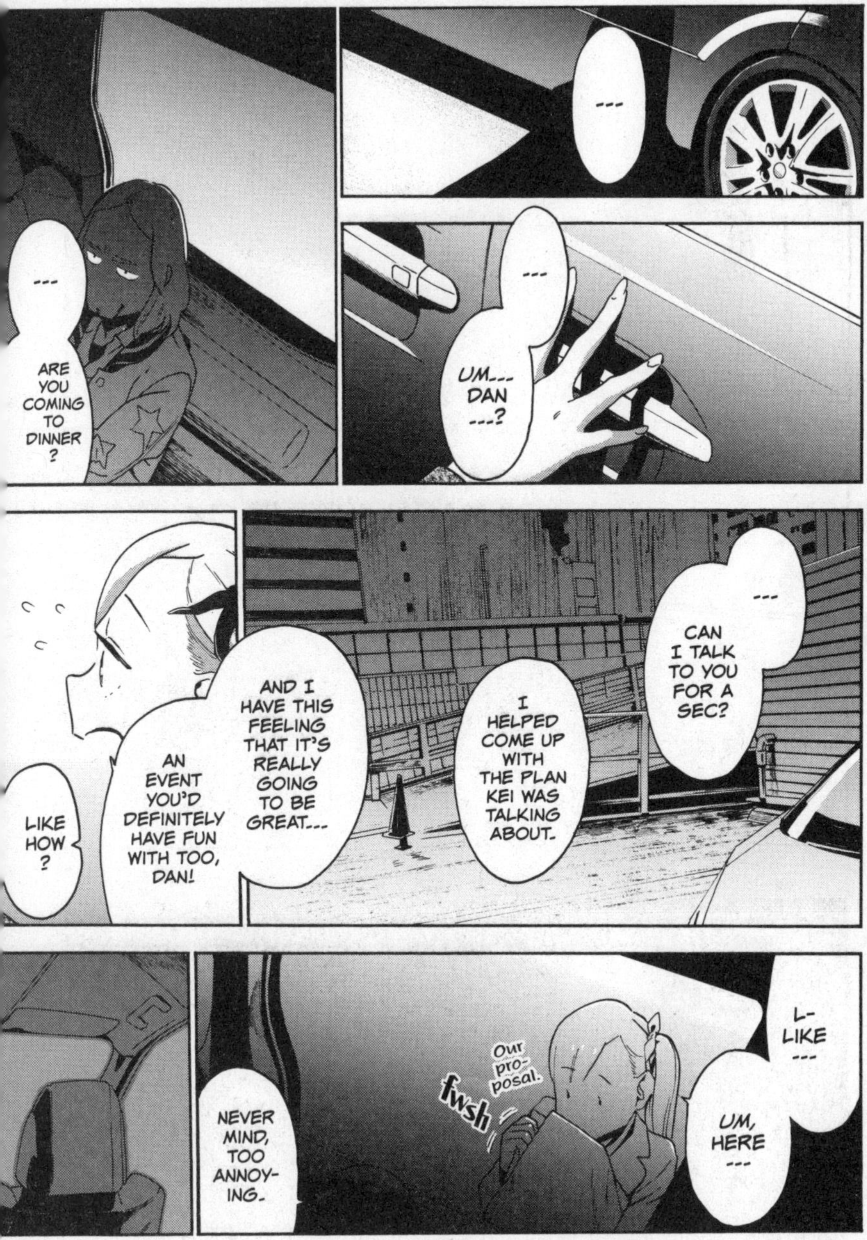
...
...
UM... DAN ...?
...
ARE YOU COMING TO DINNER?
...
CAN I TALK TO YOU FOR A SEC?
I HELPED COME UP WITH THE PLAN KEI WAS TALKING ABOUT.
AND I HAVE THIS FEELING THAT IT'S REALLY GOING TO BE GREAT...
AN EVENT YOU'D DEFINITELY HAVE FUN WITH TOO, DAN!
LIKE HOW?
L-LIKE ...
UM, HERE ...
fwsh
Our pro-posal.
NEVER MIND, TOO ANNOY-ING.

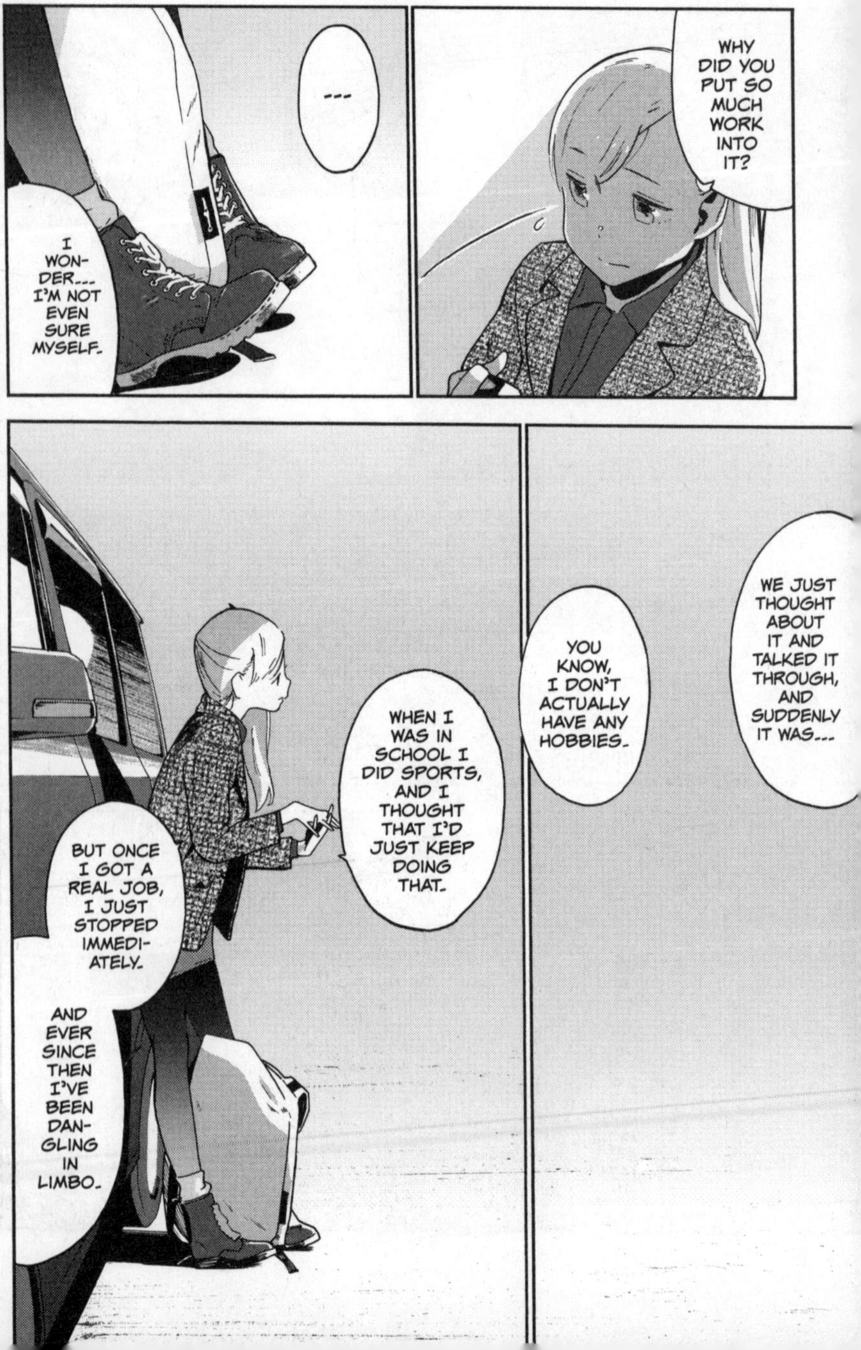
WHY DID YOU PUT SO MUCH WORK INTO IT?
...
I WONDER... I'M NOT EVEN SURE MYSELF.
WE JUST THOUGHT ABOUT IT AND TALKED IT THROUGH, AND SUDDENLY IT WAS...
YOU KNOW, I DON'T ACTUALLY HAVE ANY HOBBIES.
WHEN I WAS IN SCHOOL I DID SPORTS, AND I THOUGHT THAT I'D JUST KEEP DOING THAT.
BUT ONCE I GOT A REAL JOB, I JUST STOPPED IMMEDIATELY.
AND EVER SINCE THEN I'VE BEEN DANGLING IN LIMBO.

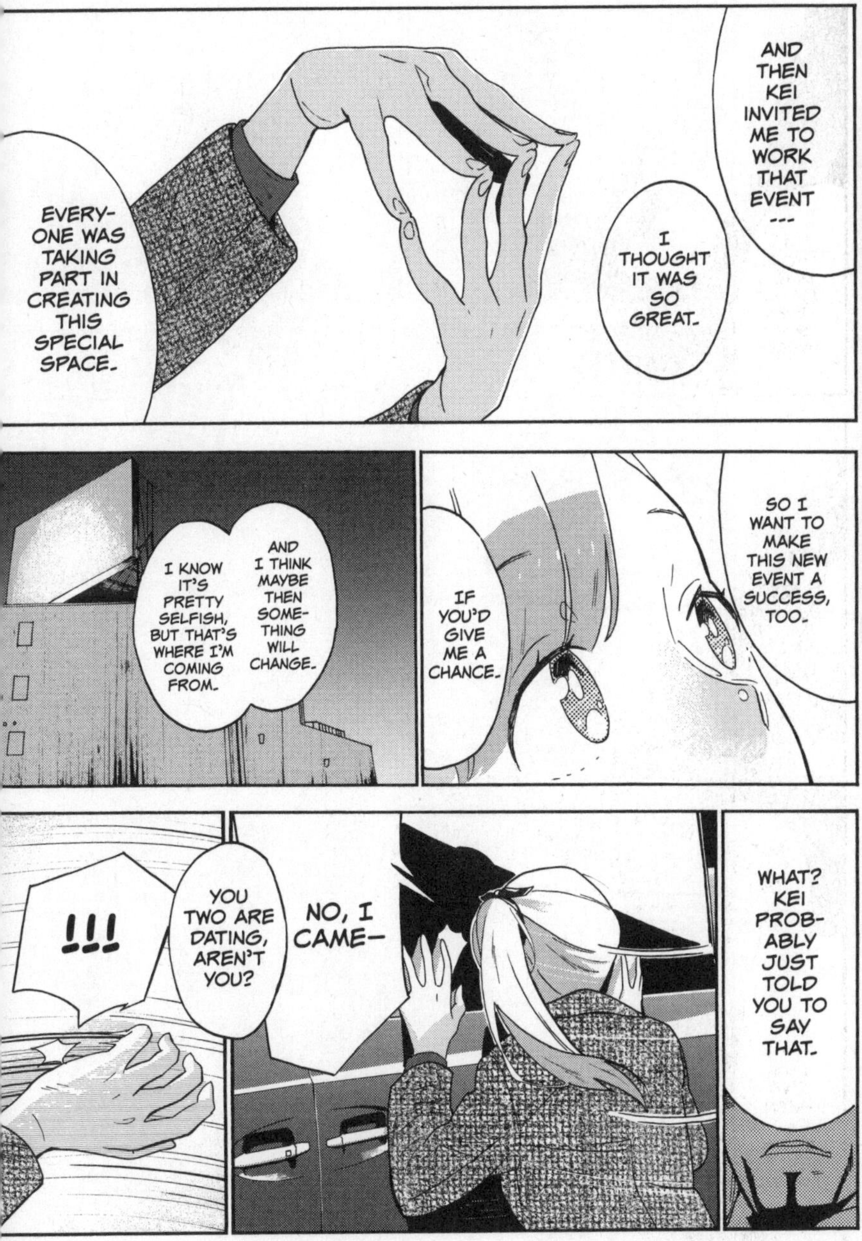
AND THEN KEI INVITED ME TO WORK THAT EVENT---
I THOUGHT IT WAS SO GREAT.
EVERY-ONE WAS TAKING PART IN CREATING THIS SPECIAL SPACE.
SO I WANT TO MAKE THIS NEW EVENT A SUCCESS, TOO.
IF YOU'D GIVE ME A CHANCE.
AND I THINK MAYBE THEN SOME-THING WILL CHANGE.
I KNOW IT'S PRETTY SELFISH, BUT THAT'S WHERE I'M COMING FROM.
WHAT? KEI PROB-ABLY JUST TOLD YOU TO SAY THAT.
NO, I CAME—
YOU TWO ARE DATING, AREN'T YOU?
!!!

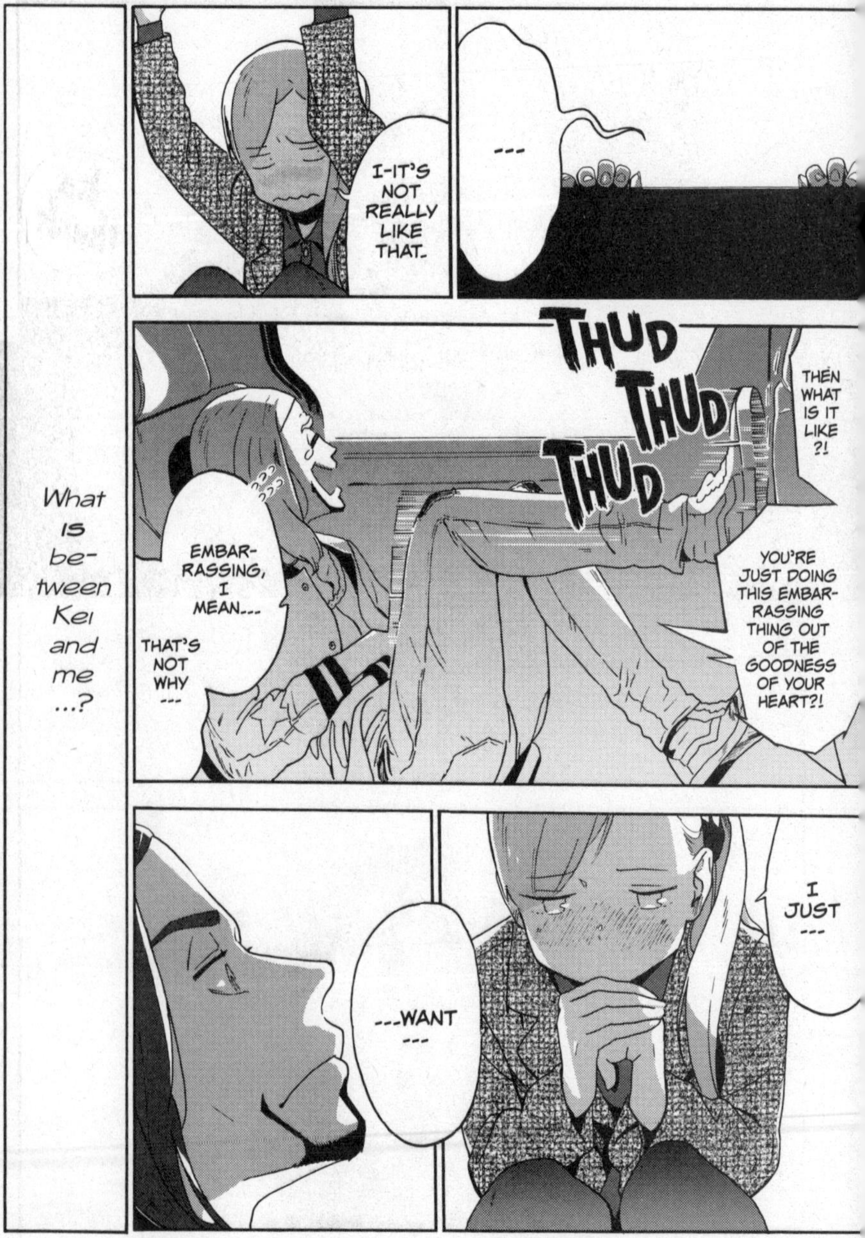

I-IT'S NOT REALLY LIKE THAT...
THUD THUD THUD
THEN WHAT IS IT LIKE ?!
YOU'RE JUST DOING THIS EMBAR-RASSING THING OUT OF THE GOODNESS OF YOUR HEART?!
EMBAR-RASSING, I MEAN...
THAT'S NOT WHY ---
I JUST ---
---WANT ---
What is be-tween Kei and me ...?

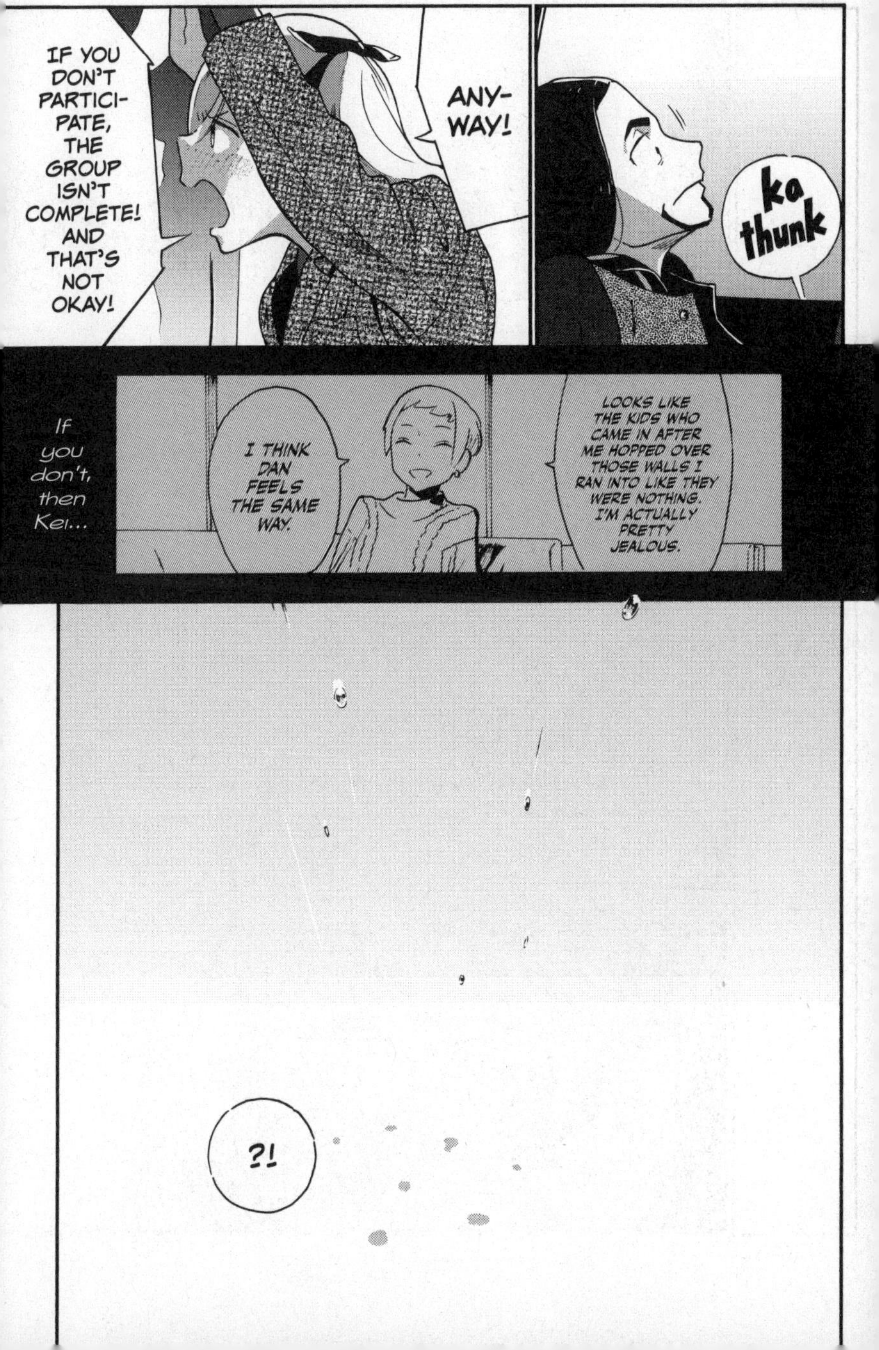
ka thunk
ANY-WAY!
IF YOU DON'T PARTICI-PATE, THE GROUP ISN'T COMPLETE! AND THAT'S NOT OKAY!
LOOKS LIKE THE KIDS WHO CAME IN AFTER ME HOPPED OVER THOSE WALLS I RAN INTO LIKE THEY WERE NOTHING. I'M ACTUALLY PRETTY JEALOUS.
I THINK DAN FEELS THE SAME WAY.
If you don't, then Kei...
?!

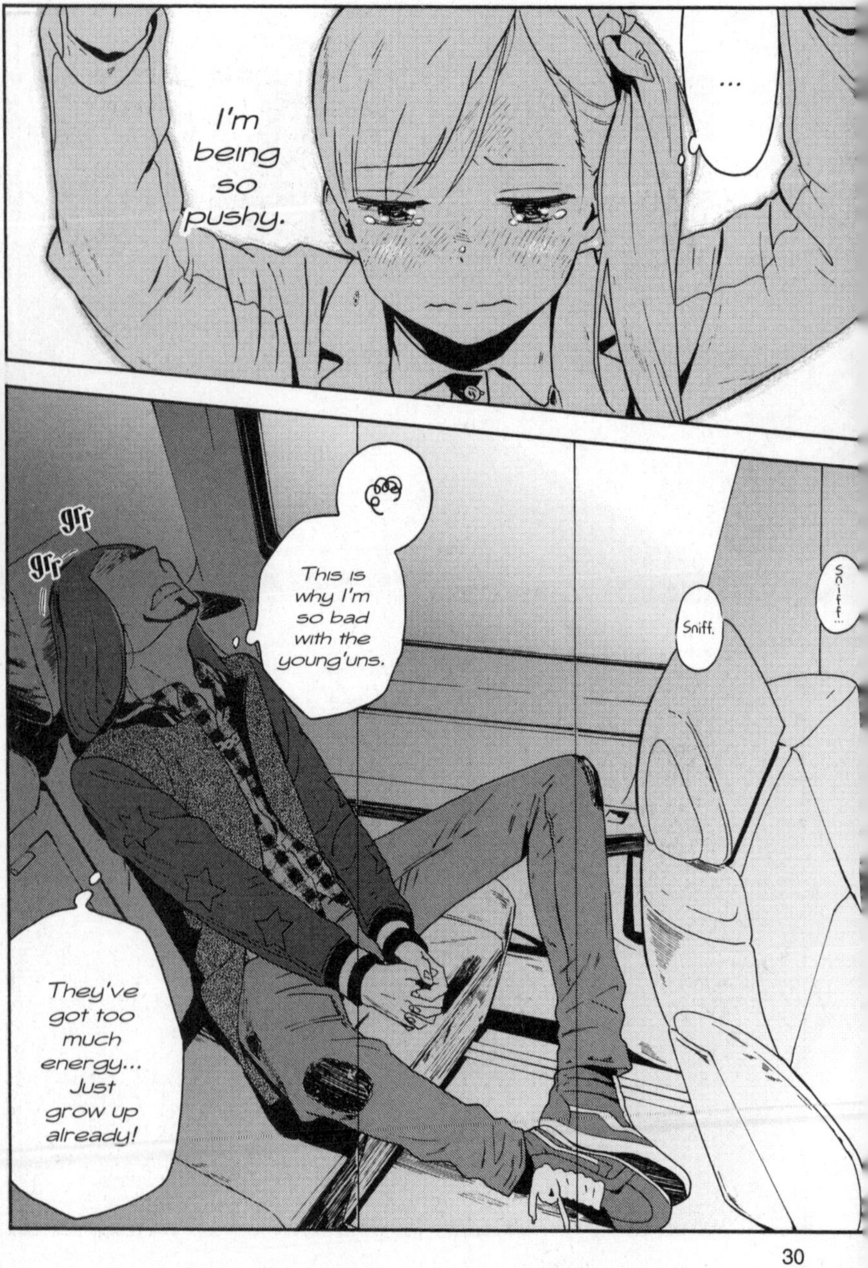
...
I'm being so pushy.
Sniff...
Sniff.
This is why I'm so bad with the young'uns.
grr
grr
They've got too much energy... Just grow up already!

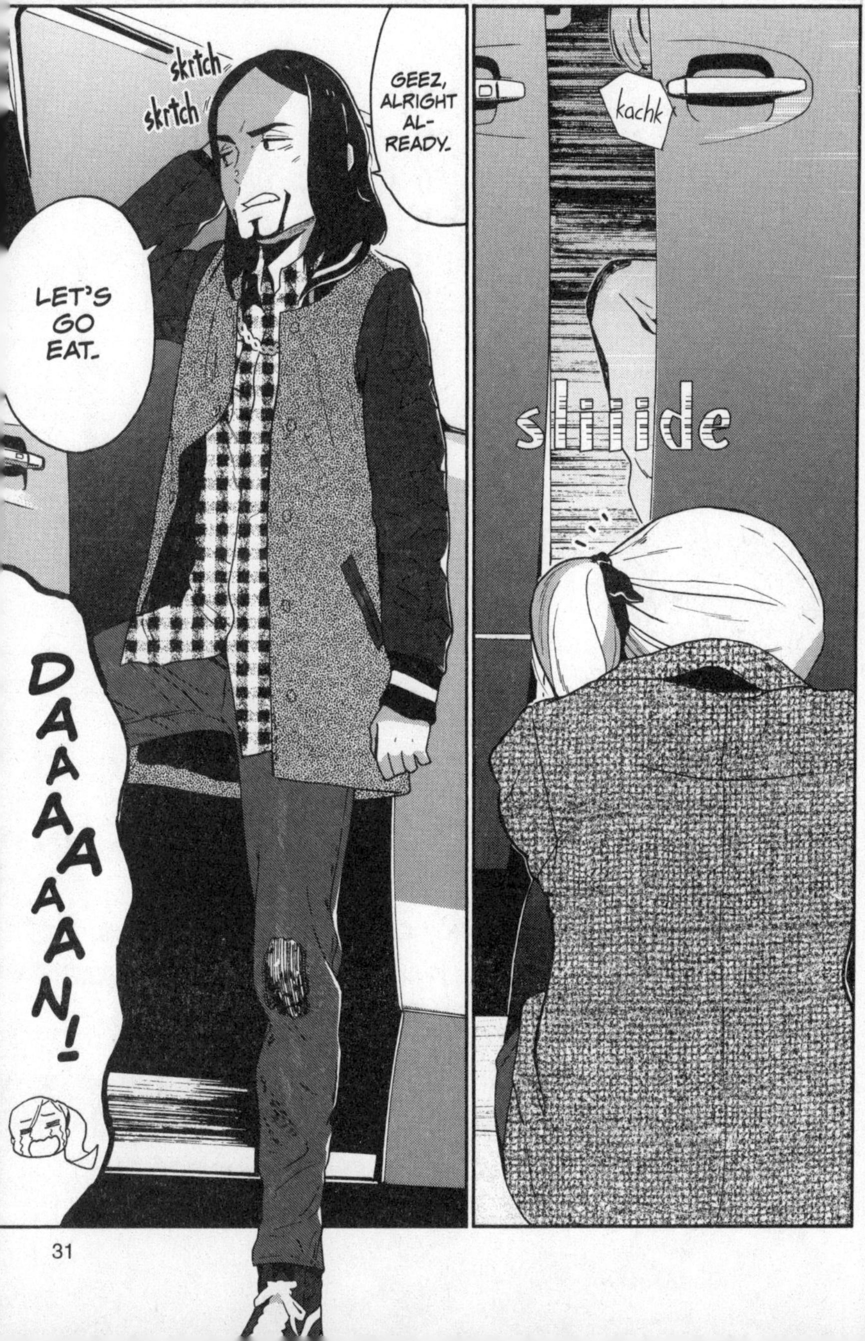
kachk
sliiide
GEEZ, ALRIGHT AL-READY.
skrtch
skrtch
LET'S GO EAT.
DAAAAAAN!

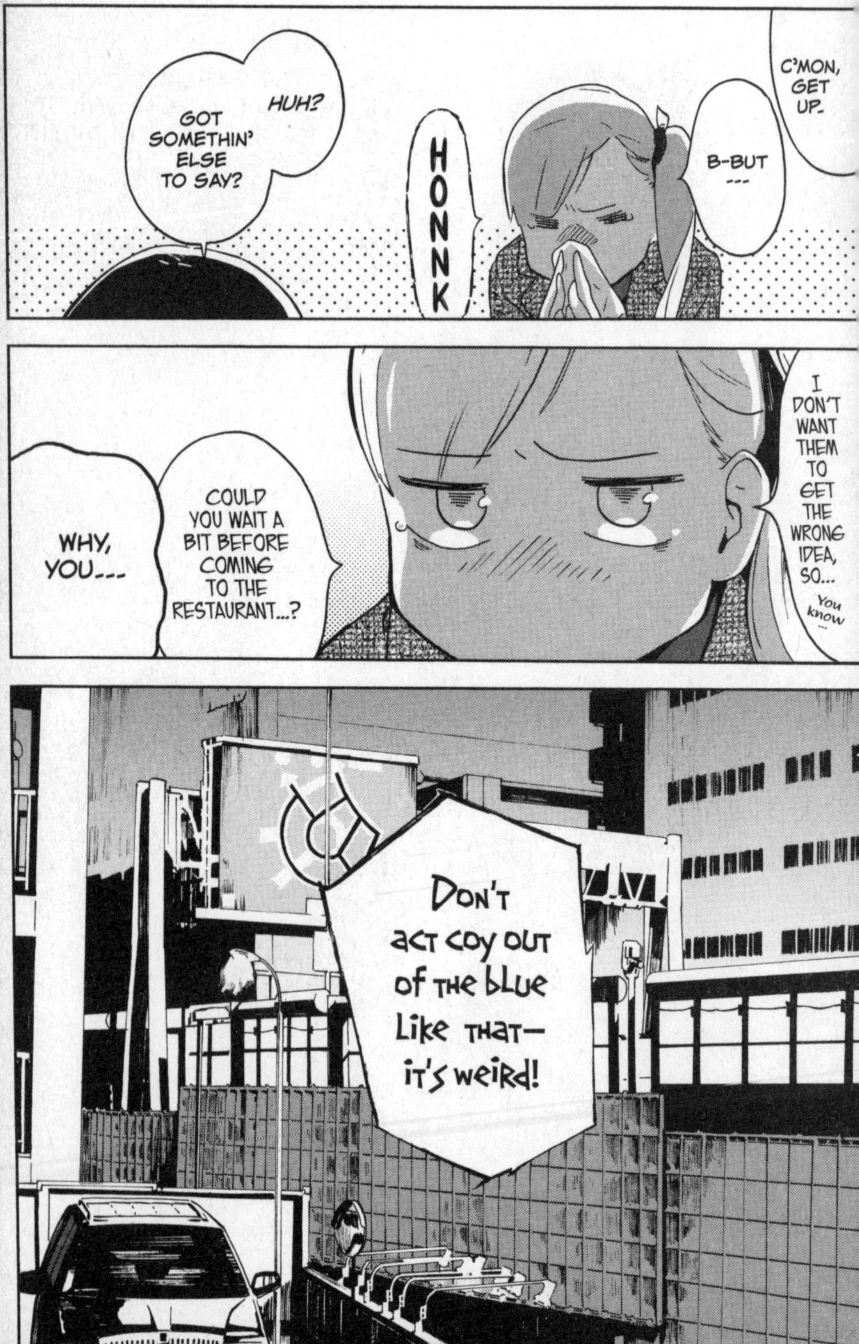
C'MON, GET UP.
B-BUT ---
HONNK
HUH?
GOT SOMETHIN' ELSE TO SAY?
I DON'T WANT THEM TO GET THE WRONG IDEA, SO...
You know ...
COULD YOU WAIT A BIT BEFORE COMING TO THE RESTAURANT...?
WHY, YOU---
Don't act coy out of the blue like that— it's weird!

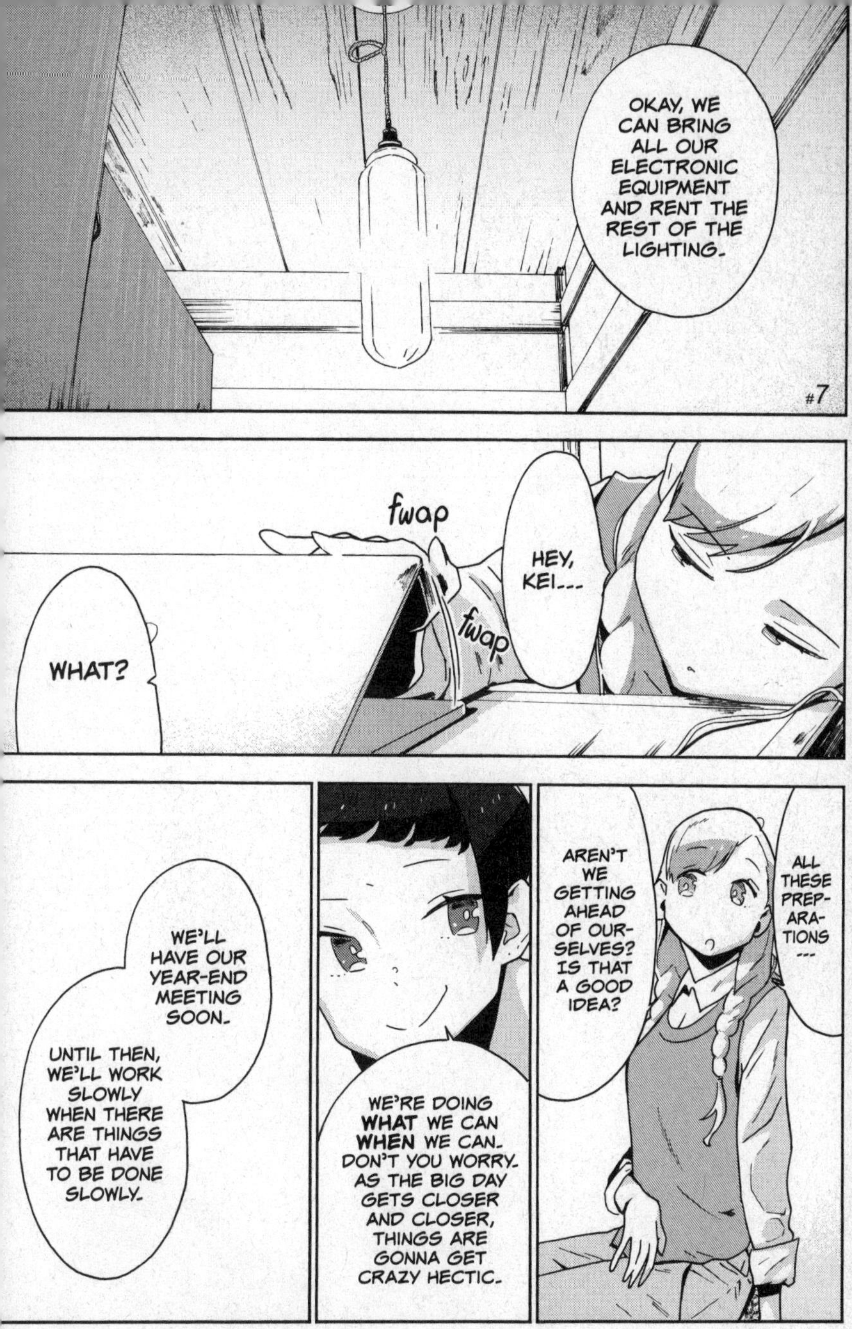
OKAY, WE CAN BRING ALL OUR ELECTRONIC EQUIPMENT AND RENT THE REST OF THE LIGHTING.
#7
HEY, KEI...
fwap
fwap
WHAT?
ALL THESE PREPARATIONS...
AREN'T WE GETTING AHEAD OF OURSELVES? IS THAT A GOOD IDEA?
WE'RE DOING **WHAT** WE CAN **WHEN** WE CAN. DON'T YOU WORRY. AS THE BIG DAY GETS CLOSER AND CLOSER, THINGS ARE GONNA GET CRAZY HECTIC.
WE'LL HAVE OUR YEAR-END MEETING SOON.
UNTIL THEN, WE'LL WORK SLOWLY WHEN THERE ARE THINGS THAT HAVE TO BE DONE SLOWLY.

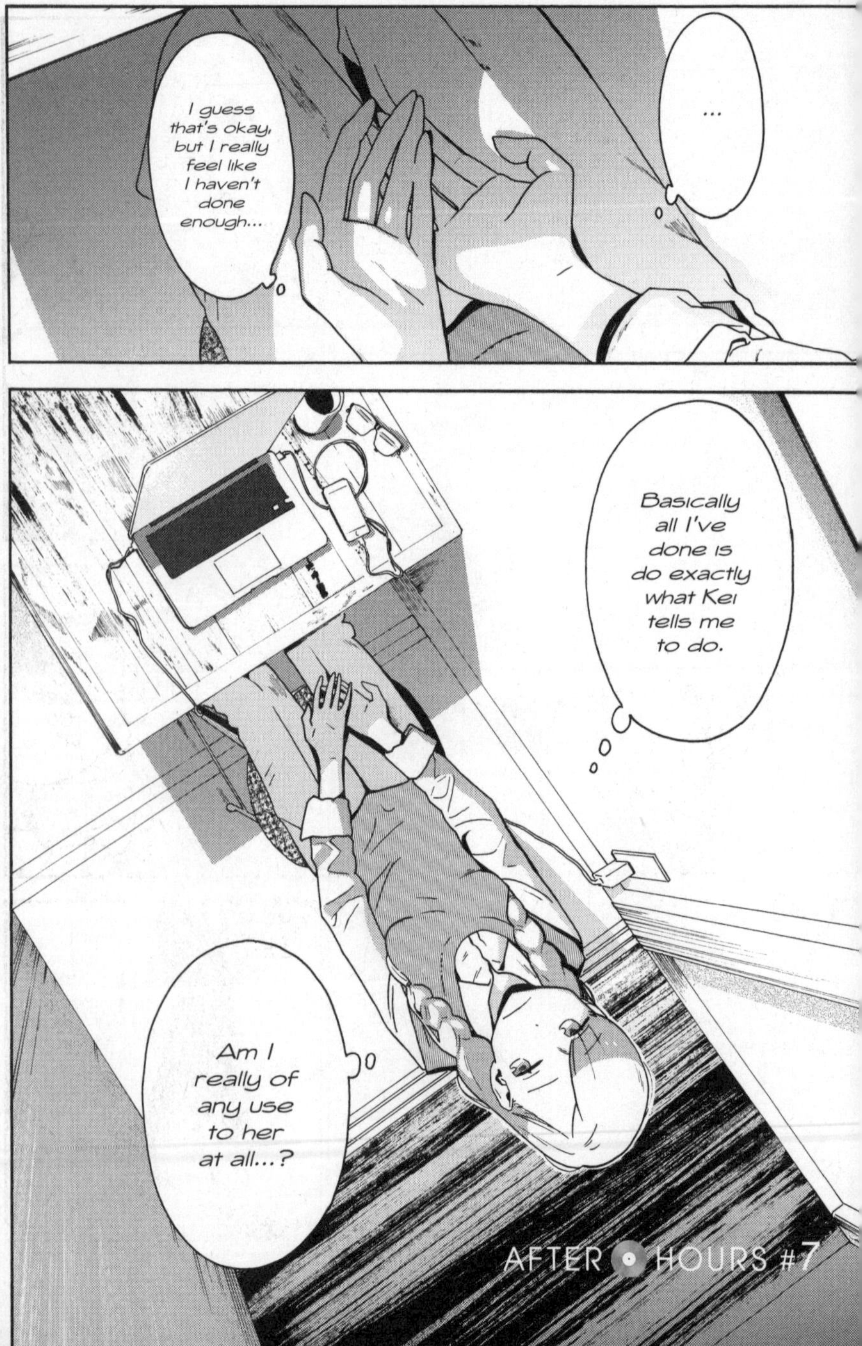
...
I guess that's okay, but I really feel like I haven't done enough...
Basically all I've done is do exactly what Kei tells me to do.
Am I really of any use to her at all...?
AFTER HOURS #7

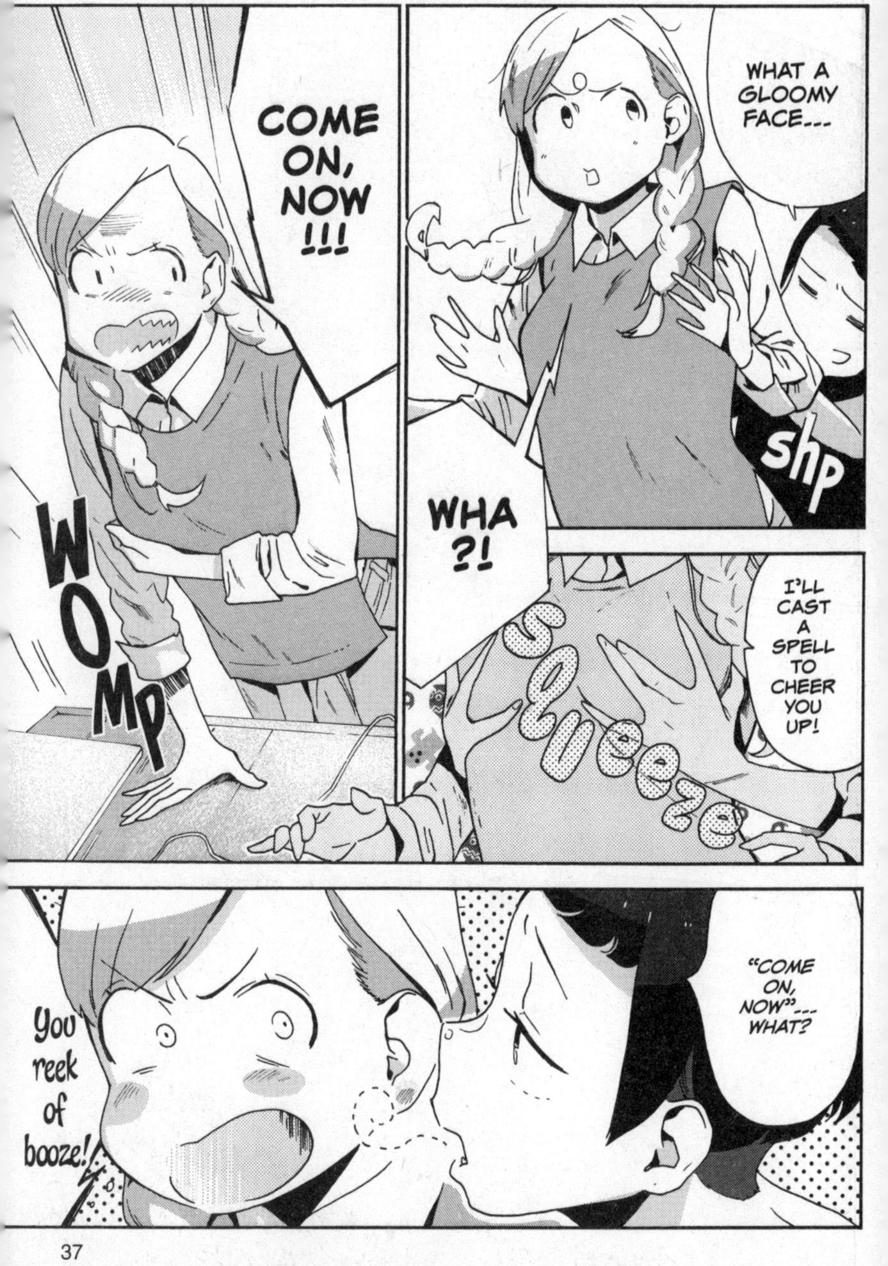
WHAT A GLOOMY FACE...
shp
WHA ?!
I'LL CAST A SPELL TO CHEER YOU UP!
Squeeze
COME ON, NOW !!!
WOMP
"COME ON, NOW"... WHAT?
You reek of booze!

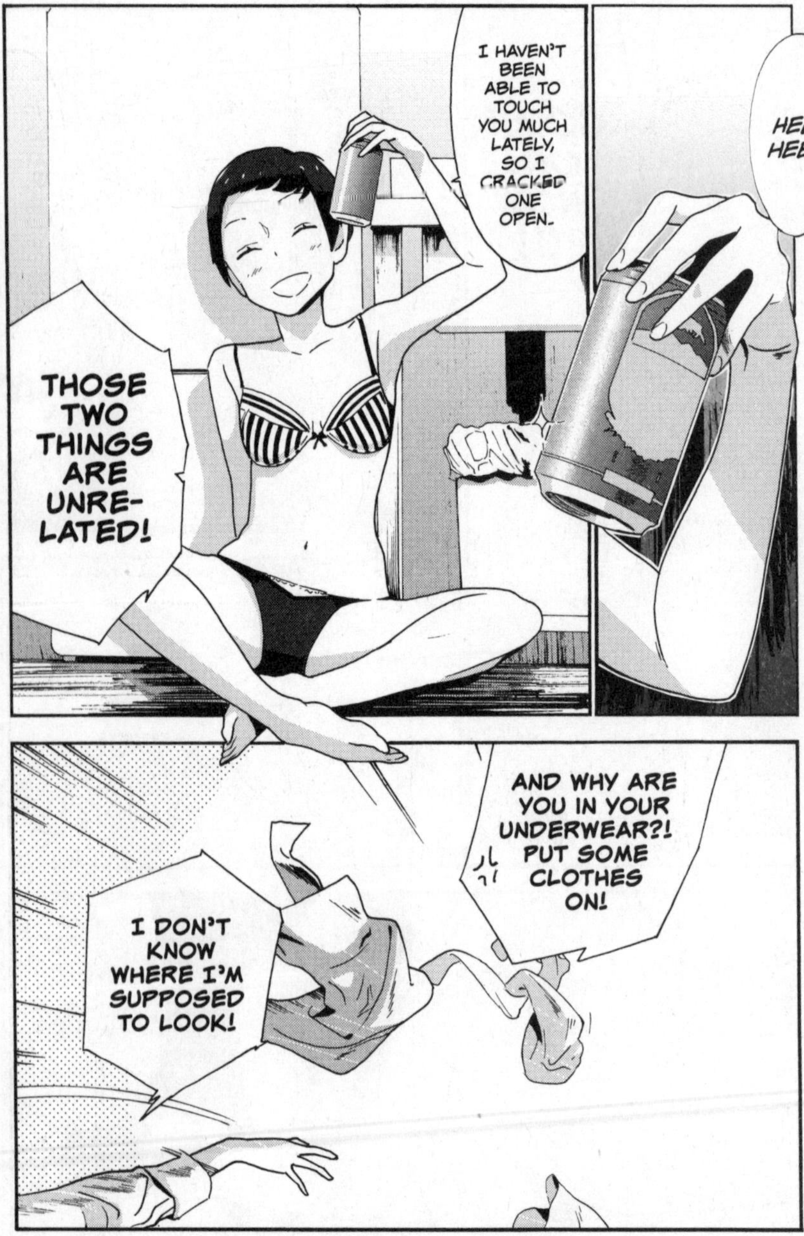
HEE HEE...
I HAVEN'T BEEN ABLE TO TOUCH YOU MUCH LATELY, SO I CRACKED ONE OPEN...
THOSE TWO THINGS ARE UNRE-LATED!
AND WHY ARE YOU IN YOUR UNDERWEAR?! PUT SOME CLOTHES ON!
I DON'T KNOW WHERE I'M SUPPOSED TO LOOK!

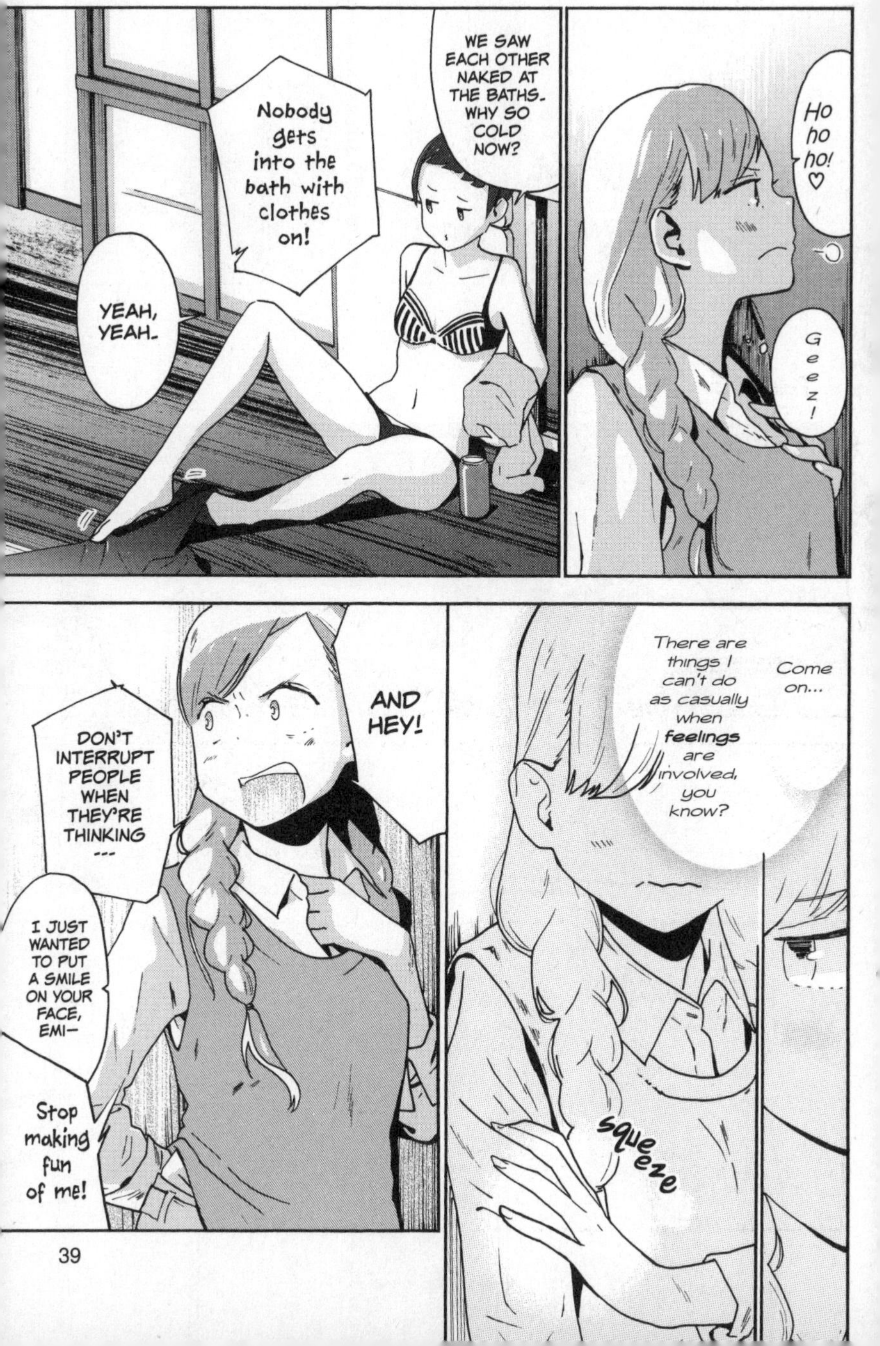
Ho ho ho! ♡
Geez!
WE SAW EACH OTHER NAKED AT THE BATHS. WHY SO COLD NOW?
Nobody gets into the bath with clothes on!
YEAH, YEAH.
Come on...
There are things I can't do as casually when **feelings** are involved, you know?
squeeze
AND HEY!
DON'T INTERRUPT PEOPLE WHEN THEY'RE THINKING---
I JUST WANTED TO PUT A SMILE ON YOUR FACE, EMI—
Stop making fun of me!

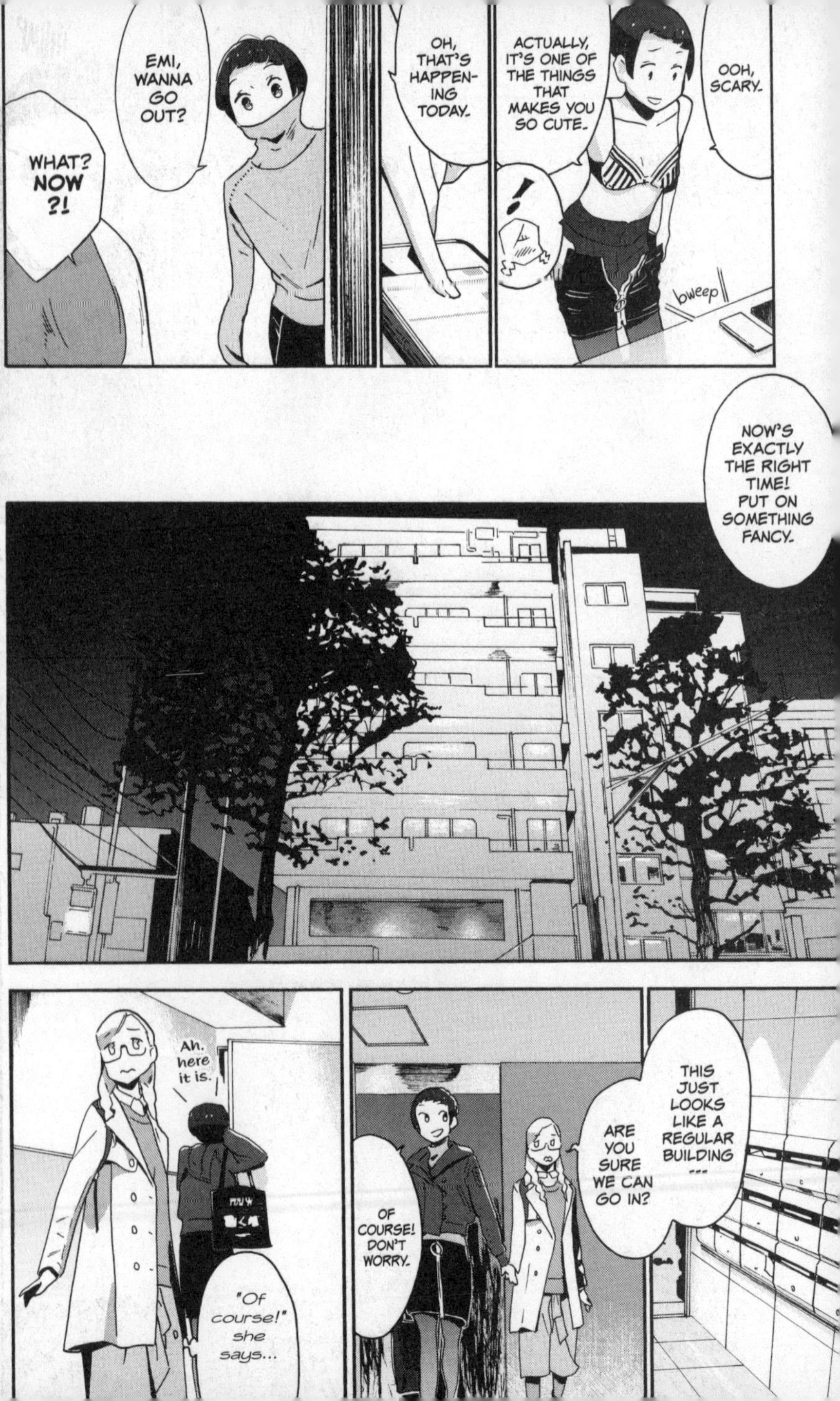
OOH, SCARY.
ACTUALLY, IT'S ONE OF THE THINGS THAT MAKES YOU SO CUTE.
!
bweep
OH, THAT'S HAPPENING TODAY.
EMI, WANNA GO OUT?
WHAT? NOW?!
NOW'S EXACTLY THE RIGHT TIME! PUT ON SOMETHING FANCY.
THIS JUST LOOKS LIKE A REGULAR BUILDING...
ARE YOU SURE WE CAN GO IN?
OF COURSE! DON'T WORRY.
Ah. here it is.
"Of course!" she says...

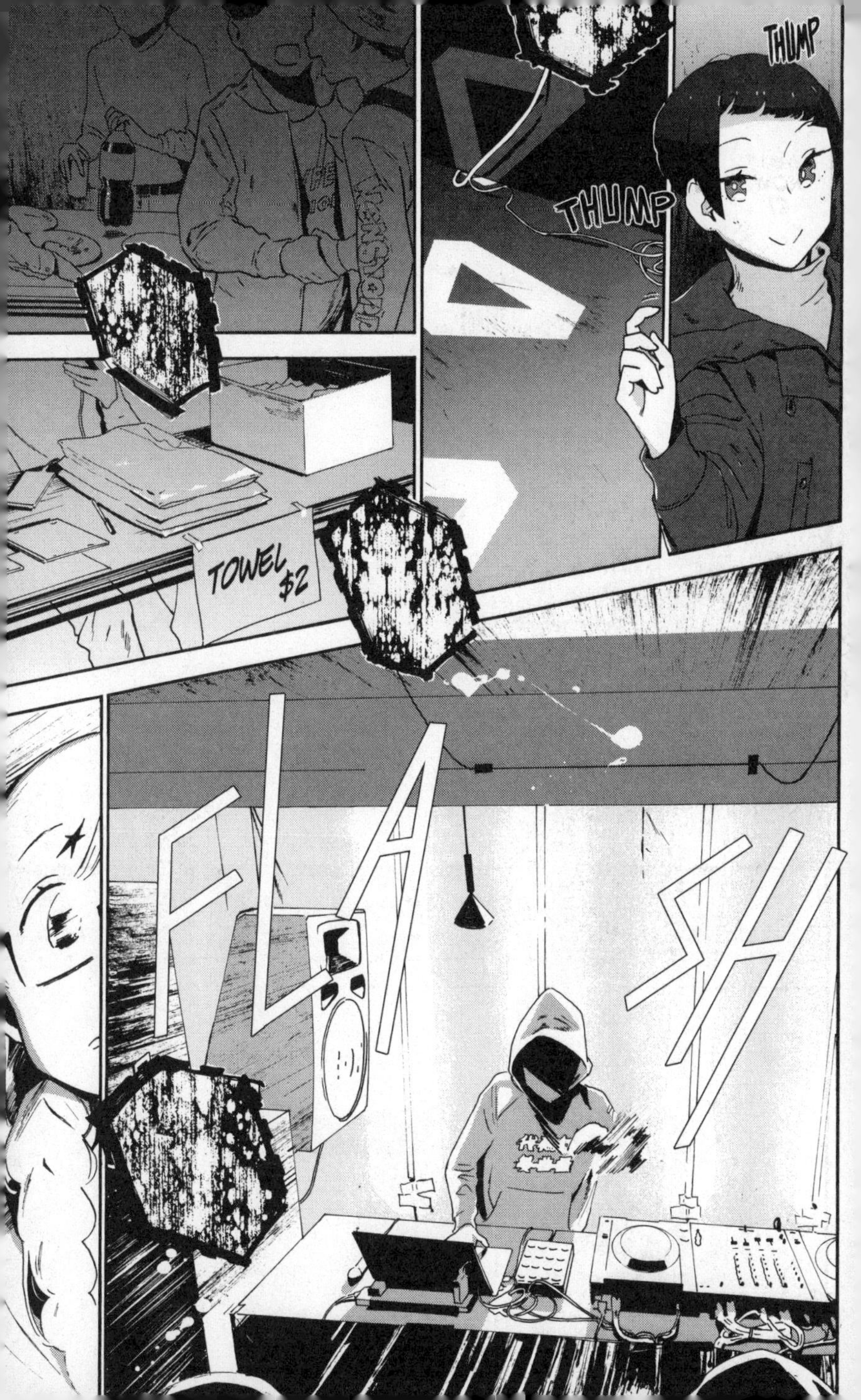
THUMP
THUMP
TOWEL $2
FLASH

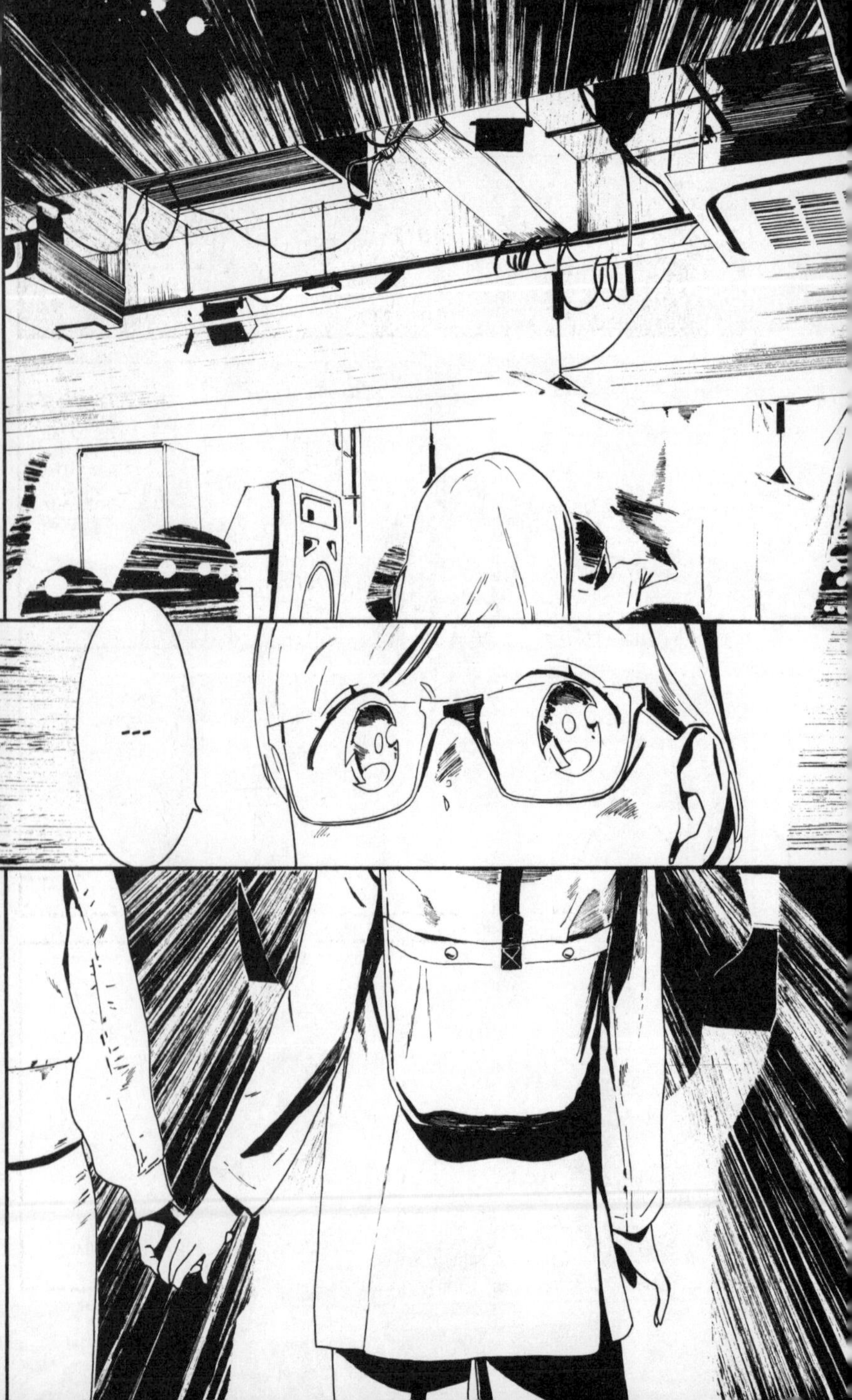
...

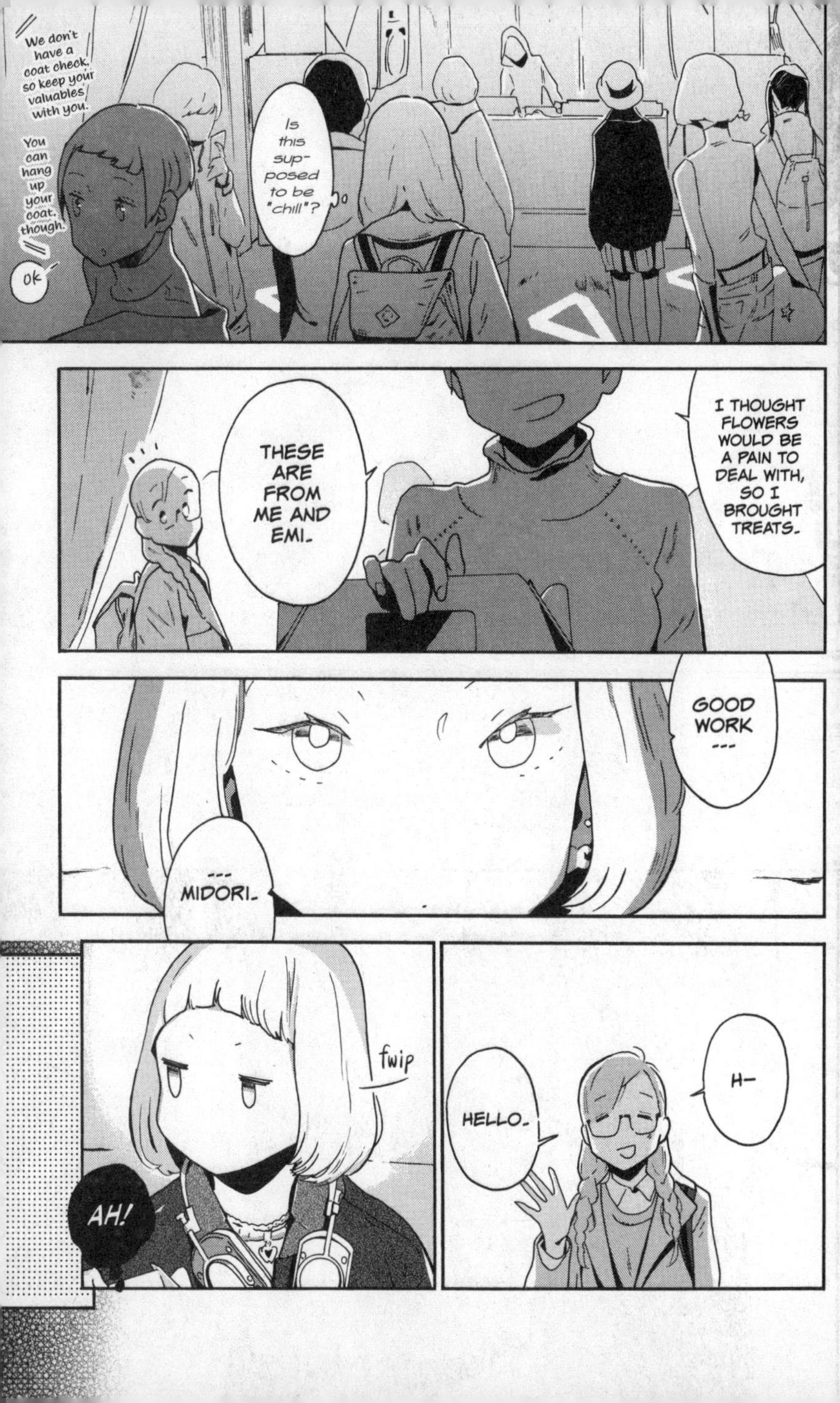
Is this sup-posed to be "chill"?
We don't have a coat check, so keep your valuables with you.
You can hang up your coat, though.
ok
I THOUGHT FLOWERS WOULD BE A PAIN TO DEAL WITH, SO I BROUGHT TREATS.
THESE ARE FROM ME AND EMI.
GOOD WORK ---
--- MIDORI.
H-
HELLO.
fwip
AH!

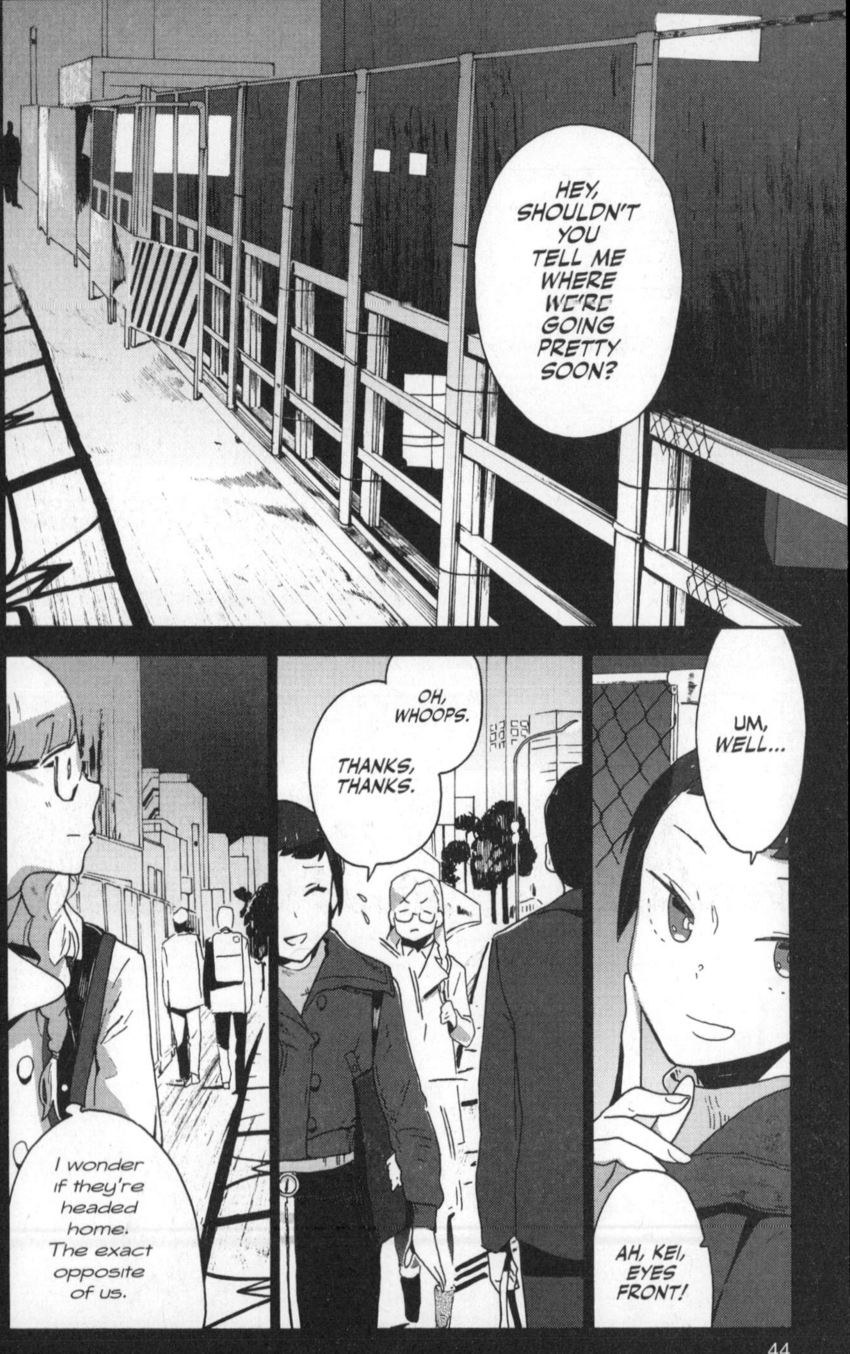
HEY, SHOULDN'T YOU TELL ME WHERE WE'RE GOING PRETTY SOON?
UM, WELL...
AH, KEI, EYES FRONT!
OH, WHOOPS.
THANKS, THANKS.
I wonder if they're headed home. The exact opposite of us.

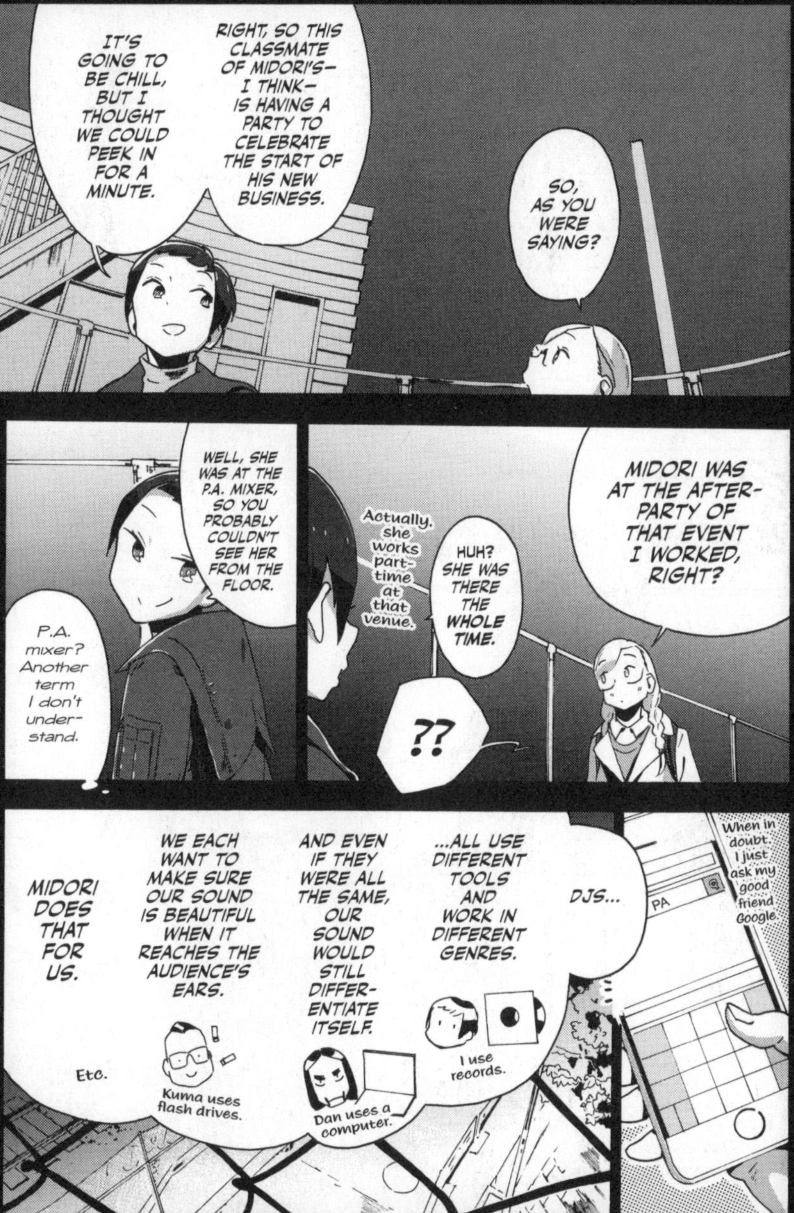

SO, AS YOU WERE SAYING?
RIGHT, SO THIS CLASSMATE OF MIDORI'S—I THINK—IS HAVING A PARTY TO CELEBRATE THE START OF HIS NEW BUSINESS.
IT'S GOING TO BE CHILL, BUT I THOUGHT WE COULD PEEK IN FOR A MINUTE.
MIDORI WAS AT THE AFTER-PARTY OF THAT EVENT I WORKED, RIGHT?
HUH? SHE WAS THERE THE WHOLE TIME.
Actually, she works part-time at that venue.
??
WELL, SHE WAS AT THE P.A. MIXER, SO YOU PROBABLY COULDN'T SEE HER FROM THE FLOOR.
P.A. mixer? Another term I don't under-stand.
When in doubt, I just ask my good friend Google.
PA
DJS...
...ALL USE DIFFERENT TOOLS AND WORK IN DIFFERENT GENRES.
I use records.
AND EVEN IF THEY WERE ALL THE SAME, OUR SOUND WOULD STILL DIFFER-ENTIATE ITSELF.
Dan uses a computer.
WE EACH WANT TO MAKE SURE OUR SOUND IS BEAUTIFUL WHEN IT REACHES THE AUDIENCE'S EARS.
Kuma uses flash drives.
MIDORI DOES THAT FOR US.
Etc.

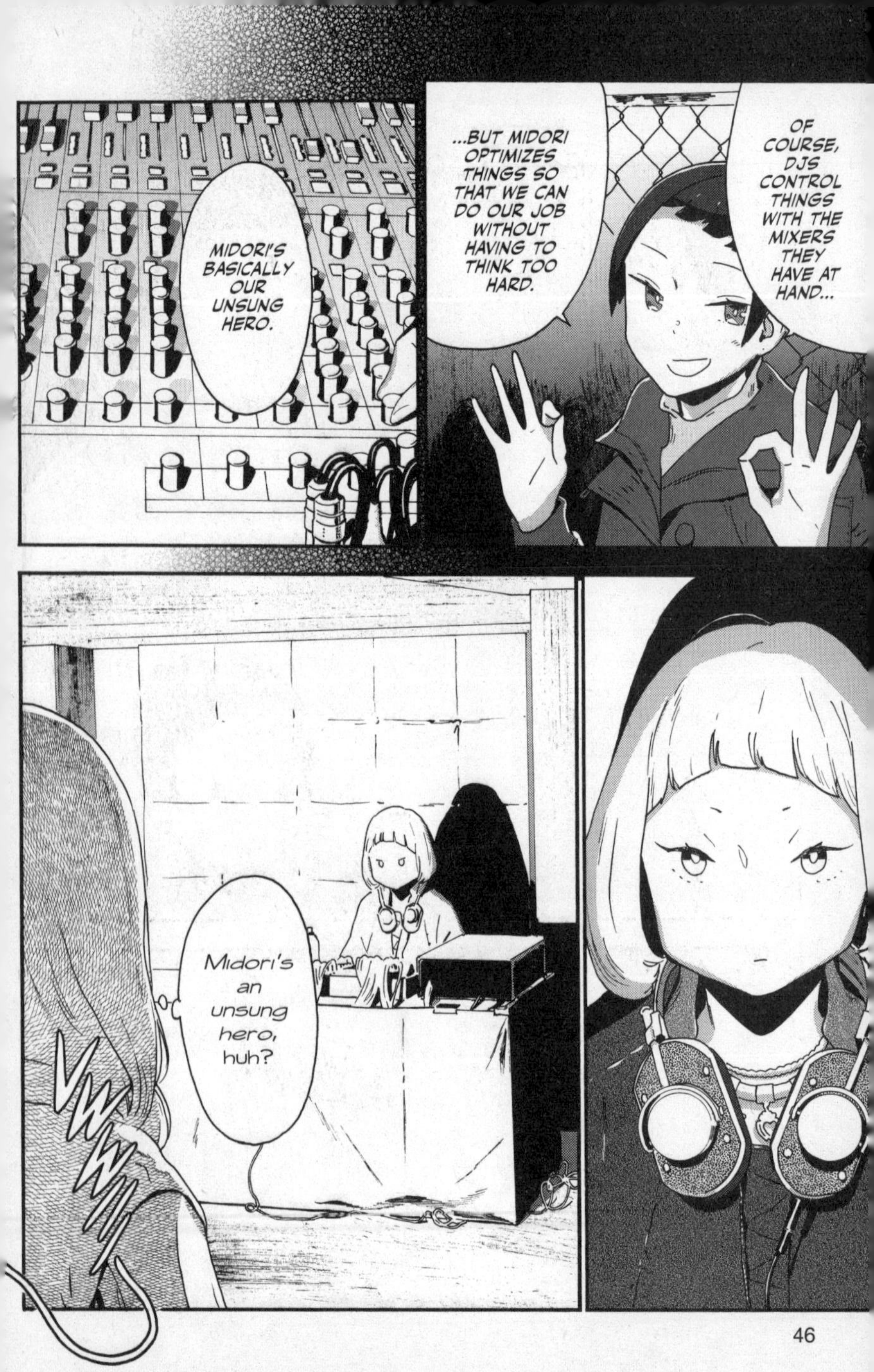
OF COURSE, DJS CONTROL THINGS WITH THE MIXERS THEY HAVE AT HAND...
...BUT MIDORI OPTIMIZES THINGS SO THAT WE CAN DO OUR JOB WITHOUT HAVING TO THINK TOO HARD.
MIDORI'S BASICALLY OUR UNSUNG HERO.
Midori's an unsung hero, huh?

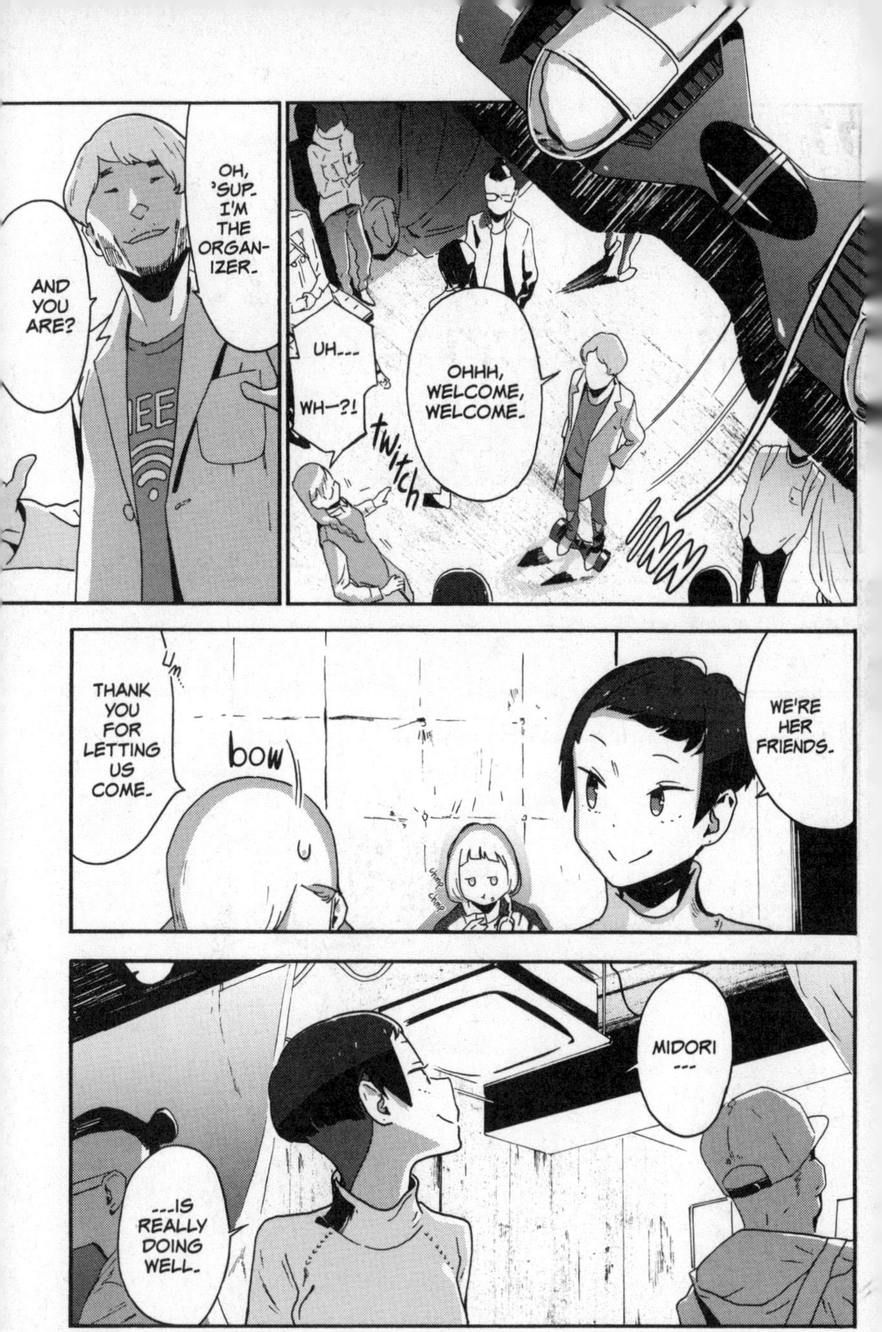
OHHH, WELCOME, WELCOME.
UH...
WH—?!
twitch
OH, 'SUP. I'M THE ORGANIZER.
AND YOU ARE?
WE'RE HER FRIENDS.
Um...
THANK YOU FOR LETTING US COME.
bow
chomp chomp
MIDORI...
...IS REALLY DOING WELL.

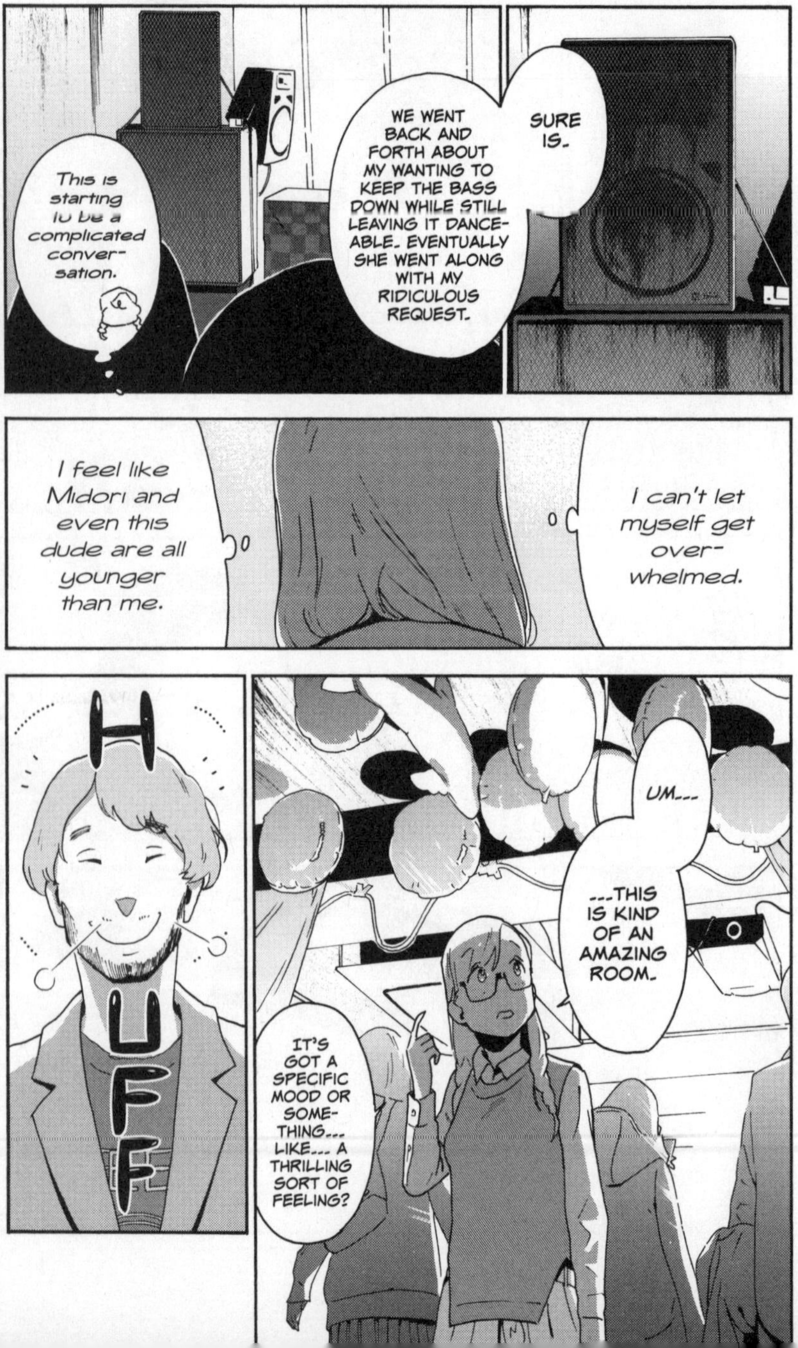
SURE IS.
WE WENT BACK AND FORTH ABOUT MY WANTING TO KEEP THE BASS DOWN WHILE STILL LEAVING IT DANCE-ABLE. EVENTUALLY SHE WENT ALONG WITH MY RIDICULOUS REQUEST.
This is starting to be a complicated conver-sation.
I feel like Midori and even this dude are all younger than me.
I can't let myself get over-whelmed.
UM...
...THIS IS KIND OF AN AMAZING ROOM.
IT'S GOT A SPECIFIC MOOD OR SOME-THING... LIKE... A THRILLING SORT OF FEELING?
HUFF

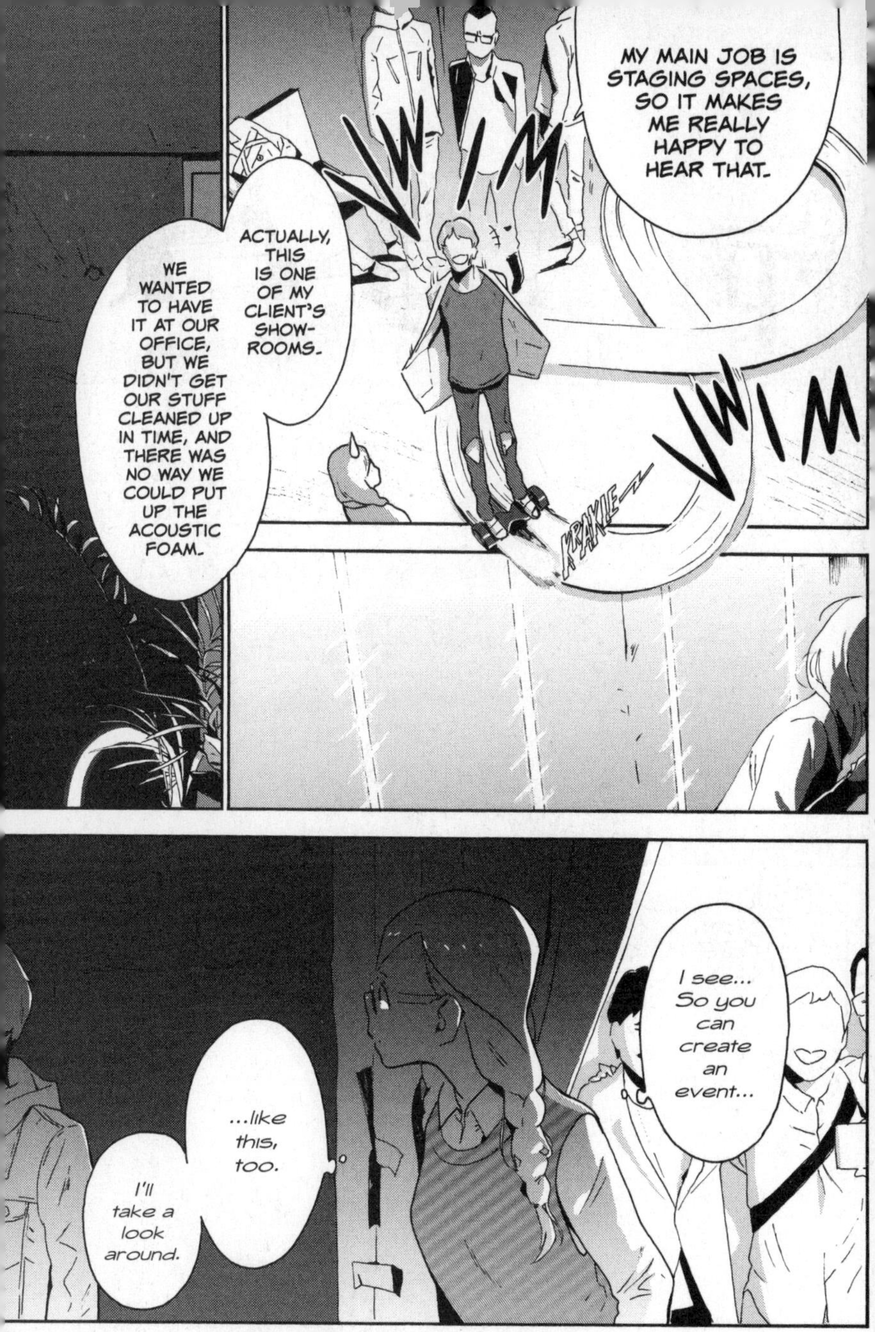
MY MAIN JOB IS STAGING SPACES, SO IT MAKES ME REALLY HAPPY TO HEAR THAT.
VWIM
VWIM
ACTUALLY, THIS IS ONE OF MY CLIENT'S SHOW-ROOMS.
WE WANTED TO HAVE IT AT OUR OFFICE, BUT WE DIDN'T GET OUR STUFF CLEANED UP IN TIME, AND THERE WAS NO WAY WE COULD PUT UP THE ACOUSTIC FOAM.
KRAKLE
I see... So you can create an event...
...like this, too.
I'll take a look around.

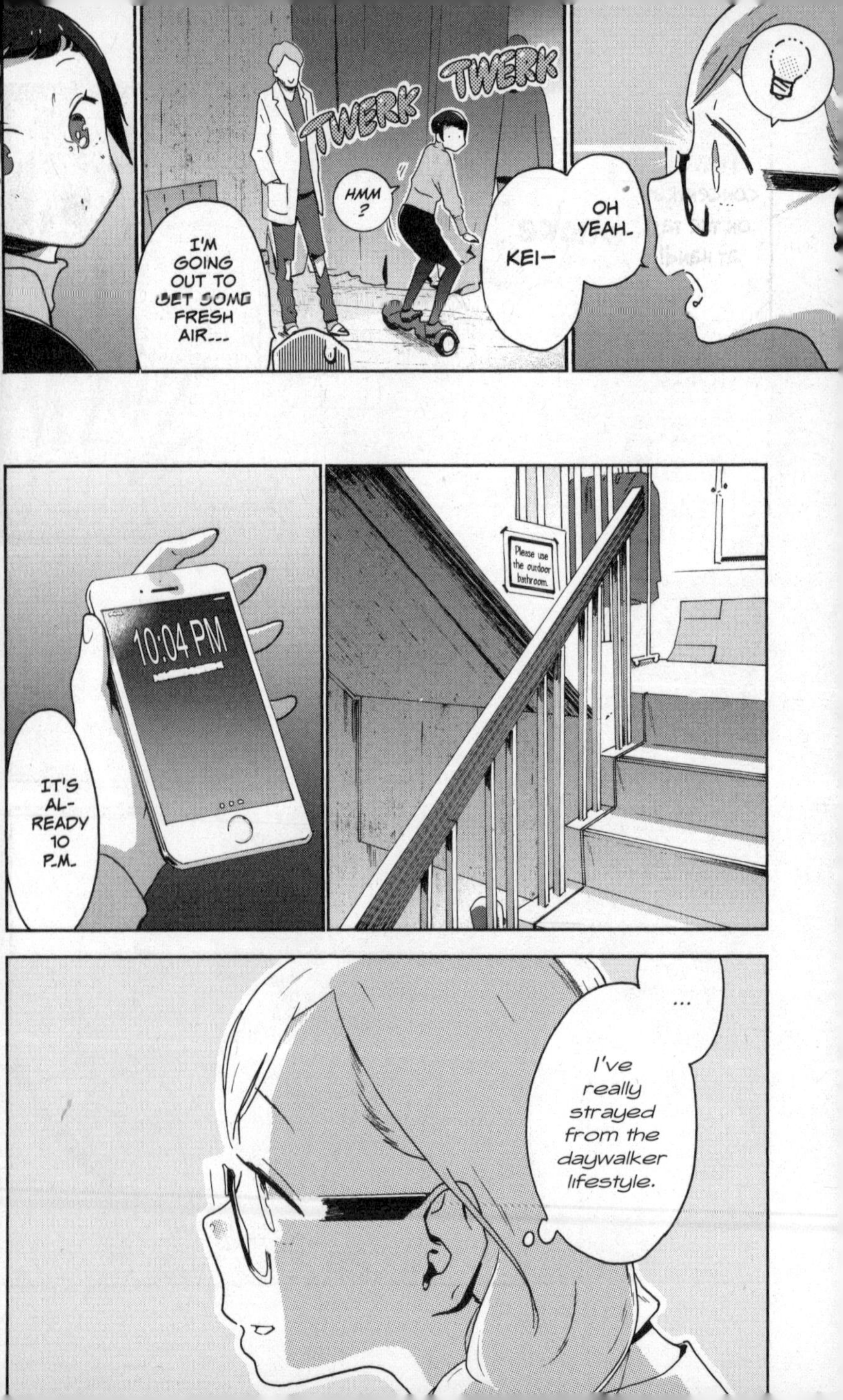

OH YEAH.
KEI—
TWERK TWERK
HMM?
I'M GOING OUT TO GET SOME FRESH AIR...
Please use the outdoor bathroom.
10:04 PM
IT'S ALREADY 10 P.M.
...
I've really strayed from the daywalker lifestyle.

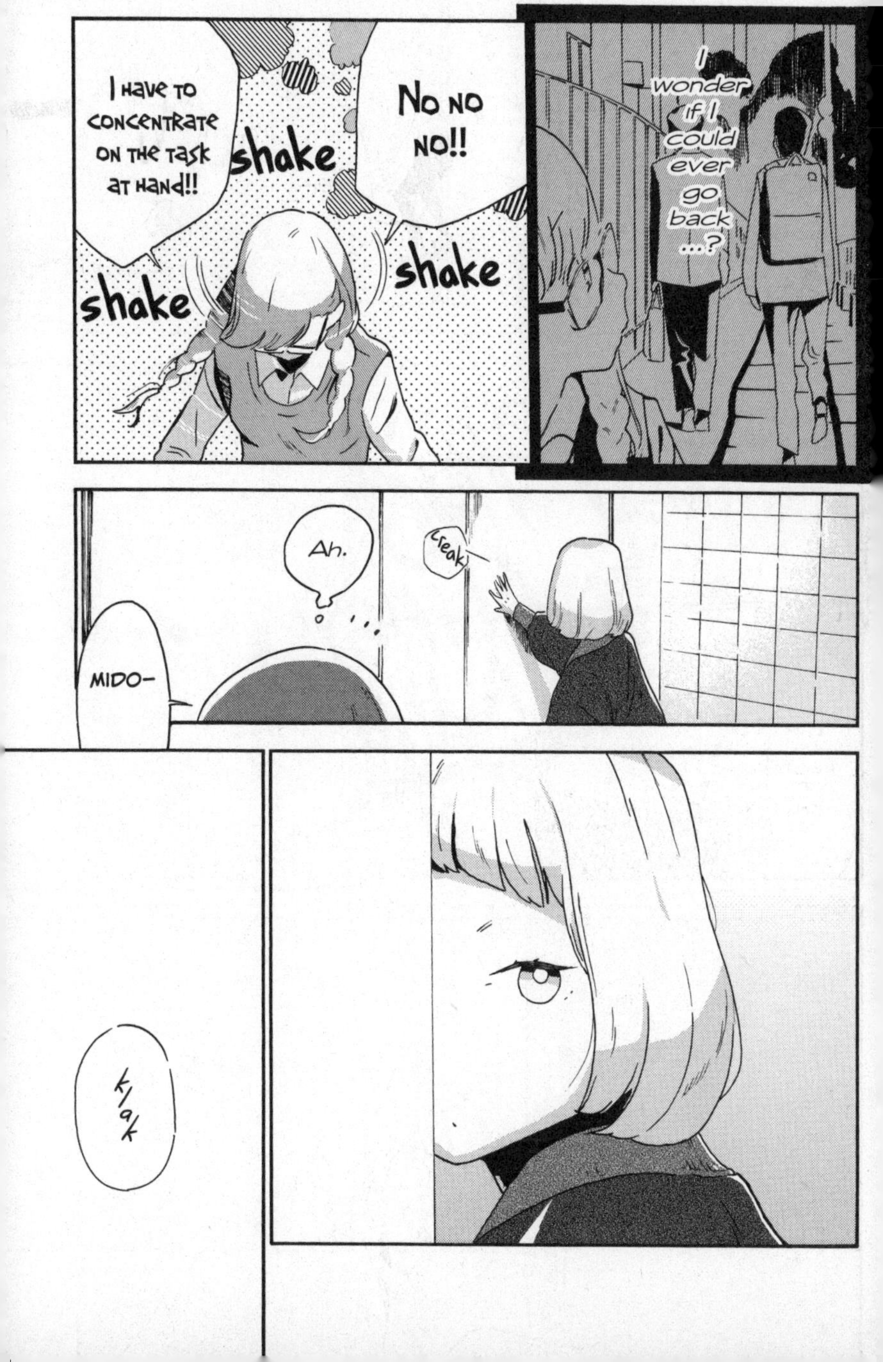
I wonder if I could ever go back ...?
No no no!!
shake
I have to concentrate on the task at hand!!
shake
shake
creak
Ah.
...
MIDO-
klak

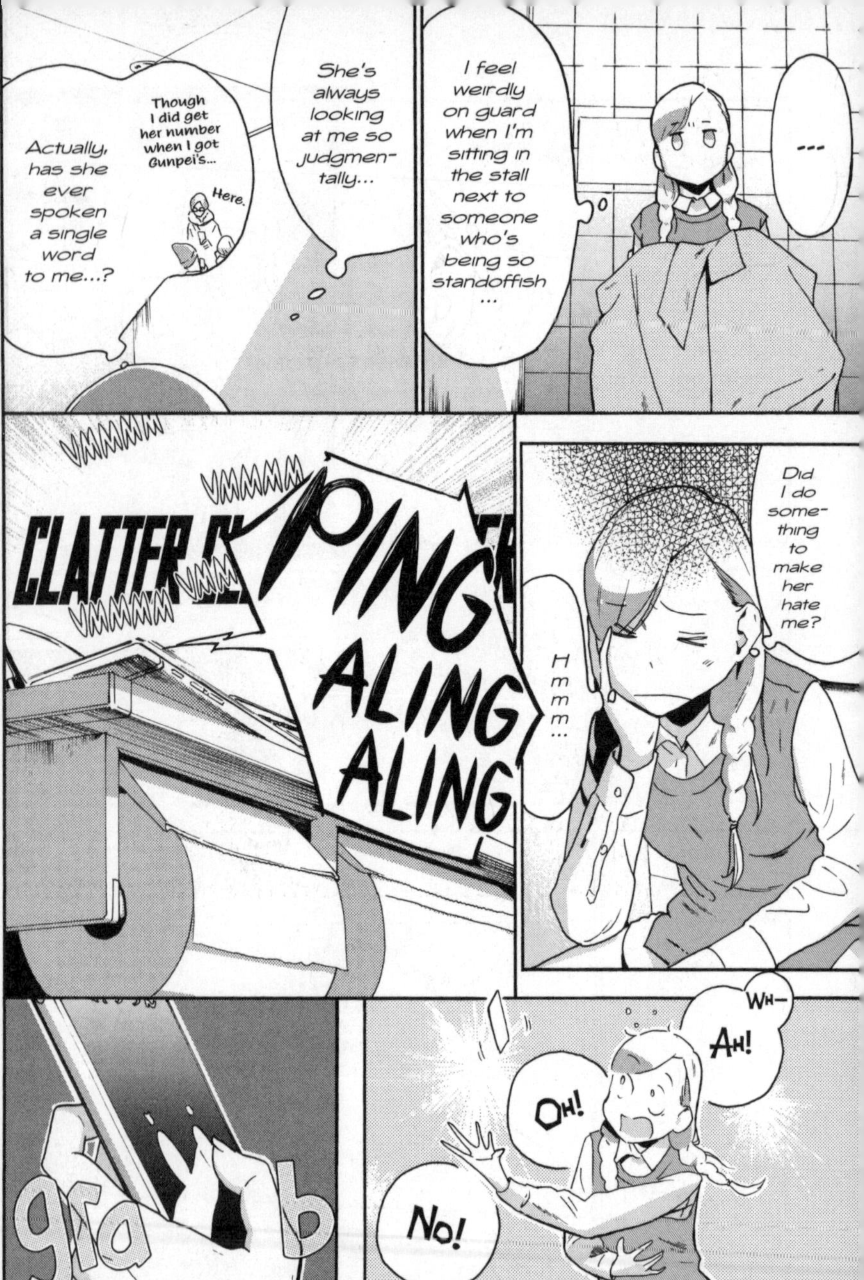
...
I feel weirdly on guard when I'm sitting in the stall next to someone who's being so standoffish...
She's always looking at me so judgmentally...
Actually, has she ever spoken a single word to me...?
Though I did get her number when I got Gunpei's...
Here.
Did I do something to make her hate me?
Hmmm...
VMMMM
VMMMM
PING ALING ALING
CLATTER
VMMMM
VMMMM
WH- AH!
OH!
NO!
grab

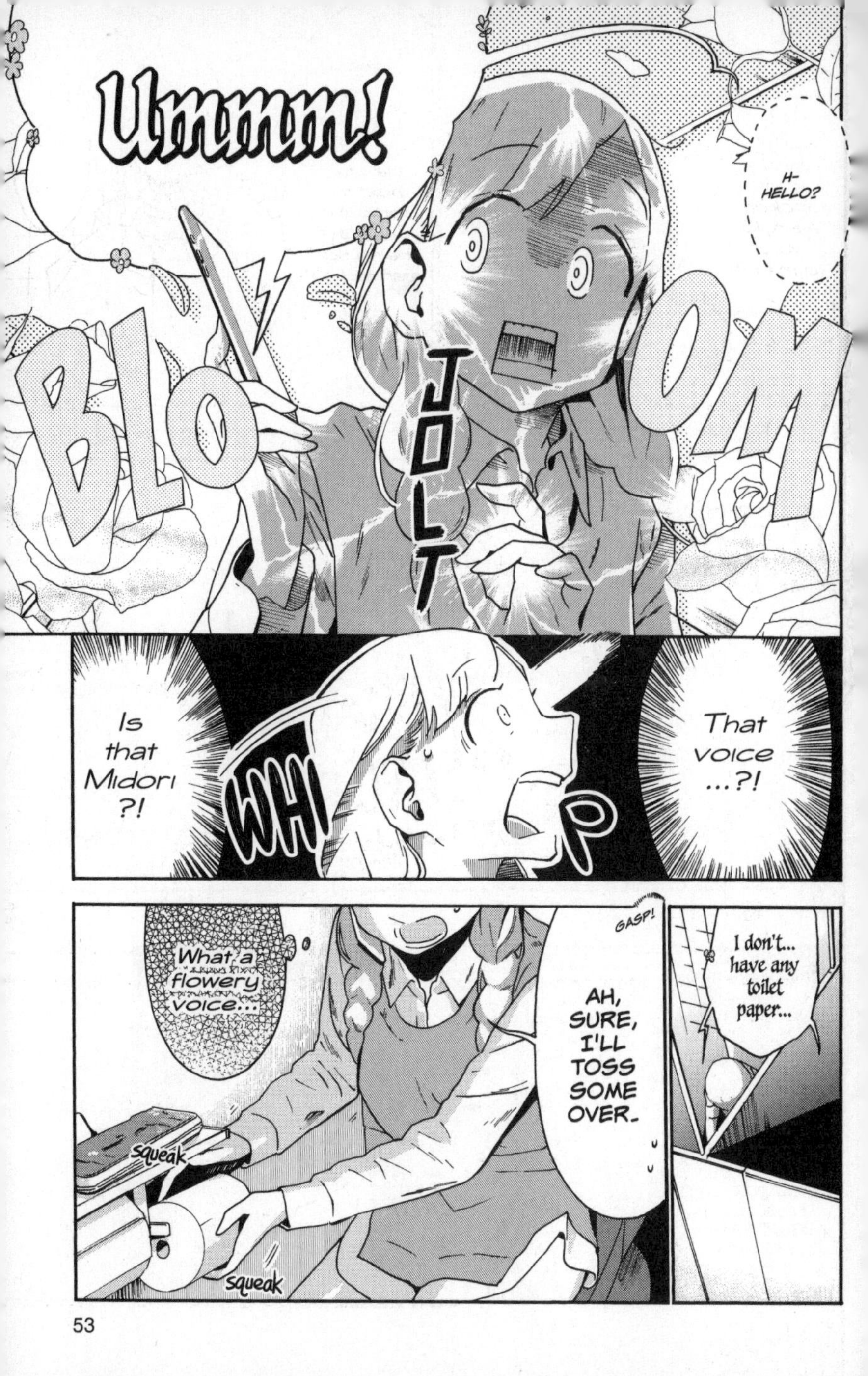
H-HELLO?
Ummmm!
BLOOM
JOLT
That voice ...?!
WHIP
Is that Midori ?!
I don't... have any toilet paper...
GASP!
AH, SURE, I'LL TOSS SOME OVER.
What a flowery voice...
squeak
squeak

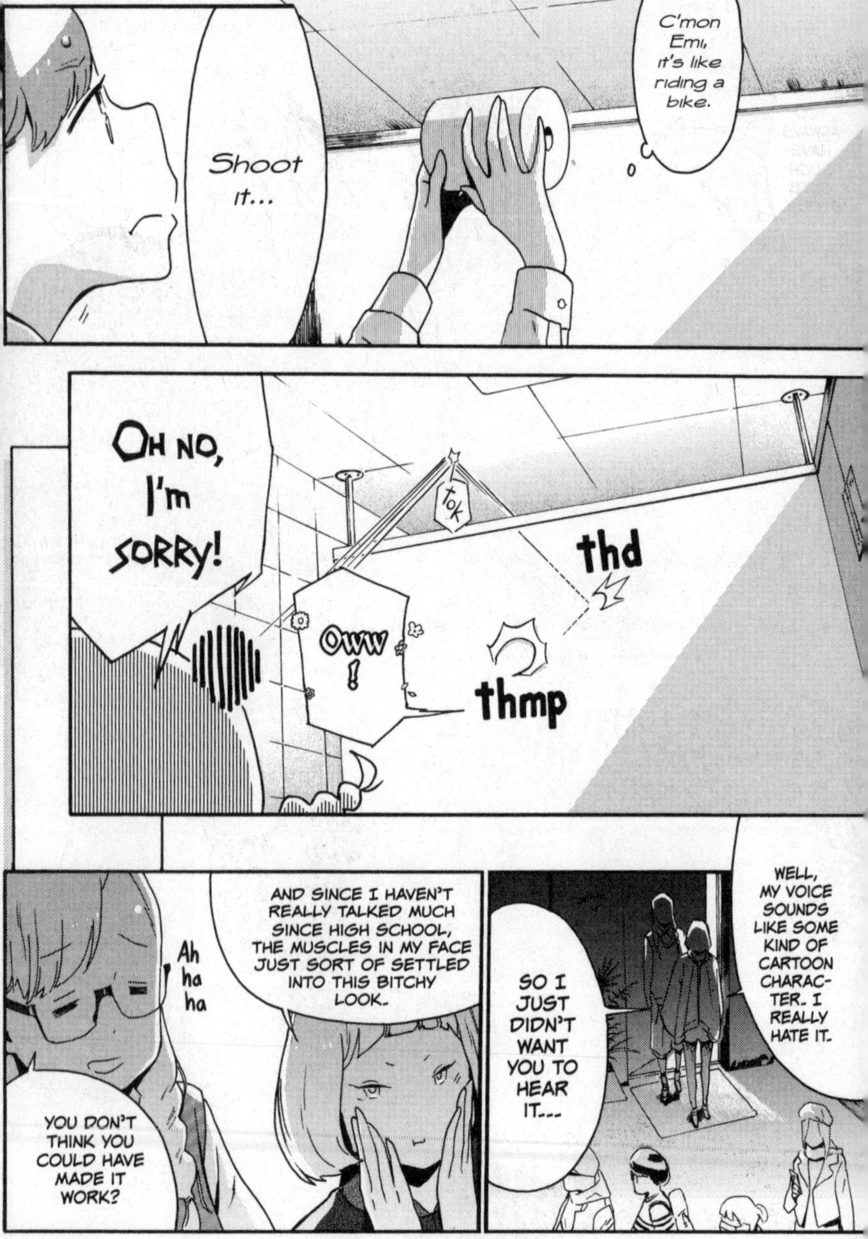
C'mon Emi, it's like riding a bike.
Shoot it...
tok
thd
Oww!
thmp
OH NO, I'm SORRY!
WELL, MY VOICE SOUNDS LIKE SOME KIND OF CARTOON CHARACTER. I REALLY HATE IT.
SO I JUST DIDN'T WANT YOU TO HEAR IT...
AND SINCE I HAVEN'T REALLY TALKED MUCH SINCE HIGH SCHOOL, THE MUSCLES IN MY FACE JUST SORT OF SETTLED INTO THIS BITCHY LOOK.
Ah ha ha
YOU DON'T THINK YOU COULD HAVE MADE IT WORK?

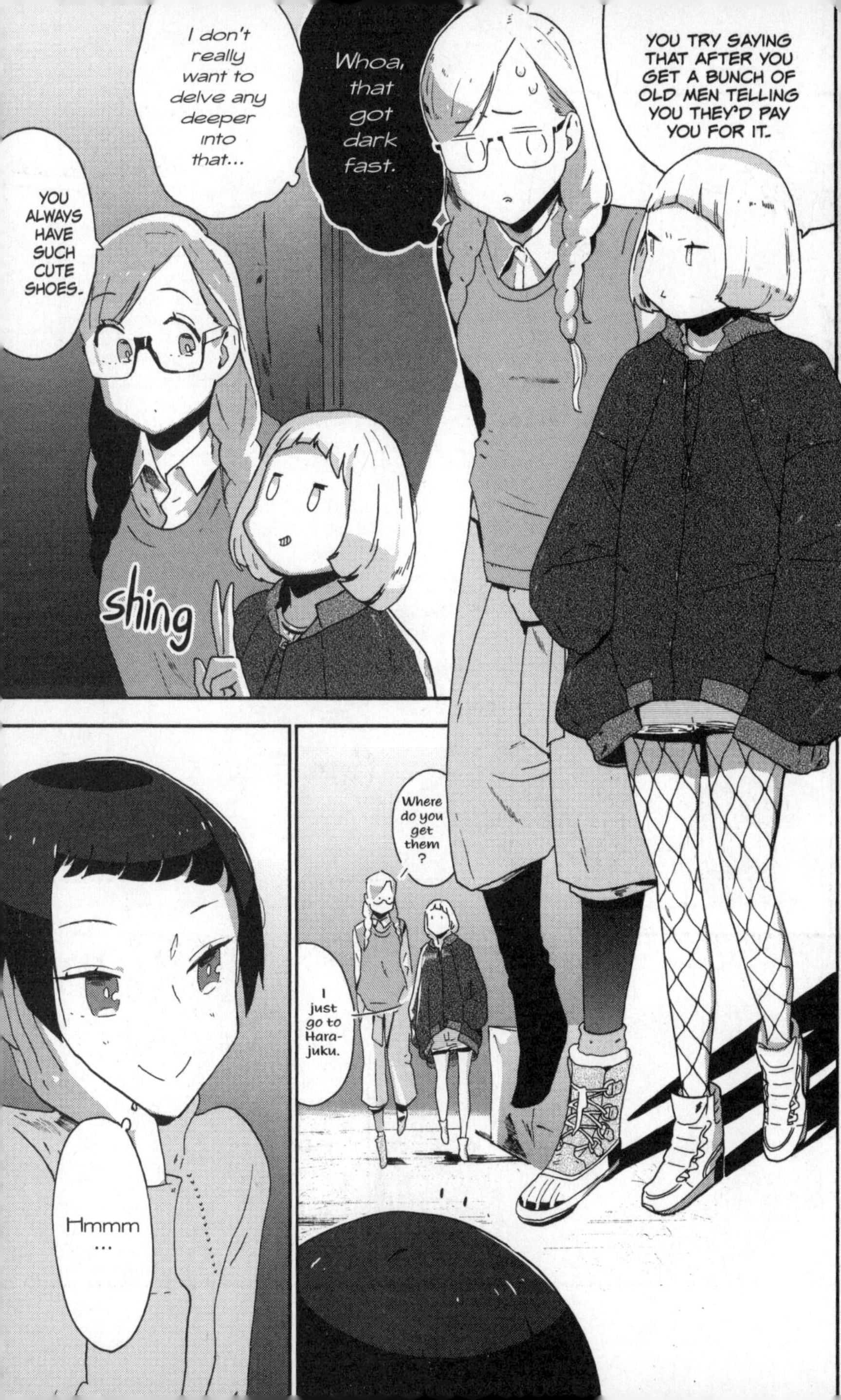
YOU TRY SAYING THAT AFTER YOU GET A BUNCH OF OLD MEN TELLING YOU THEY'D PAY YOU FOR IT.
Whoa, that got dark fast.
I don't really want to delve any deeper into that...
YOU ALWAYS HAVE SUCH CUTE SHOES.
shing
Where do you get them?
I just go to Harajuku.
Hmmm ...

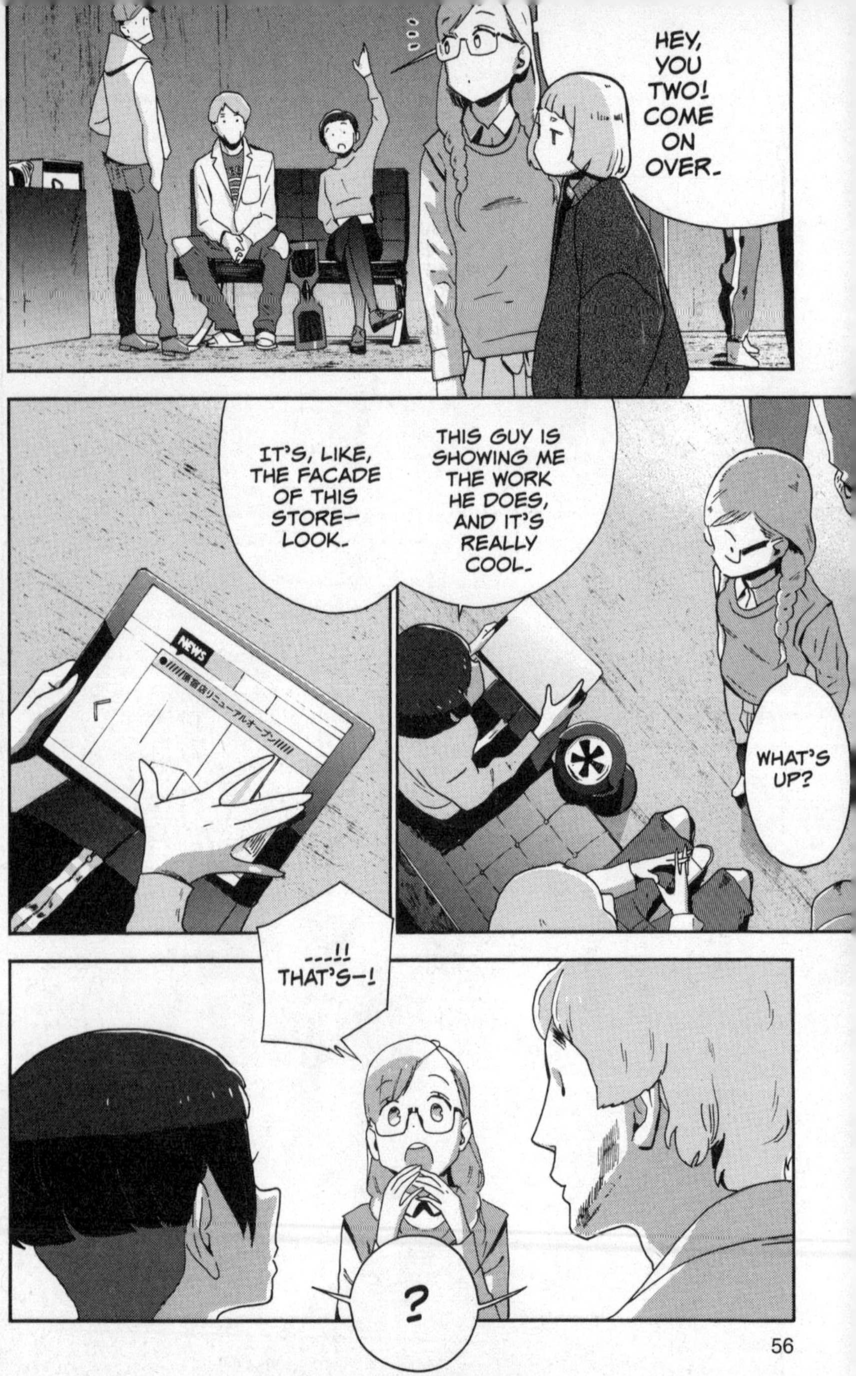
HEY, YOU TWO! COME ON OVER.
WHAT'S UP?
THIS GUY IS SHOWING ME THE WORK HE DOES, AND IT'S REALLY COOL.
IT'S, LIKE, THE FACADE OF THIS STORE— LOOK.
NEWS
...!! THAT'S—!
?

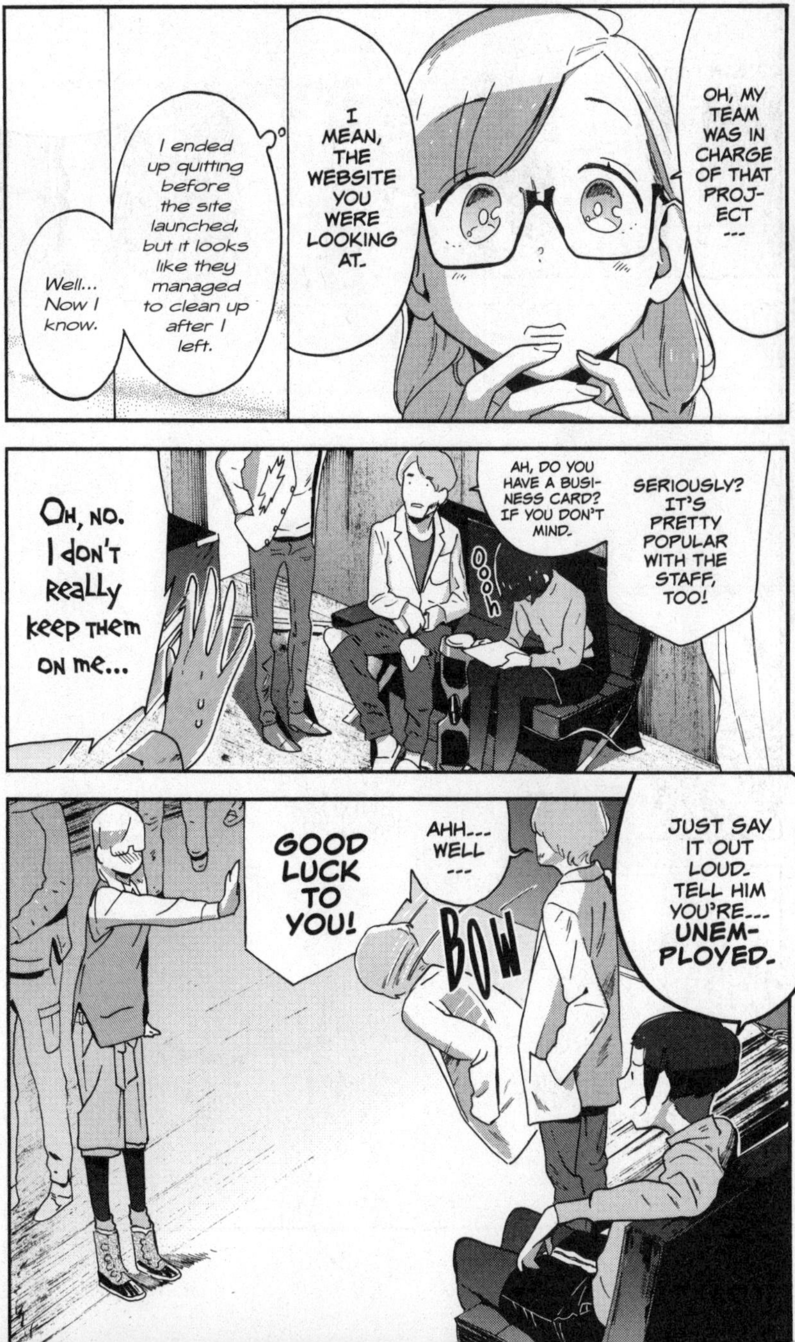
OH, MY TEAM WAS IN CHARGE OF THAT PROJ-ECT---
I MEAN, THE WEBSITE YOU WERE LOOKING AT.
I ended up quitting before the site launched, but it looks like they managed to clean up after I left.
Well... Now I know.
SERIOUSLY? IT'S PRETTY POPULAR WITH THE STAFF, TOO!
AH, DO YOU HAVE A BUSI-NESS CARD? IF YOU DON'T MIND.
Oooh
OH, NO. I DON'T REALLY KEEP THEM ON ME...
JUST SAY IT OUT LOUD. TELL HIM YOU'RE... UNEM-PLOYED.
AHH... WELL ---
BOW
GOOD LUCK TO YOU!

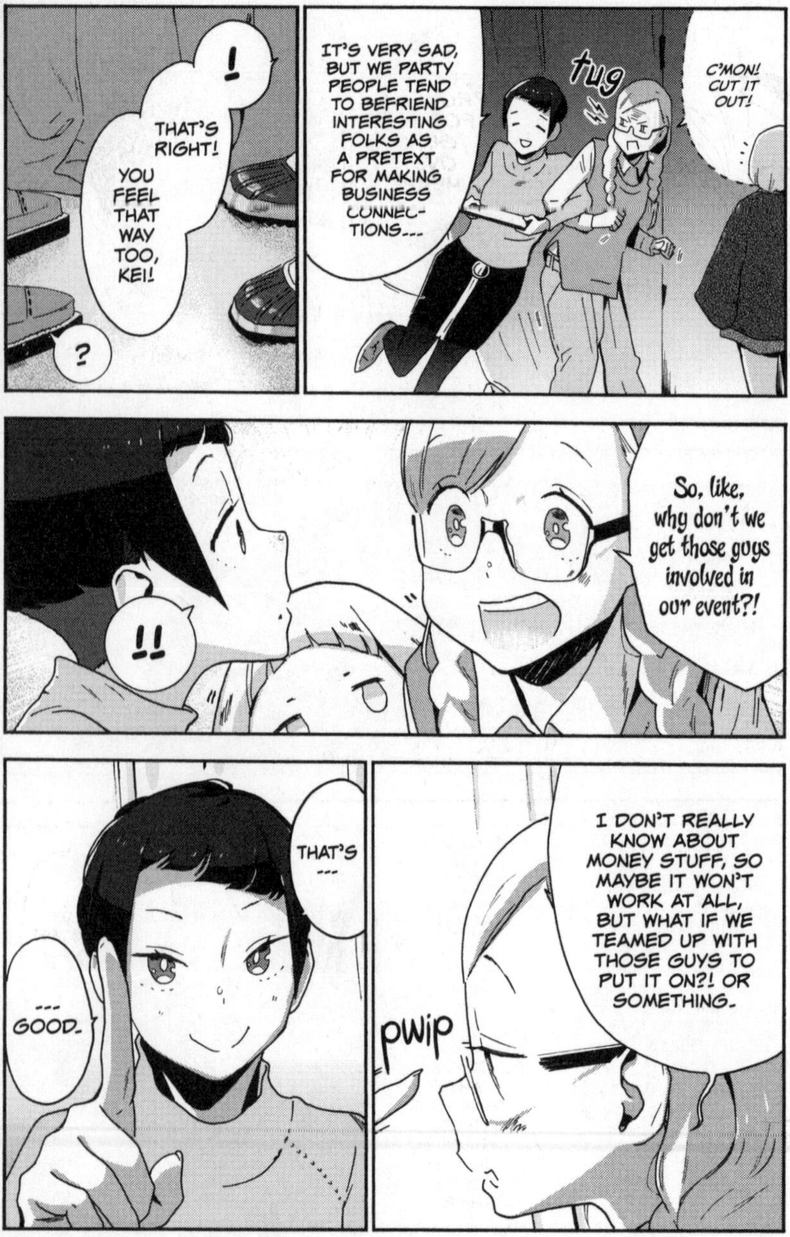
C'MON! CUT IT OUT!
tug
IT'S VERY SAD, BUT WE PARTY PEOPLE TEND TO BEFRIEND INTERESTING FOLKS AS A PRETEXT FOR MAKING BUSINESS CONNEC-TIONS...
!
THAT'S RIGHT! YOU FEEL THAT WAY TOO, KEI!
?
So, like, why don't we get those guys involved in our event?!
!!
I DON'T REALLY KNOW ABOUT MONEY STUFF, SO MAYBE IT WON'T WORK AT ALL, BUT WHAT IF WE TEAMED UP WITH THOSE GUYS TO PUT IT ON?! OR SOMETHING.
pwip
THAT'S...
...GOOD.

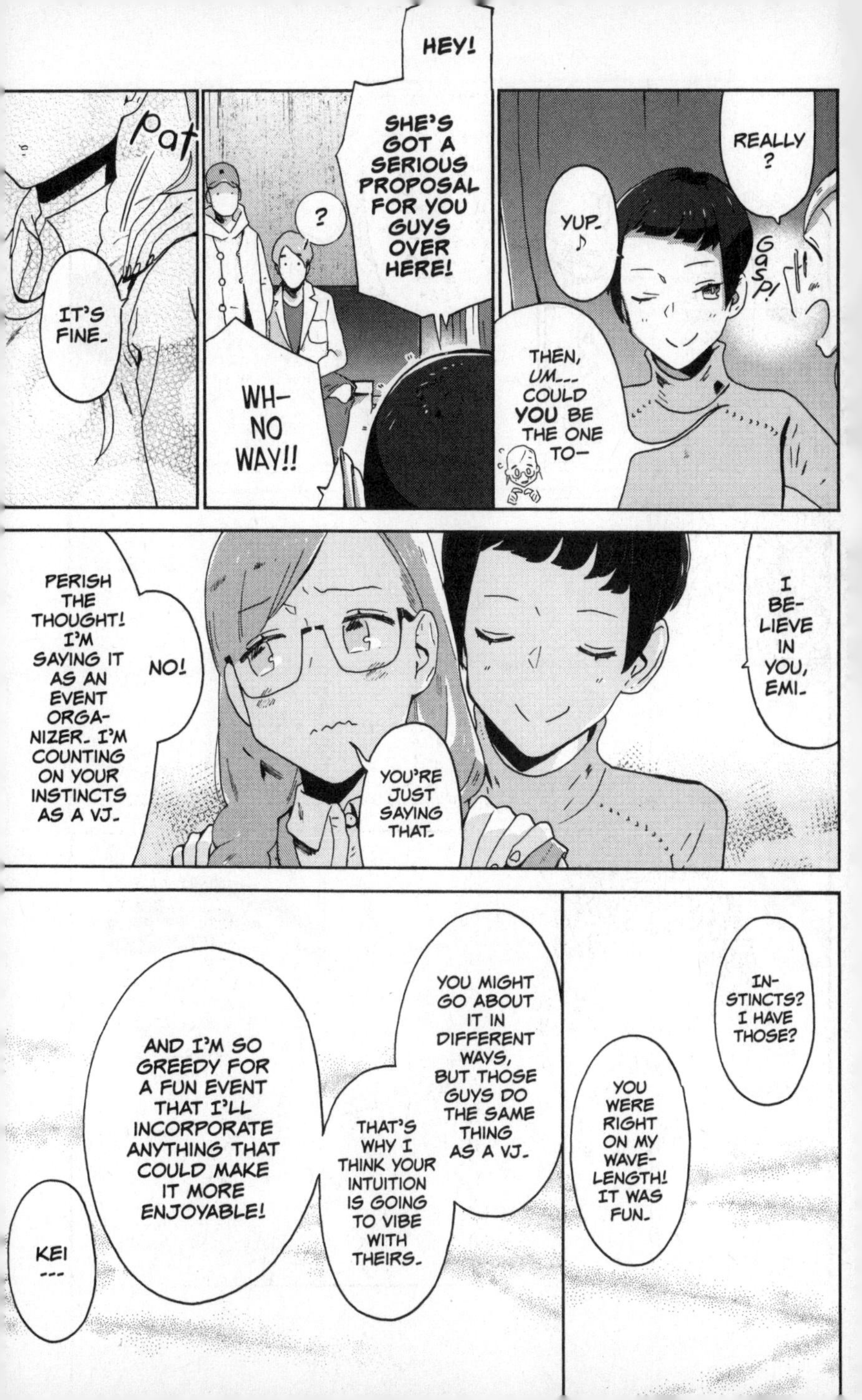
REALLY?
Gasp!
YUP. ♪
THEN, UM... COULD YOU BE THE ONE TO—
HEY!
SHE'S GOT A SERIOUS PROPOSAL FOR YOU GUYS OVER HERE!
?
WH— NO WAY!!
pat
IT'S FINE.
I BELIEVE IN YOU, EMI.
YOU'RE JUST SAYING THAT.
NO!
PERISH THE THOUGHT! I'M SAYING IT AS AN EVENT ORGANIZER. I'M COUNTING ON YOUR INSTINCTS AS A VJ.
INSTINCTS? I HAVE THOSE?
YOU WERE RIGHT ON MY WAVELENGTH! IT WAS FUN.
YOU MIGHT GO ABOUT IT IN DIFFERENT WAYS, BUT THOSE GUYS DO THE SAME THING AS A VJ.
THAT'S WHY I THINK YOUR INTUITION IS GOING TO VIBE WITH THEIRS.
AND I'M SO GREEDY FOR A FUN EVENT THAT I'LL INCORPORATE ANYTHING THAT COULD MAKE IT MORE ENJOYABLE!
KEI...

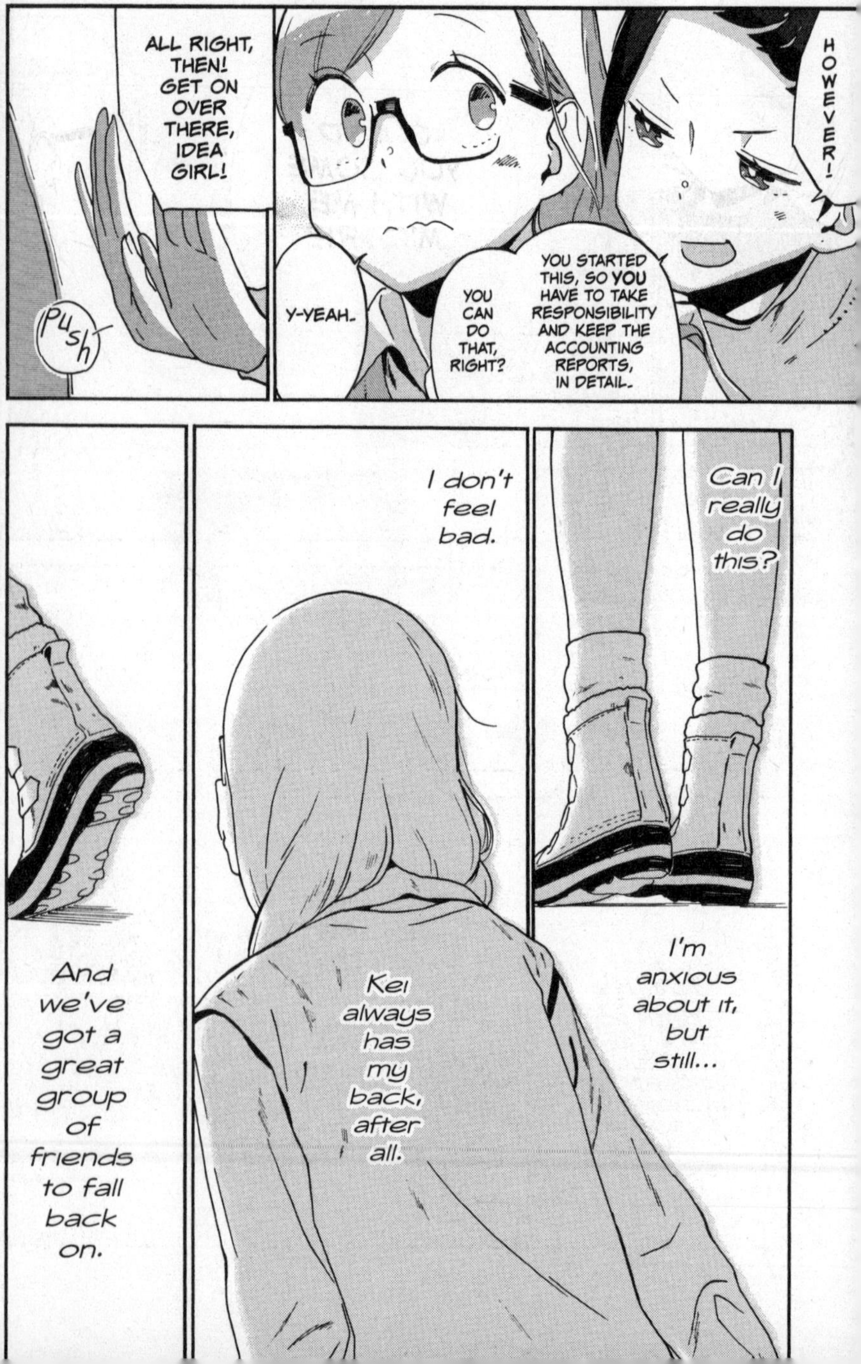
HOWEVER!
YOU STARTED THIS, SO YOU HAVE TO TAKE RESPONSIBILITY AND KEEP THE ACCOUNTING REPORTS, IN DETAIL.
YOU CAN DO THAT, RIGHT?
Y-YEAH.
ALL RIGHT, THEN! GET ON OVER THERE, IDEA GIRL!
push
Can I really do this?
I'm anxious about it, but still...
I don't feel bad.
Kei always has my back, after all.
And we've got a great group of friends to fall back on.

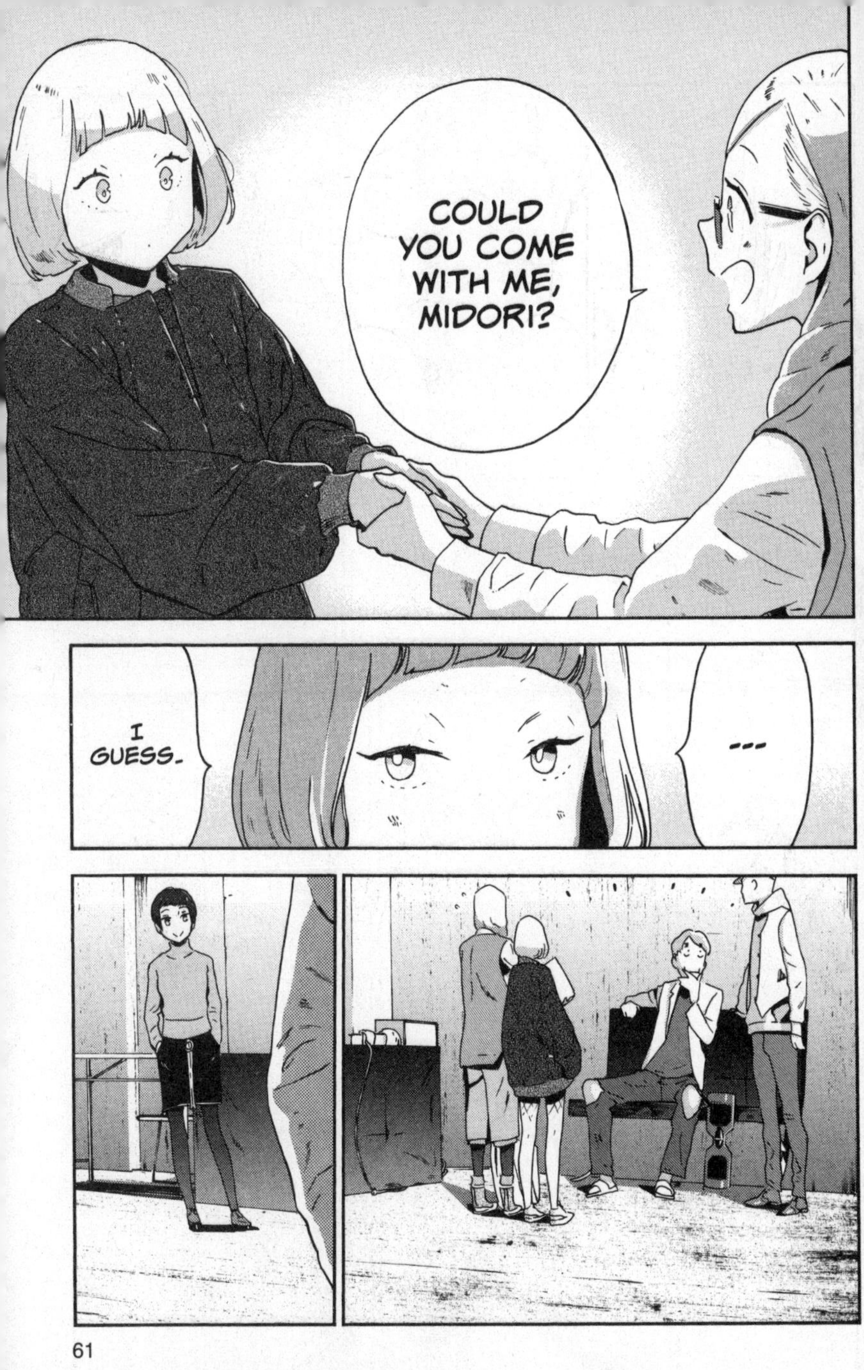
COULD YOU COME WITH ME, MIDORI?
...
I GUESS.

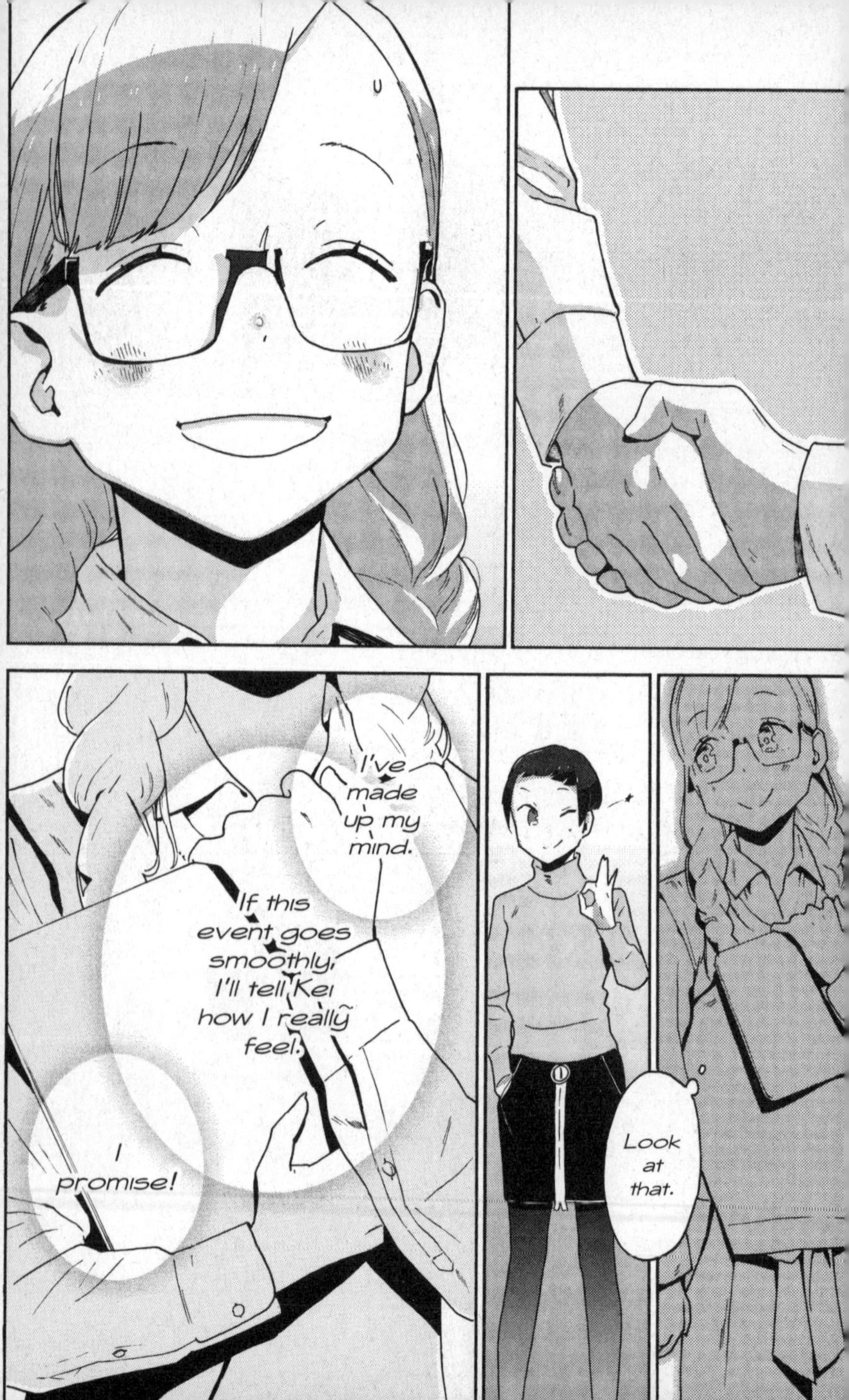
Look at that.
I've made up my mind.
If this event goes smoothly, I'll tell Kei how I really feel.
I promise!

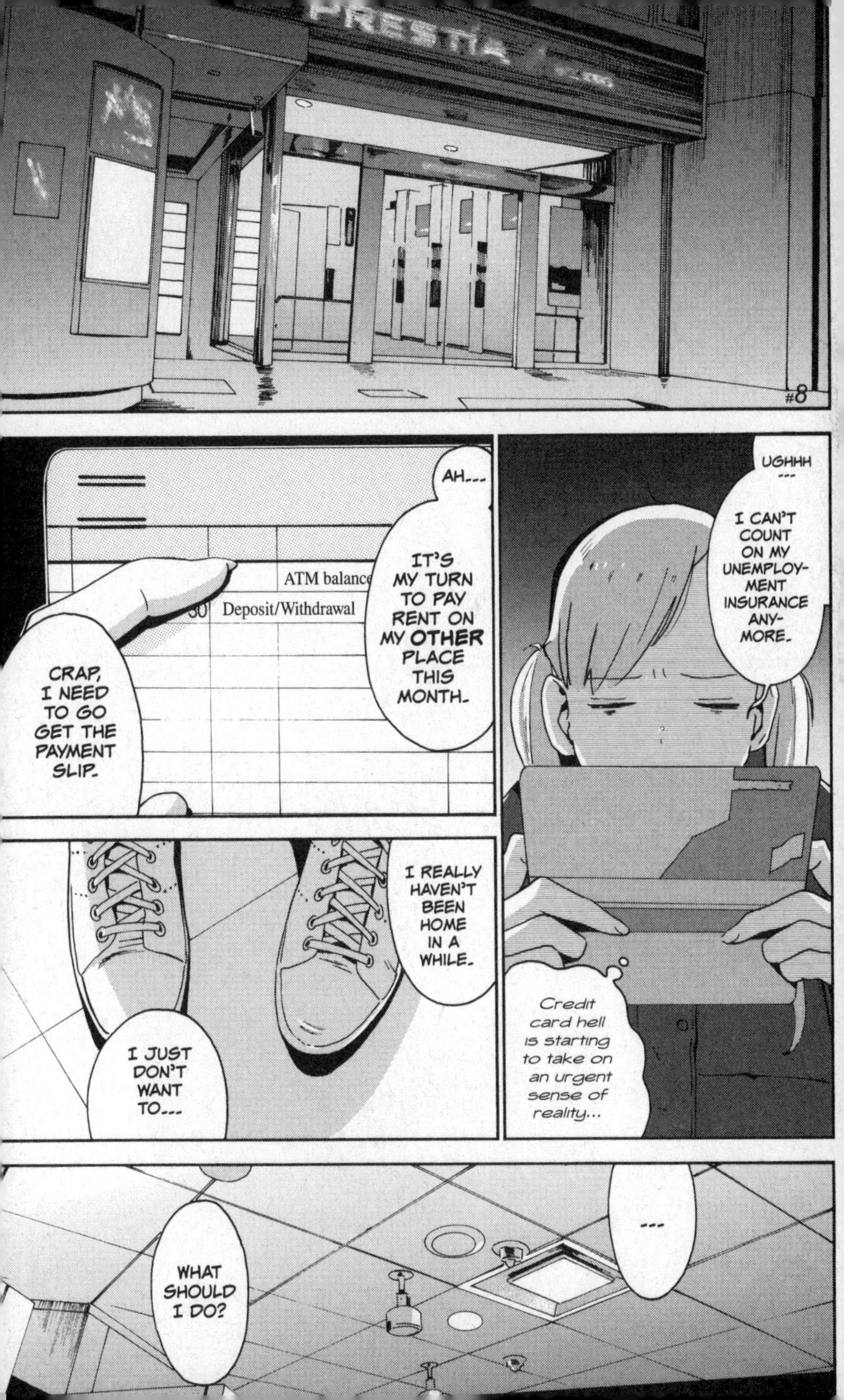
PRESTIA
#8
UGHHH ---
I CAN'T COUNT ON MY UNEMPLOYMENT INSURANCE ANYMORE.
Credit card hell is starting to take on an urgent sense of reality...
AH---
IT'S MY TURN TO PAY RENT ON MY OTHER PLACE THIS MONTH.
ATM balance
Deposit/Withdrawal
CRAP, I NEED TO GO GET THE PAYMENT SLIP.
I REALLY HAVEN'T BEEN HOME IN A WHILE.
I JUST DON'T WANT TO---

WHAT SHOULD I DO?

AFTER HOURS #8

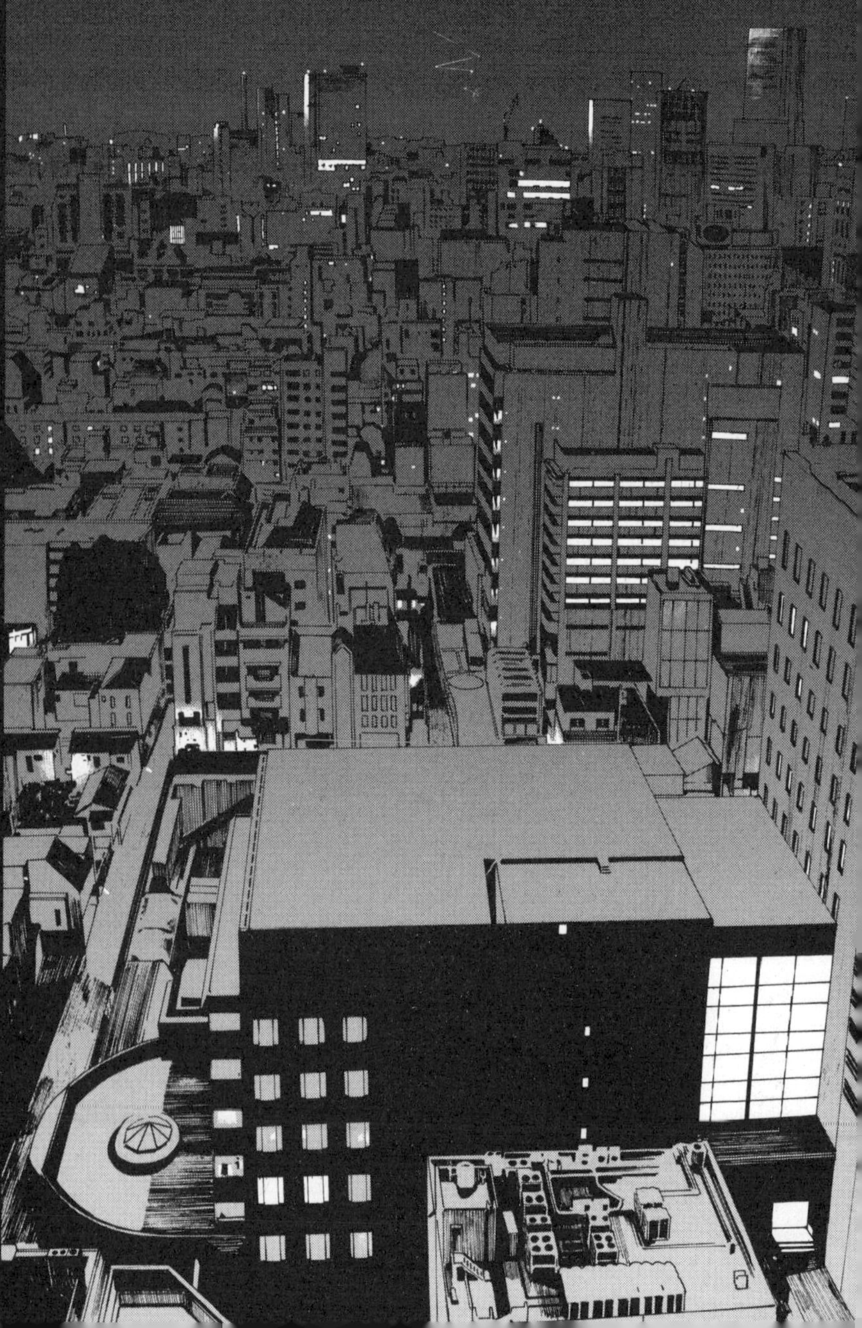

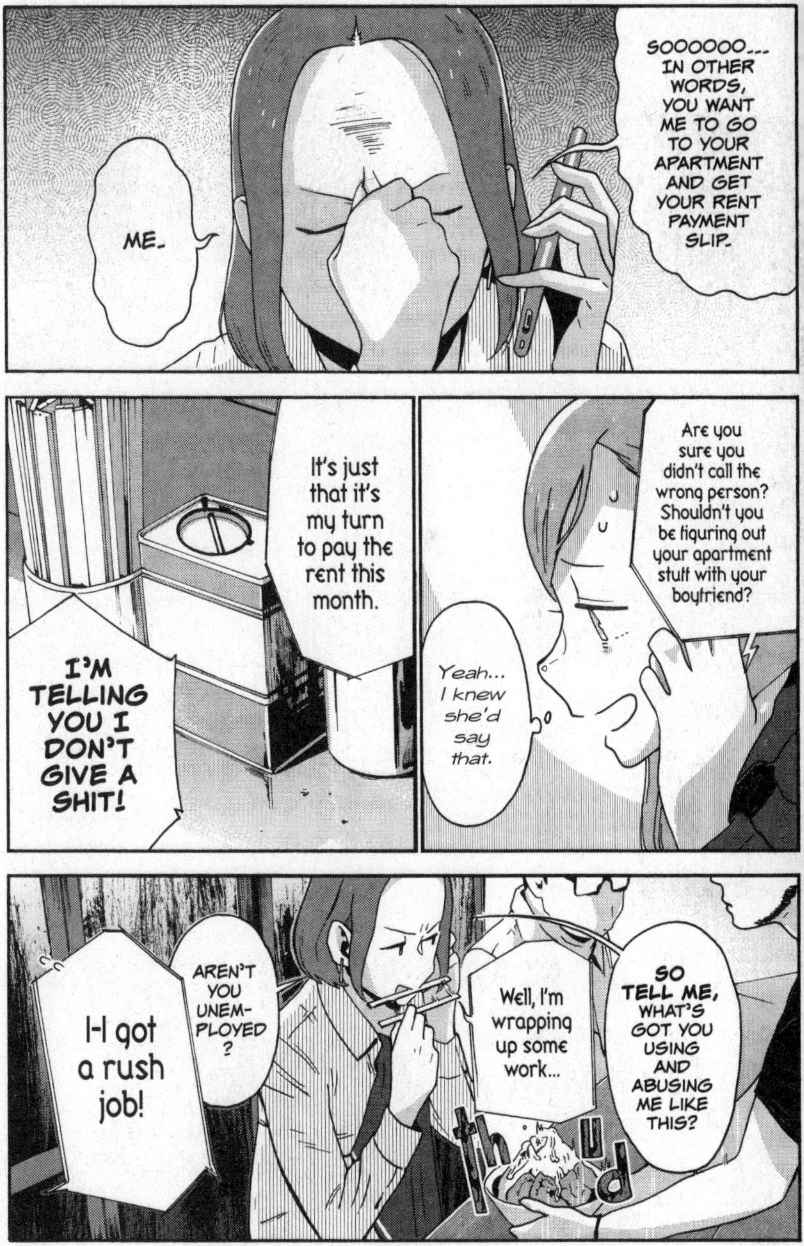
SOOOOOO... IN OTHER WORDS, YOU WANT ME TO GO TO YOUR APARTMENT AND GET YOUR RENT PAYMENT SLIP.
ME.
Are you sure you didn't call the wrong person? Shouldn't you be figuring out your apartment stuff with your boyfriend?
Yeah... I knew she'd say that.
It's just that it's my turn to pay the rent this month.
I'M TELLING YOU I DON'T GIVE A SHIT!
SO TELL ME, WHAT'S GOT YOU USING AND ABUSING ME LIKE THIS?
thud
Well, I'm wrapping up some work...
AREN'T YOU UNEMPLOYED?
I-I got a rush job!

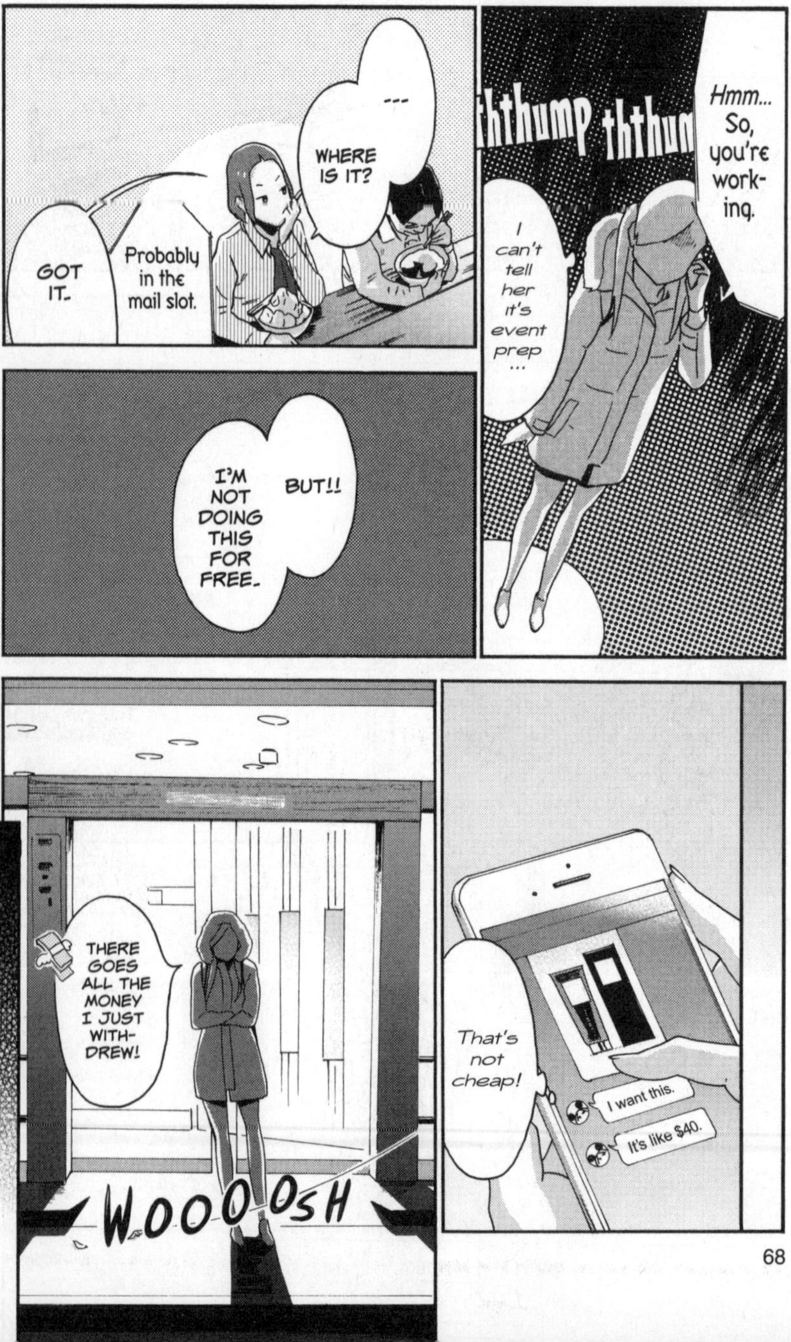
ththump ththum
Hmm... So, you're work-ing.
I can't tell her it's event prep...

WHERE IS IT?
Probably in the mail slot.
GOT IT.
BUT!!
I'M NOT DOING THIS FOR FREE.
I want this.
It's like $40.
That's not cheap!
THERE GOES ALL THE MONEY I JUST WITH-DREW!
WOOOOSH

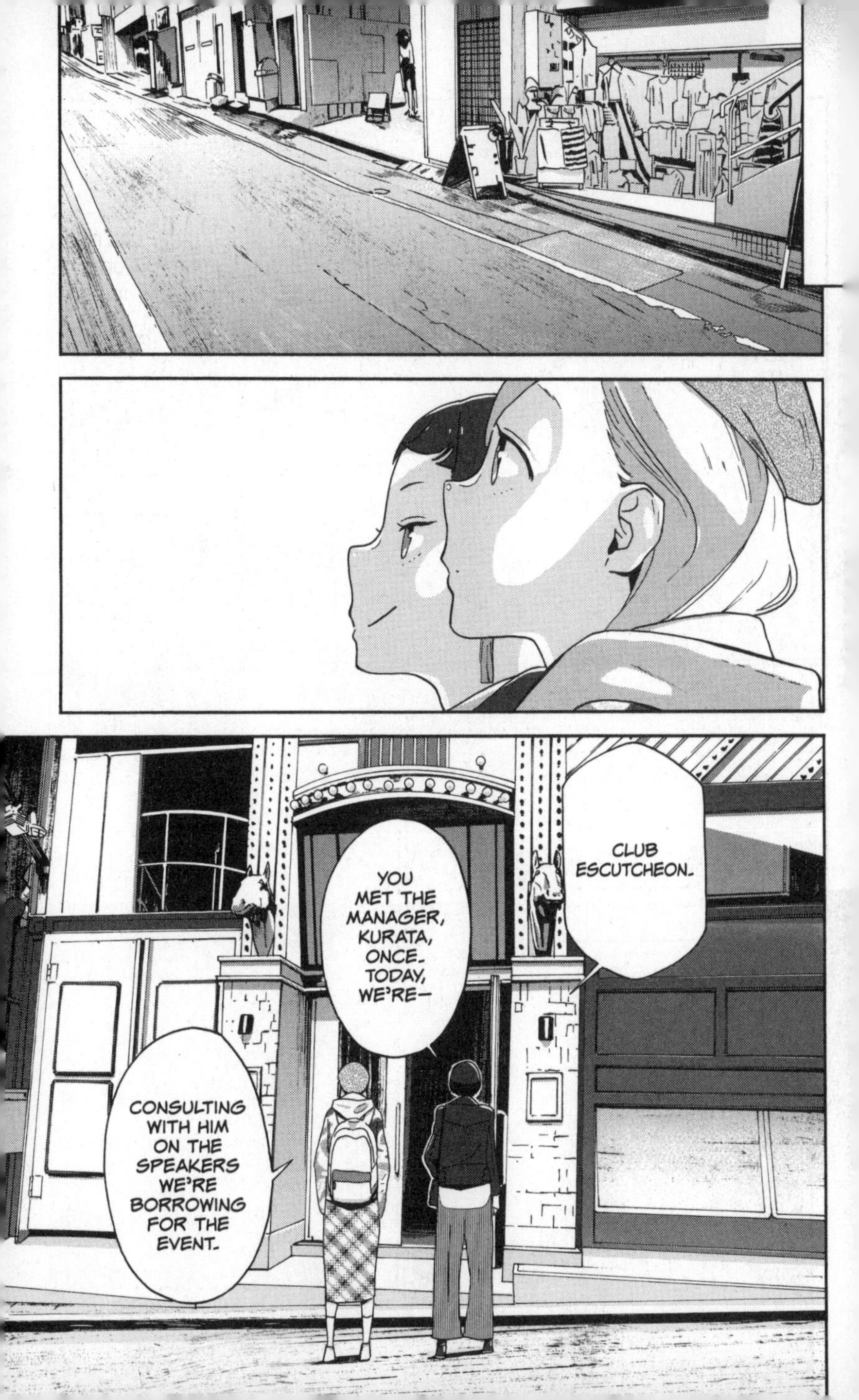
CLUB ESCUTCHEON.
YOU MET THE MANAGER, KURATA, ONCE. TODAY, WE'RE—
CONSULTING WITH HIM ON THE SPEAKERS WE'RE BORROWING FOR THE EVENT.

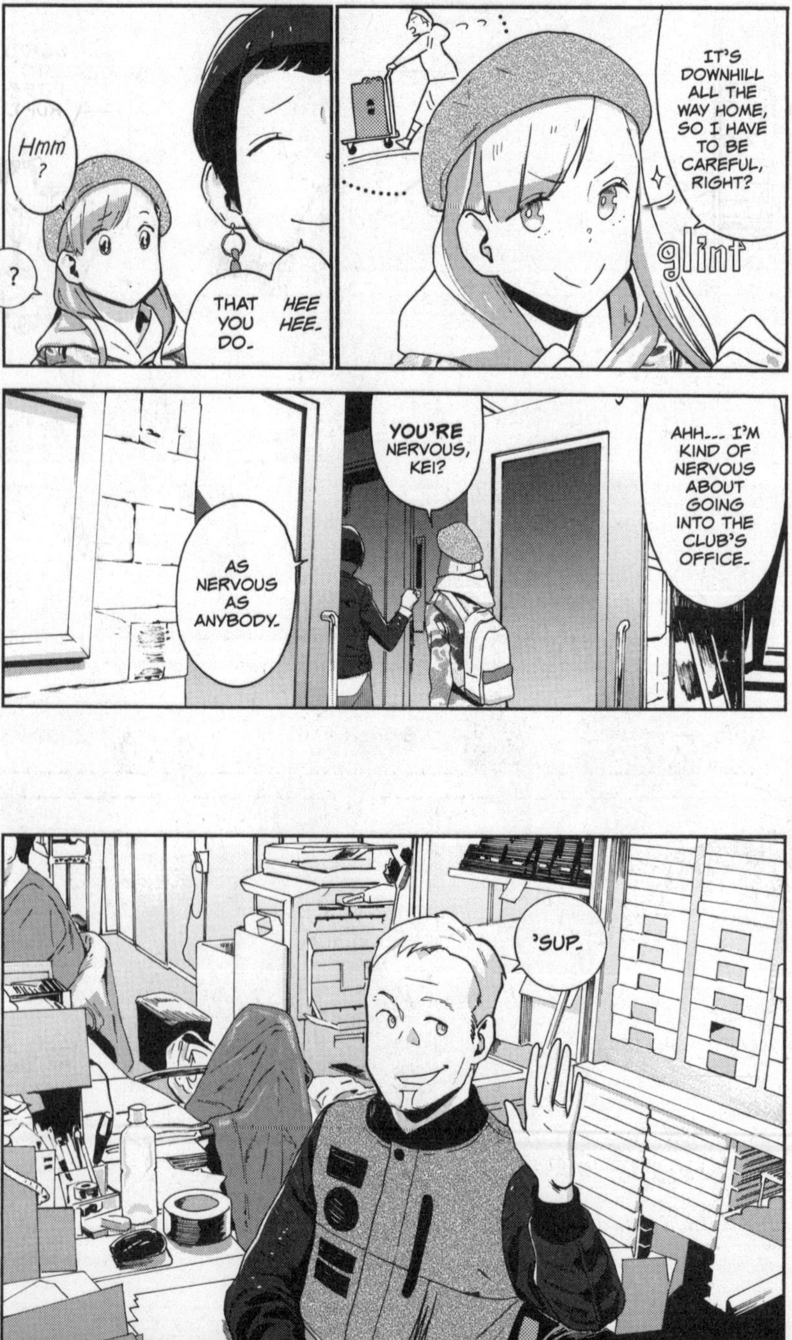
IT'S DOWNHILL ALL THE WAY HOME, SO I HAVE TO BE CAREFUL, RIGHT?
glint
HEE HEE.
THAT YOU DO.
Hmm?
?
AHH... I'M KIND OF NERVOUS ABOUT GOING INTO THE CLUB'S OFFICE.
YOU'RE NERVOUS, KEI?
AS NERVOUS AS ANYBODY.
'SUP.

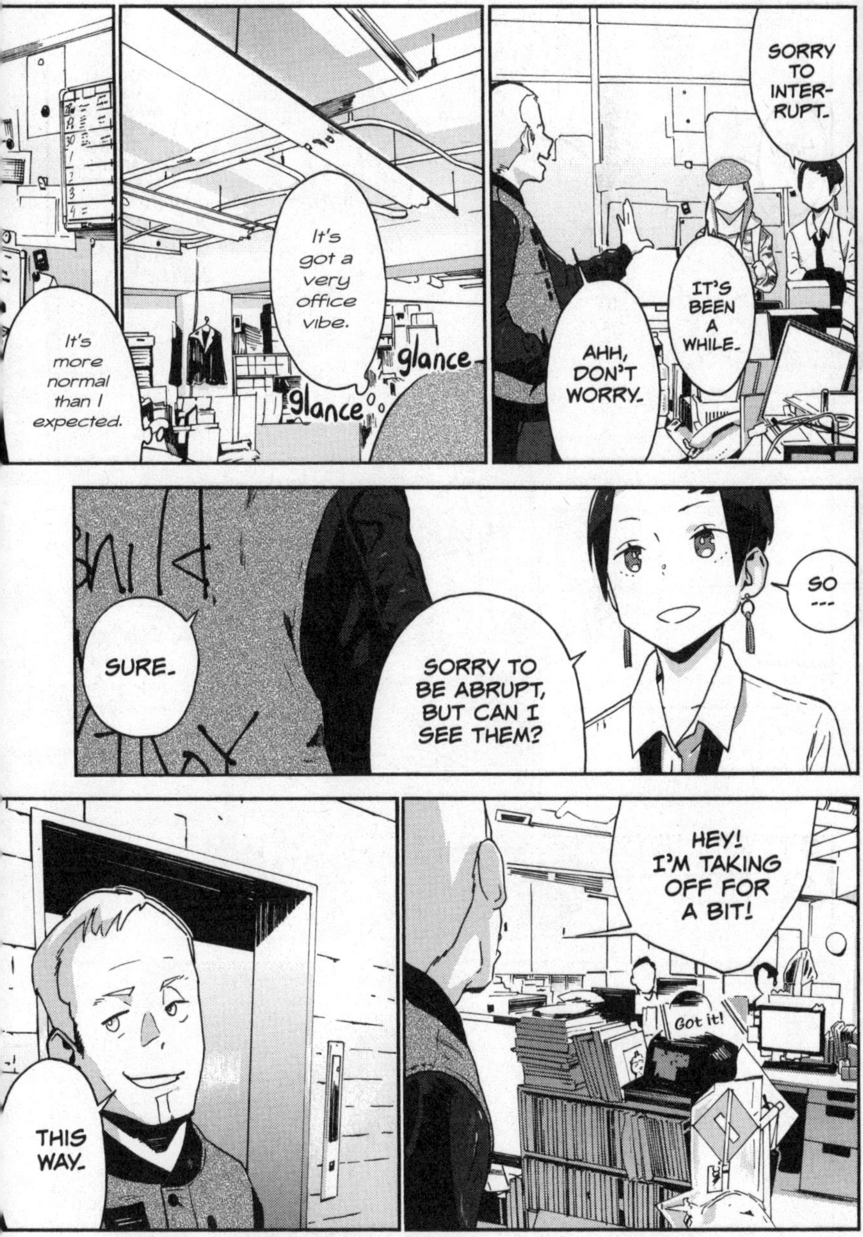
SORRY TO INTERRUPT...
IT'S BEEN A WHILE...
AHH, DON'T WORRY...
It's got a very office vibe.
glance
glance
It's more normal than I expected.
SO---
SORRY TO BE ABRUPT, BUT CAN I SEE THEM?
SURE...
HEY! I'M TAKING OFF FOR A BIT!
Got it!
THIS WAY...

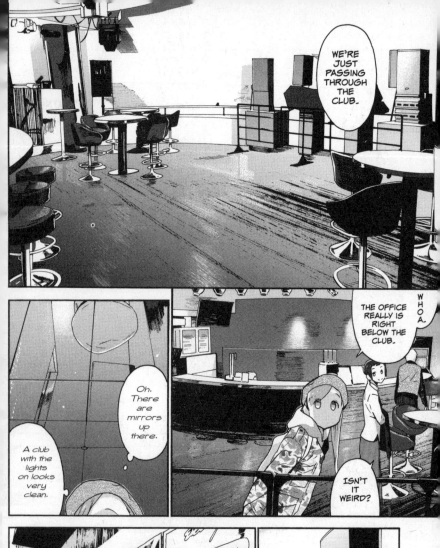

WE'RE JUST PASSING THROUGH THE CLUB.

THE OFFICE REALLY IS RIGHT BELOW THE CLUB.

W H O A.

Oh. There are mirrors up there.

A club with the lights on looks very clean.

ISN'T IT WEIRD?

SERI-OUSLY, I WAS LOST.

YEAH?

EDM SUPER ULTRA HYPER ANTHEM

❤ kids get in free! ❤

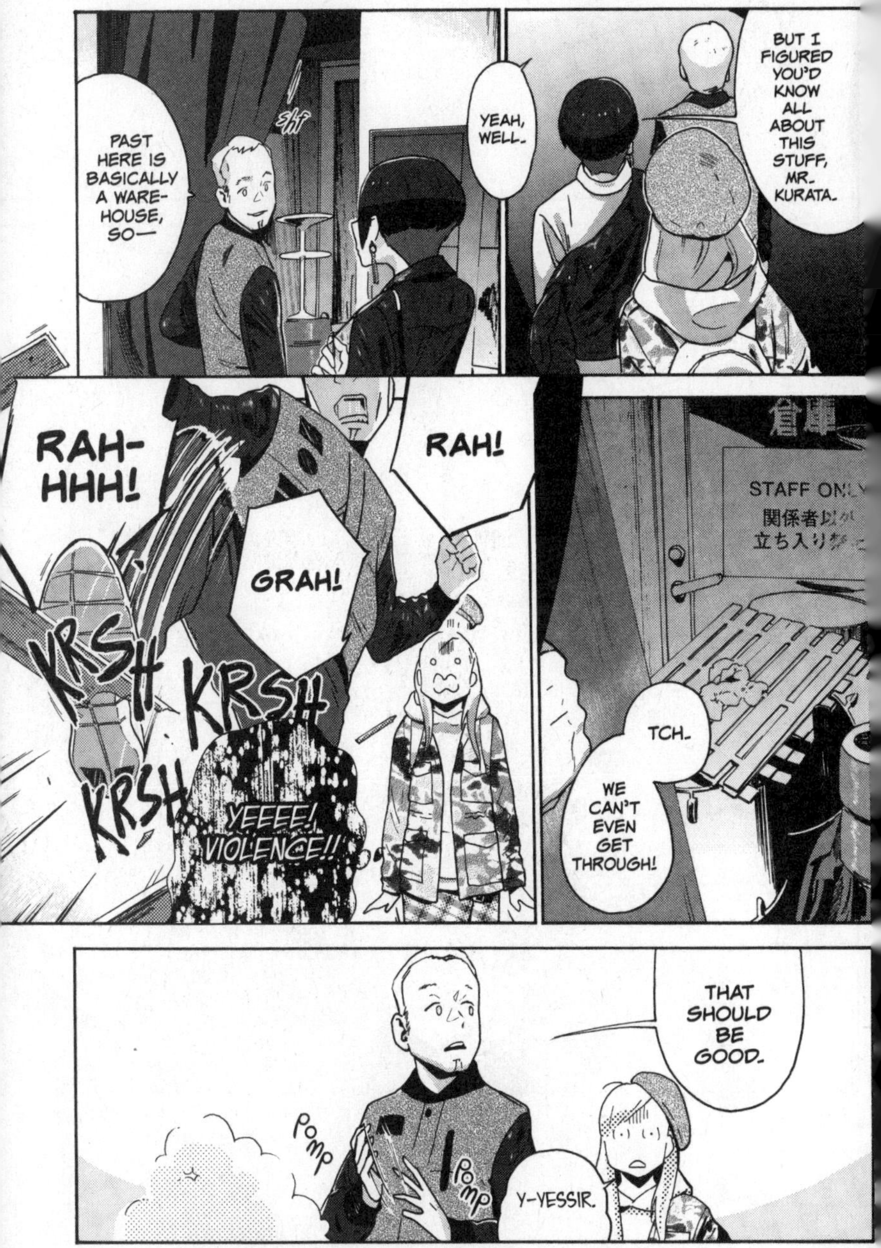
BUT I FIGURED YOU'D KNOW ALL ABOUT THIS STUFF, MR. KURATA.
YEAH, WELL.
shf
PAST HERE IS BASICALLY A WARE-HOUSE, SO—
倉庫
STAFF ONL
関係者以
立ち入り禁
TCH.
WE CAN'T EVEN GET THROUGH!
RAH!
RAH-HHH!
GRAH!
KRSH
KRSH
KRSH
YEEEEE! VIOLENCE!!
THAT SHOULD BE GOOD.
POMP
POMP
Y-YESSIR.

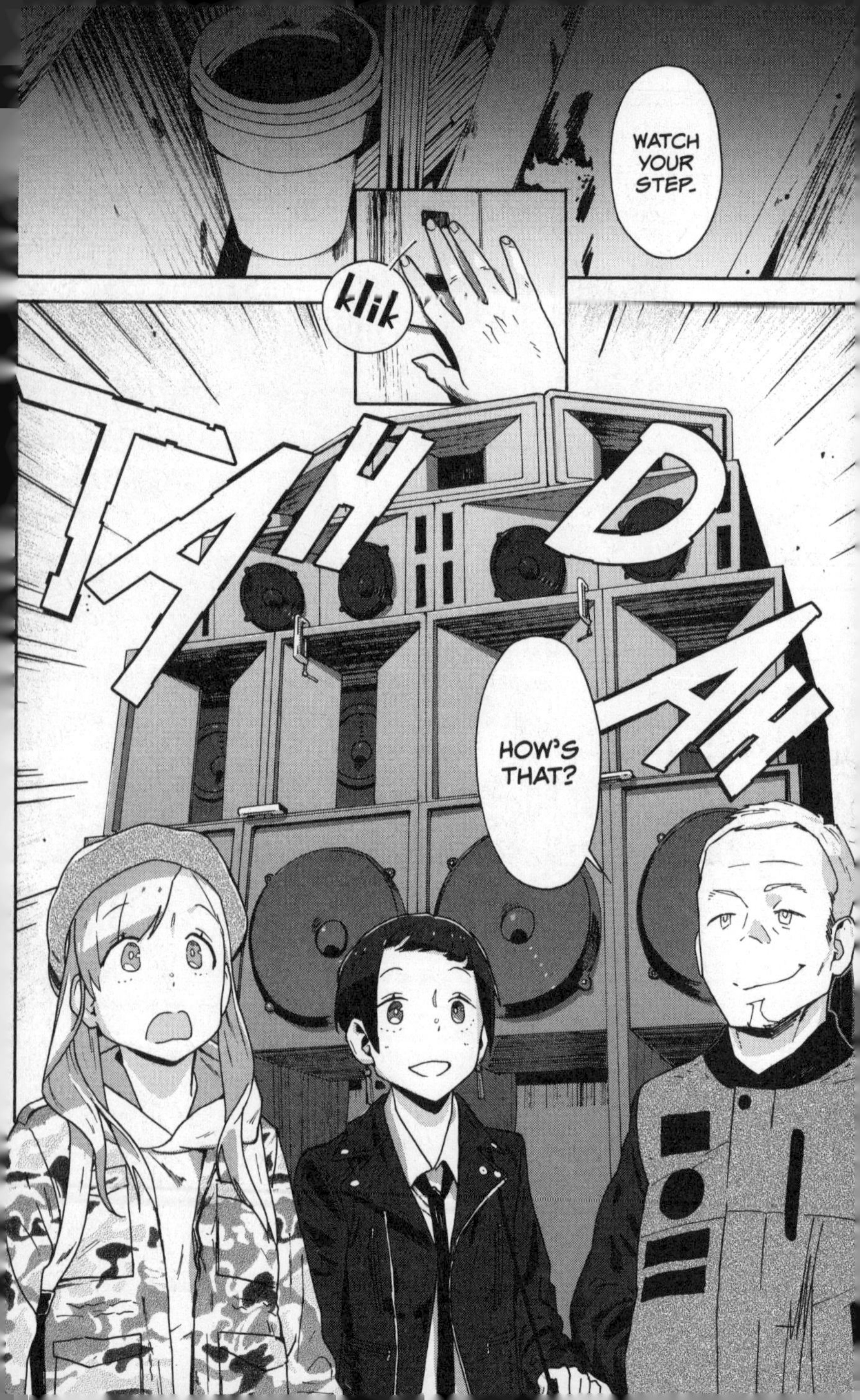
WATCH YOUR STEP...
klik
TAH DAH!
HOW'S THAT?

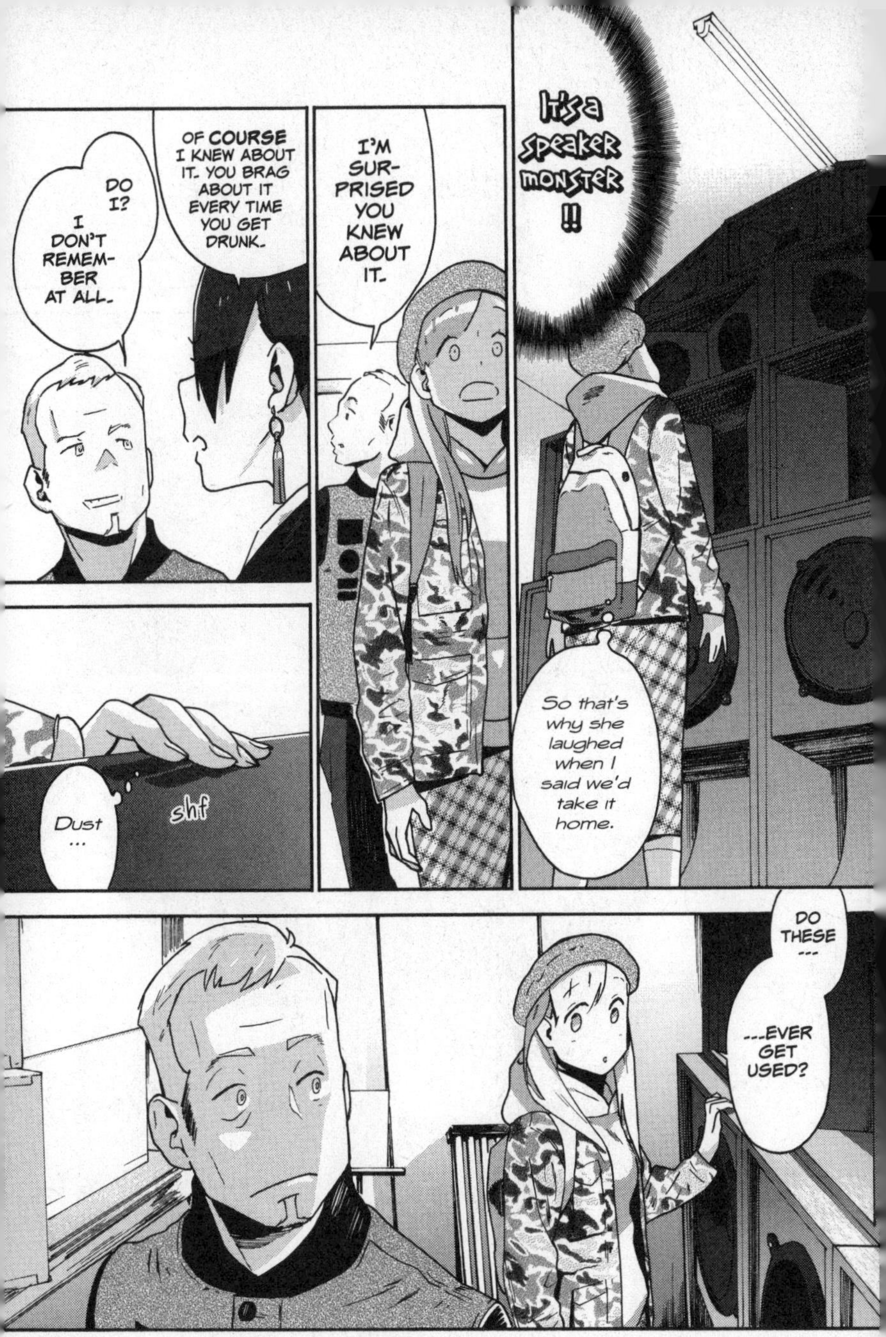
It's a speaker monster!!
So that's why she laughed when I said we'd take it home.
I'M SURPRISED YOU KNEW ABOUT IT.
OF COURSE I KNEW ABOUT IT. YOU BRAG ABOUT IT EVERY TIME YOU GET DRUNK.
DO I? I DON'T REMEMBER AT ALL.
shf
Dust...
DO THESE---
---EVER GET USED?

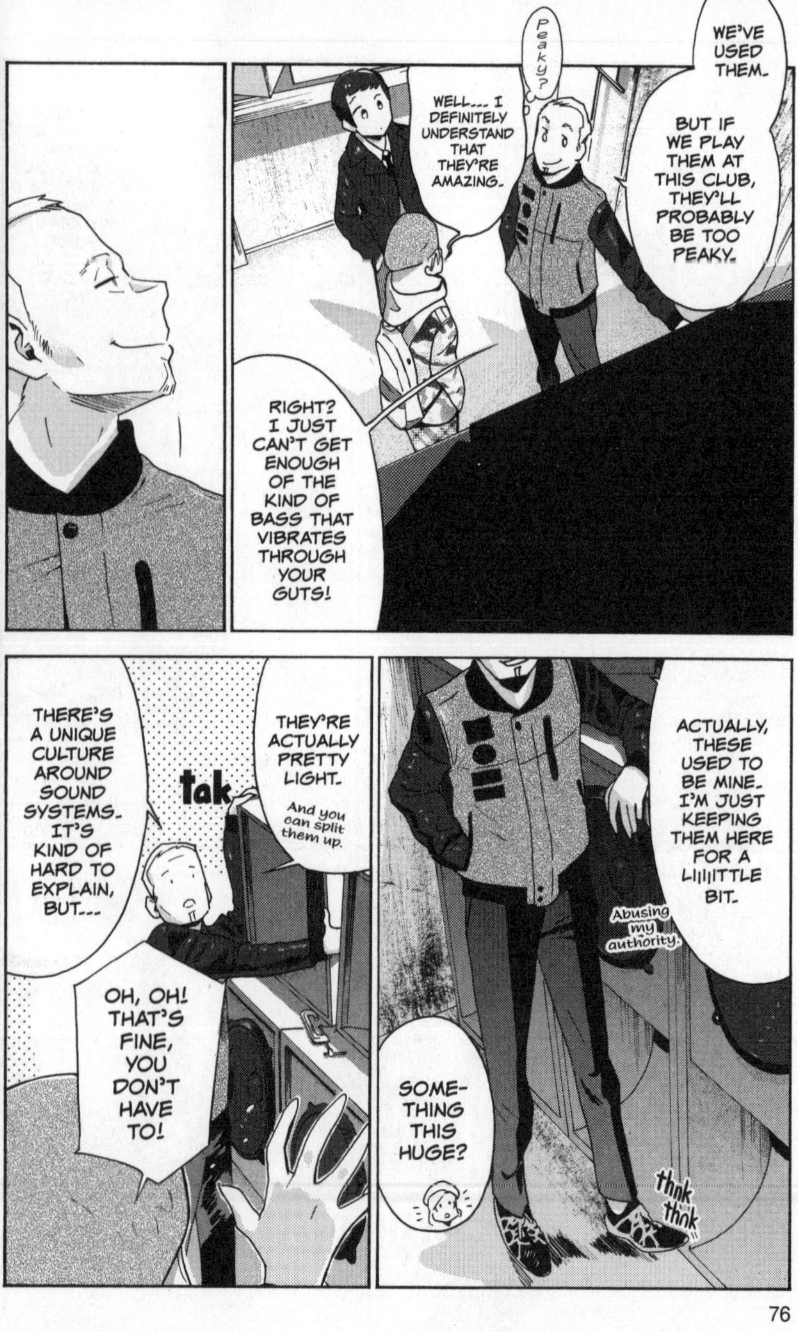
WE'VE USED THEM.
BUT IF WE PLAY THEM AT THIS CLUB, THEY'LL PROBABLY BE TOO PEAKY.
Peaky?
WELL... I DEFINITELY UNDERSTAND THAT THEY'RE AMAZING.
RIGHT? I JUST CAN'T GET ENOUGH OF THE KIND OF BASS THAT VIBRATES THROUGH YOUR GUTS!
ACTUALLY, THESE USED TO BE MINE. I'M JUST KEEPING THEM HERE FOR A LIIIITTLE BIT.
Abusing my authority.
thnk thnk
SOME-THING THIS HUGE?
THEY'RE ACTUALLY PRETTY LIGHT.
And you can split them up.
tak
THERE'S A UNIQUE CULTURE AROUND SOUND SYSTEMS. IT'S KIND OF HARD TO EXPLAIN, BUT...
OH, OH! THAT'S FINE, YOU DON'T HAVE TO!

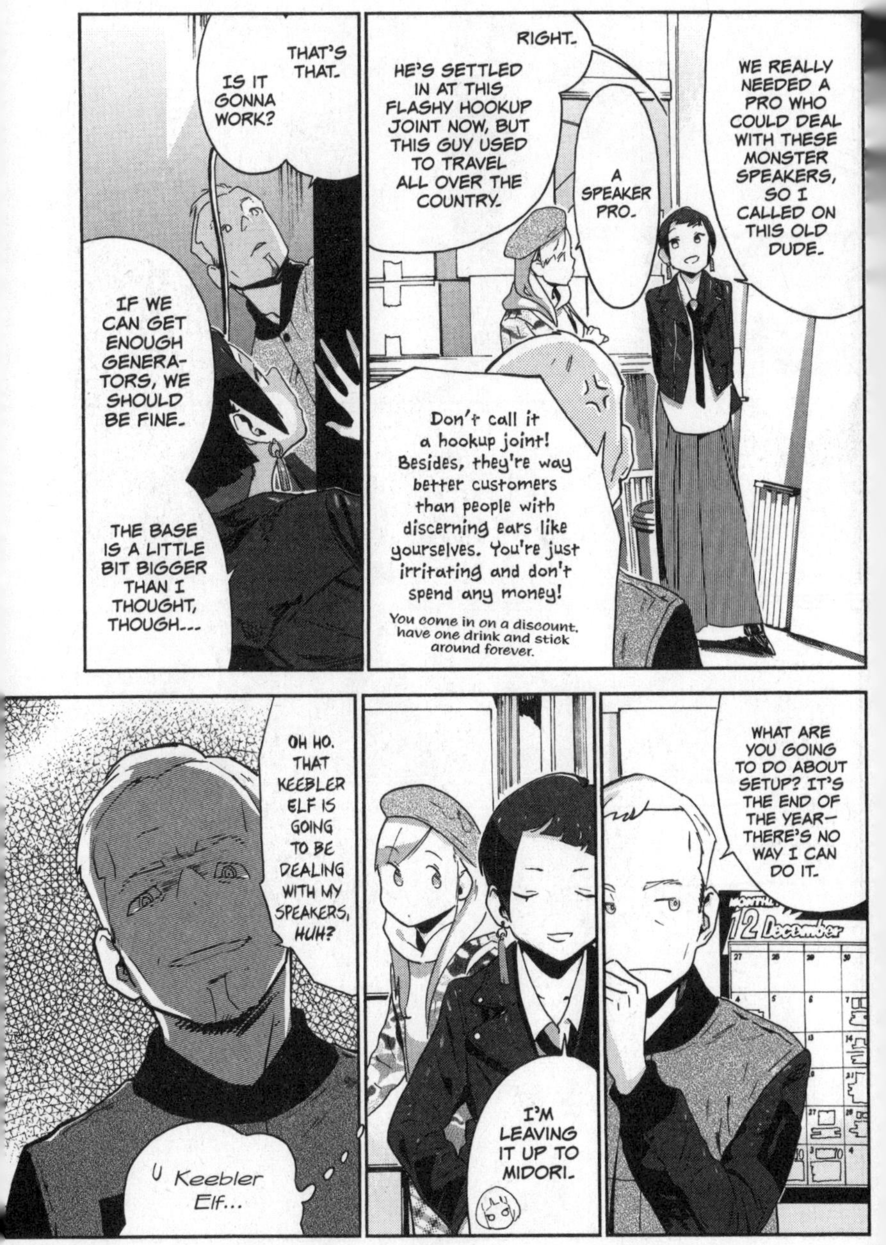
WE REALLY NEEDED A PRO WHO COULD DEAL WITH THESE MONSTER SPEAKERS, SO I CALLED ON THIS OLD DUDE.
A SPEAKER PRO.
RIGHT.
HE'S SETTLED IN AT THIS FLASHY HOOKUP JOINT NOW, BUT THIS GUY USED TO TRAVEL ALL OVER THE COUNTRY.
Don't call it a hookup joint! Besides, they're way better customers than people with discerning ears like yourselves. You're just irritating and don't spend any money!
You come in on a discount, have one drink and stick around forever.
THAT'S THAT.
IS IT GONNA WORK?
IF WE CAN GET ENOUGH GENERA-TORS, WE SHOULD BE FINE.
THE BASE IS A LITTLE BIT BIGGER THAN I THOUGHT, THOUGH...
WHAT ARE YOU GOING TO DO ABOUT SETUP? IT'S THE END OF THE YEAR—THERE'S NO WAY I CAN DO IT.
12 December
I'M LEAVING IT UP TO MIDORI.
OH HO. THAT KEEBLER ELF IS GOING TO BE DEALING WITH MY SPEAKERS, HUH?
Keebler Elf...

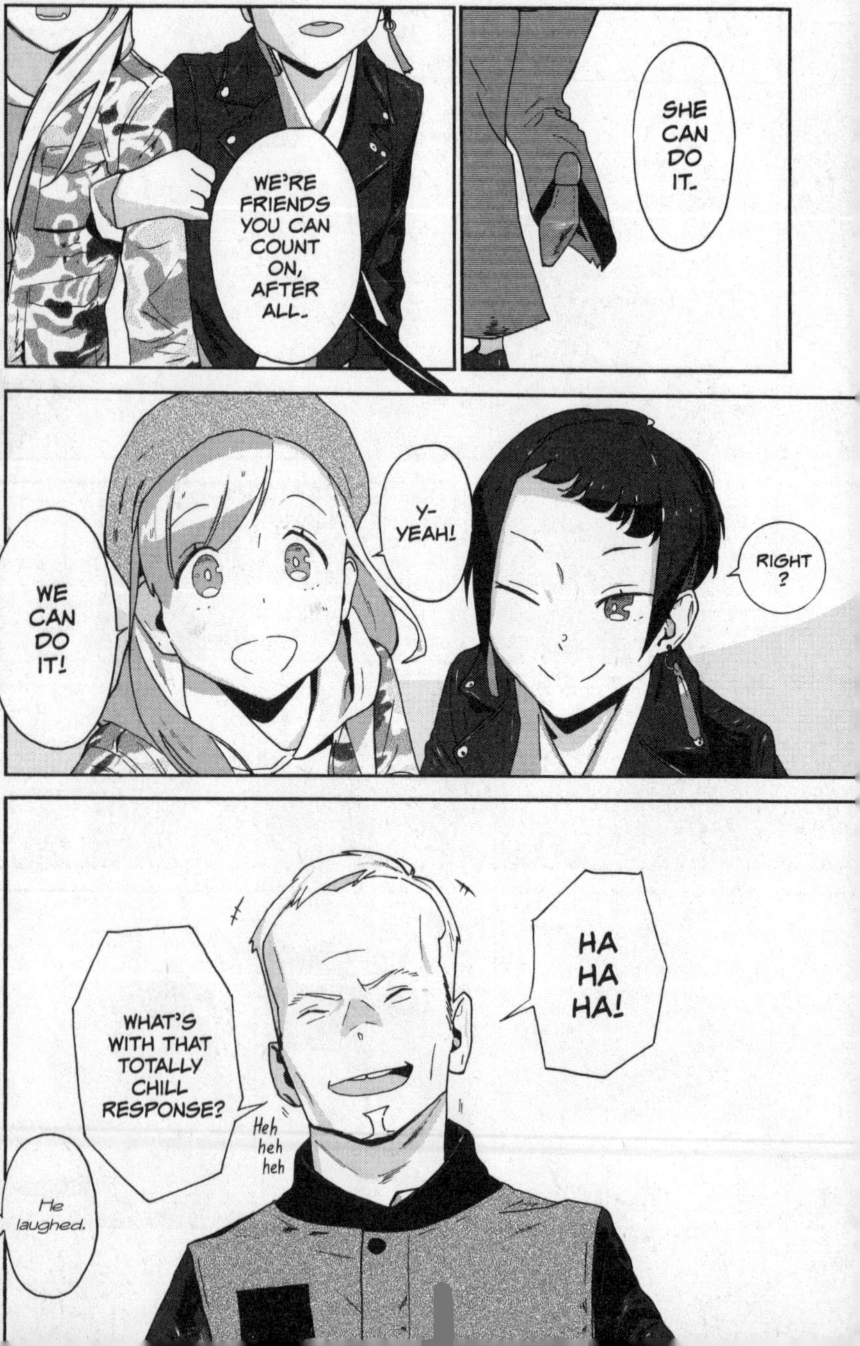
SHE CAN DO IT.
WE'RE FRIENDS YOU CAN COUNT ON, AFTER ALL.
RIGHT?
Y-YEAH!
WE CAN DO IT!
HA HA HA!
Heh heh heh
WHAT'S WITH THAT TOTALLY CHILL RESPONSE?
He laughed.

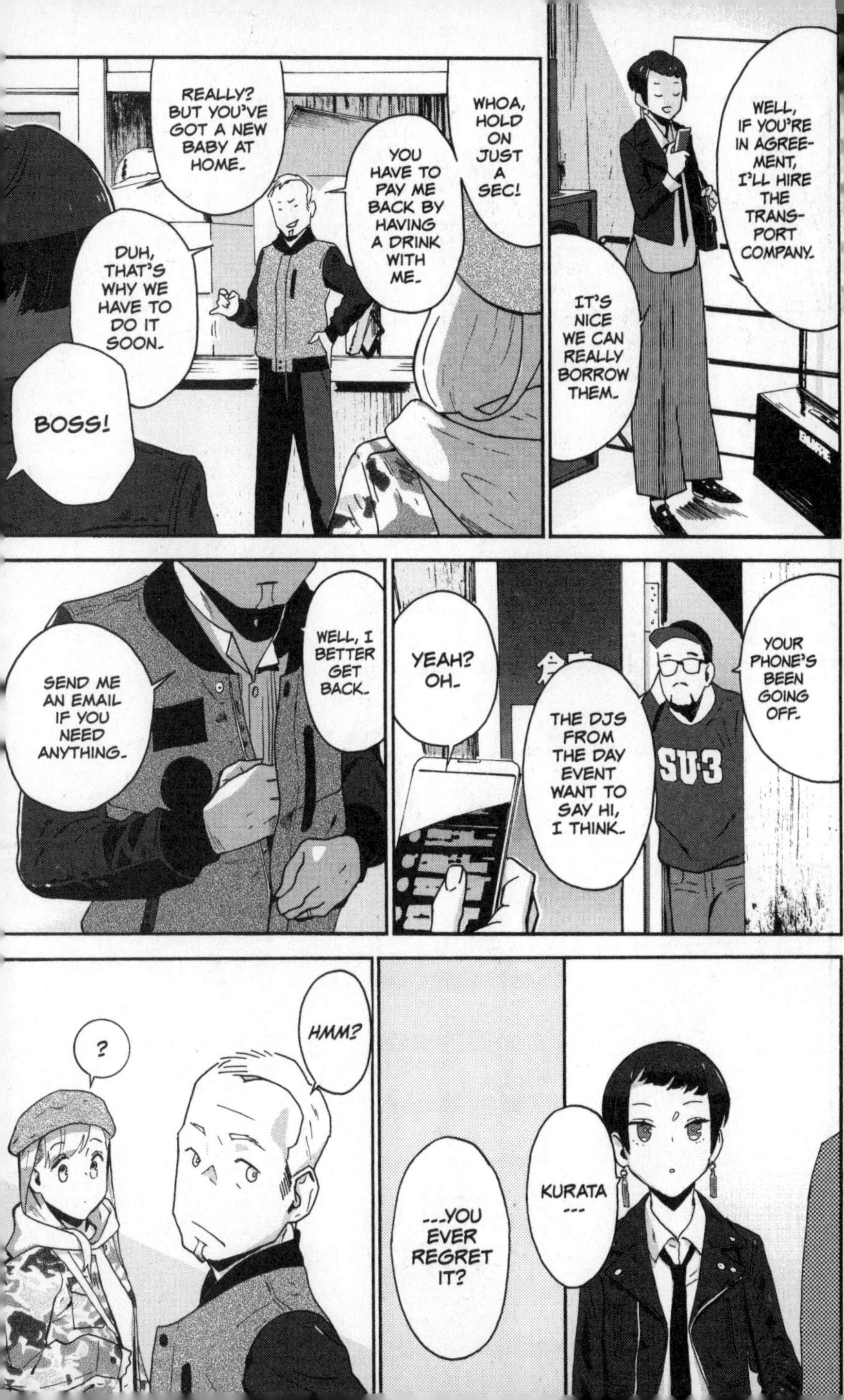
WELL, IF YOU'RE IN AGREEMENT, I'LL HIRE THE TRANSPORT COMPANY.
IT'S NICE WE CAN REALLY BORROW THEM.
WHOA, HOLD ON JUST A SEC!
YOU HAVE TO PAY ME BACK BY HAVING A DRINK WITH ME.
REALLY? BUT YOU'VE GOT A NEW BABY AT HOME.
DUH, THAT'S WHY WE HAVE TO DO IT SOON.
BOSS!
YOUR PHONE'S BEEN GOING OFF.
THE DJS FROM THE DAY EVENT WANT TO SAY HI, I THINK.
YEAH? OH.
WELL, I BETTER GET BACK.
SEND ME AN EMAIL IF YOU NEED ANYTHING.
KURATA---
---YOU EVER REGRET IT?
HMM?
?

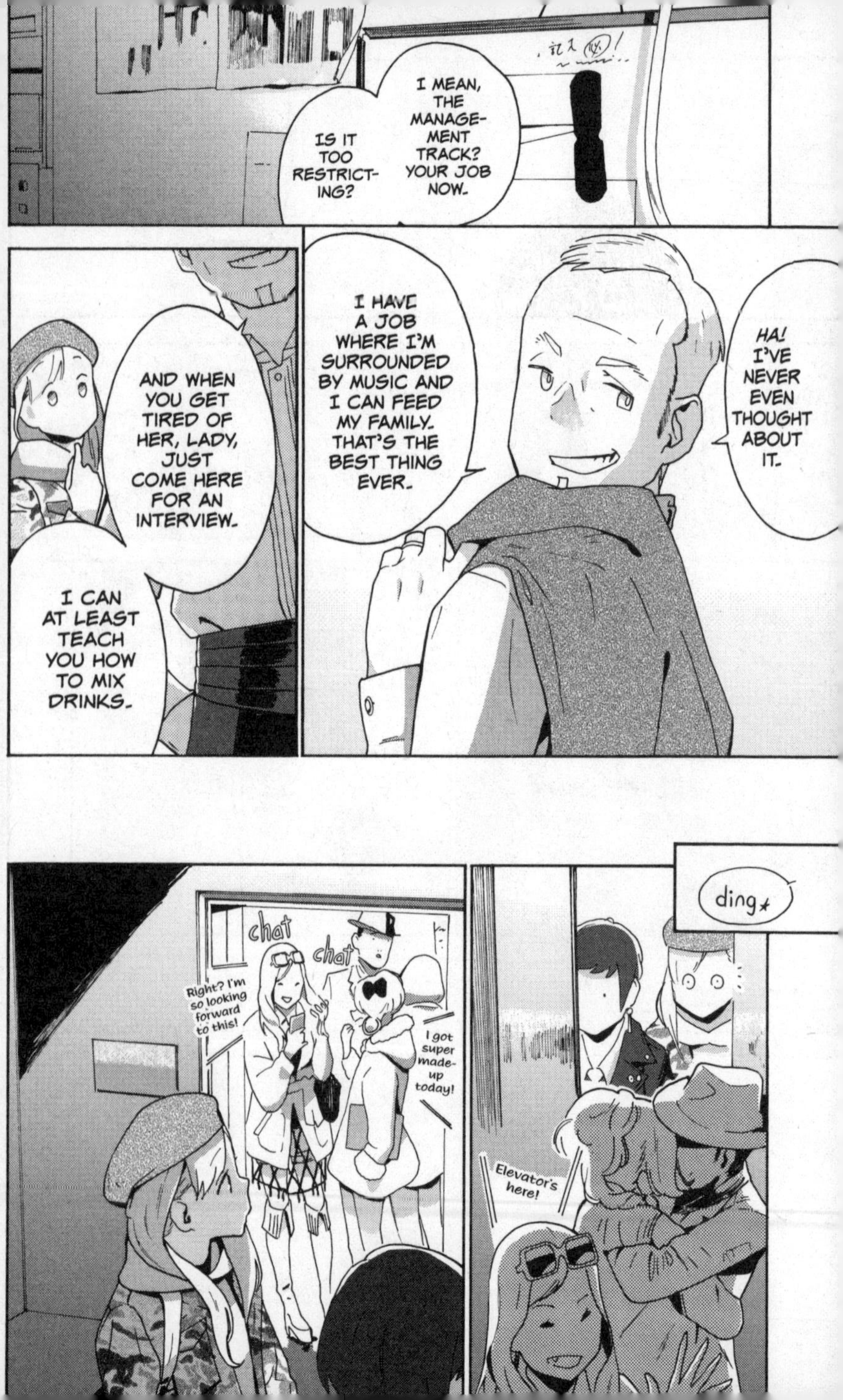
I MEAN, THE MANAGEMENT TRACK? YOUR JOB NOW.
IS IT TOO RESTRICTING?
HA! I'VE NEVER EVEN THOUGHT ABOUT IT.
I HAVE A JOB WHERE I'M SURROUNDED BY MUSIC AND I CAN FEED MY FAMILY. THAT'S THE BEST THING EVER.
AND WHEN YOU GET TIRED OF HER, LADY, JUST COME HERE FOR AN INTERVIEW.
I CAN AT LEAST TEACH YOU HOW TO MIX DRINKS.
ding★
Elevator's here!
chat
chat
Right? I'm so looking forward to this!
I got super made-up today!

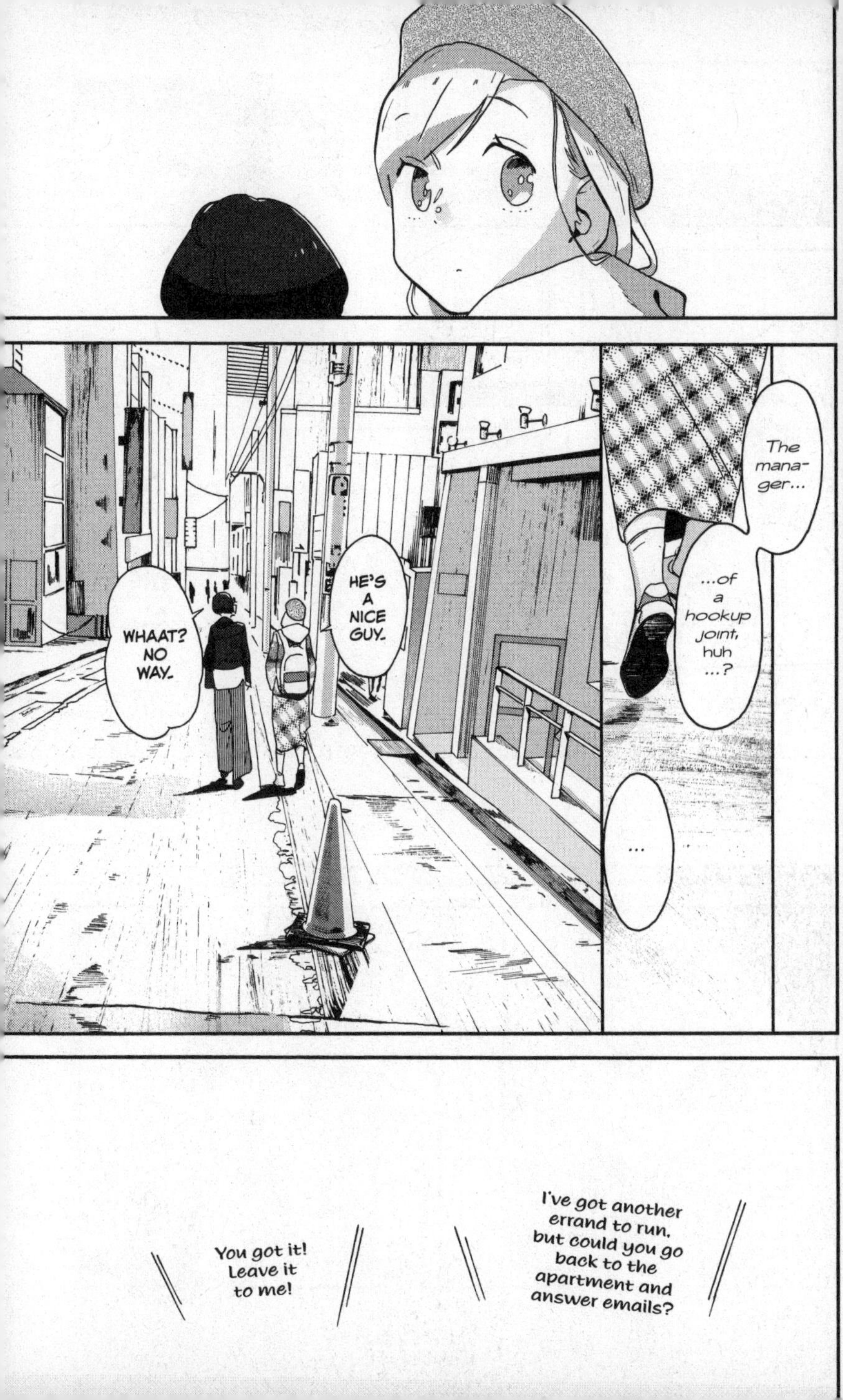
The manager...
...of a hookup joint, huh ...?
...
HE'S A NICE GUY.
WHAAT? NO WAY.
I've got another errand to run, but could you go back to the apartment and answer emails?
You got it! Leave it to me!

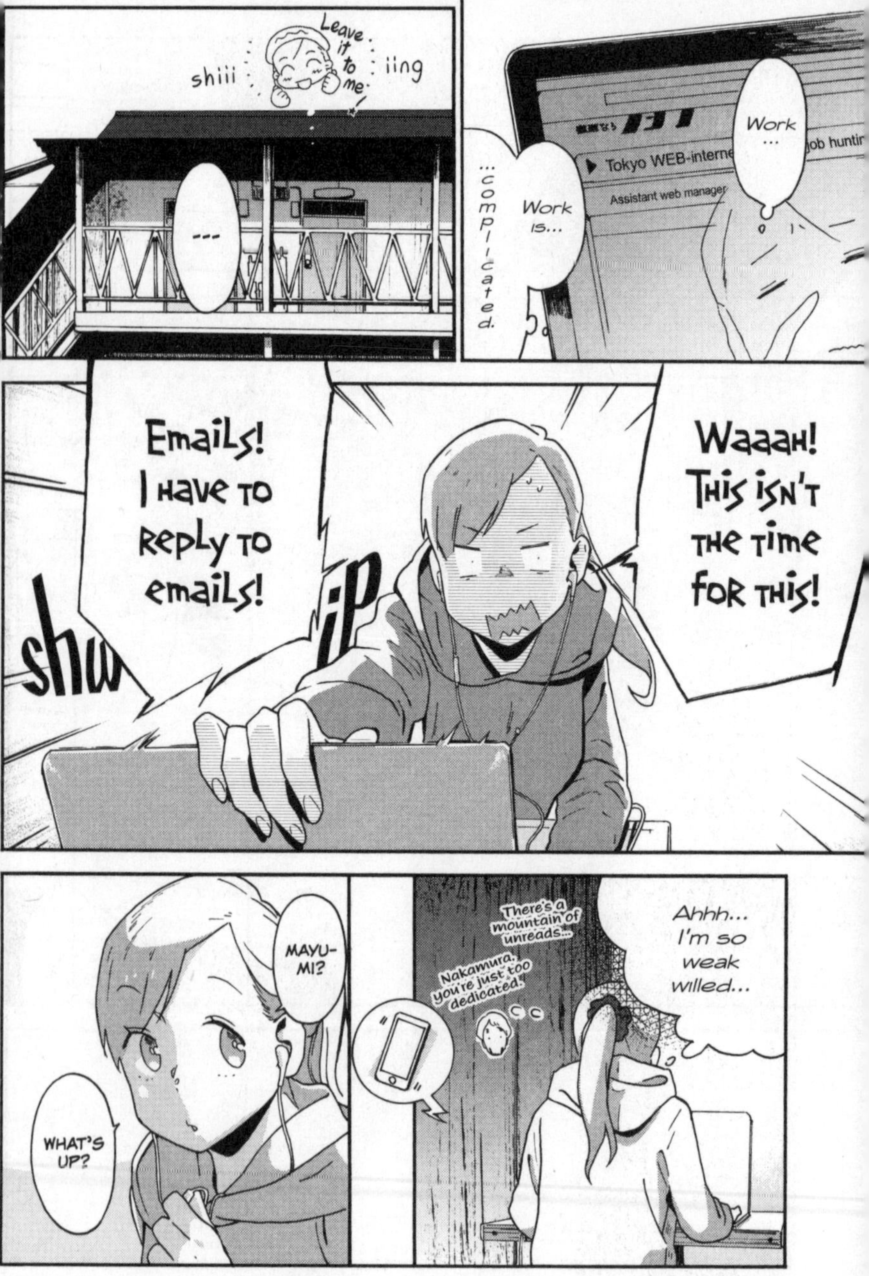
Work ...
Tokyo WEB-interne
Assistant web manager
job huntin
Work is...
...complicated.
Leave it to me!
shiii iing
...
Waaah! This isn't the time for this!
Emails! I have to reply to emails!
Ahhh... I'm so weak willed...
There's a mountain of unreads...
Nakamura, you're just too dedicated!
MAYU-MI?
...
WHAT'S UP?

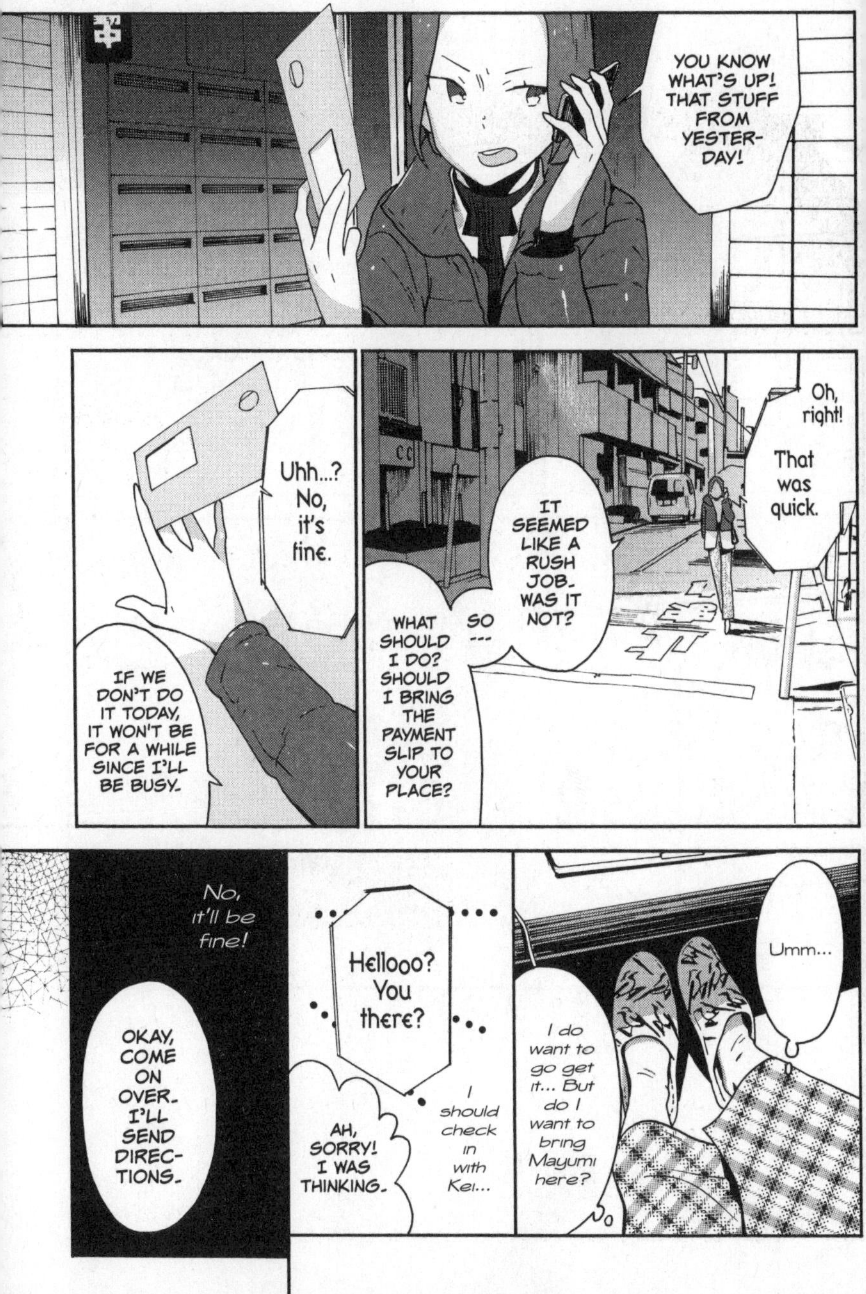
YOU KNOW WHAT'S UP! THAT STUFF FROM YESTER-DAY!
Oh, right! That was quick.
IT SEEMED LIKE A RUSH JOB. WAS IT NOT?
SO ... WHAT SHOULD I DO? SHOULD I BRING THE PAYMENT SLIP TO YOUR PLACE?
Uhh...? No, it's fine.
IF WE DON'T DO IT TODAY, IT WON'T BE FOR A WHILE SINCE I'LL BE BUSY.
Umm...
I do want to go get it... But do I want to bring Mayumi here?
Hellooo? You there?
I should check in with Kei...
AH, SORRY! I WAS THINKING.
No, it'll be fine!
OKAY, COME ON OVER. I'LL SEND DIRECTIONS.

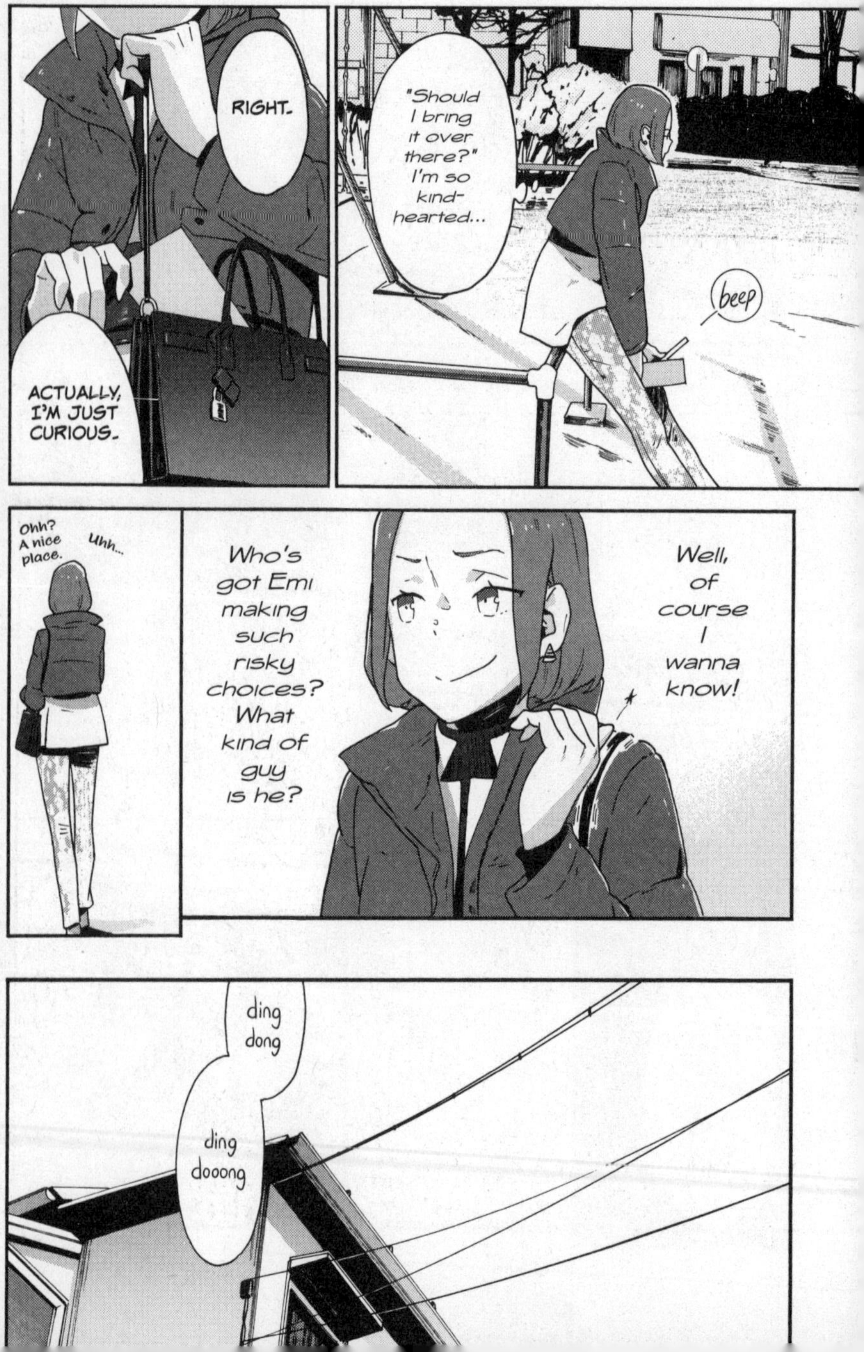
"Should I bring it over there?" I'm so kind-hearted...
beep
RIGHT.
ACTUALLY, I'M JUST CURIOUS.
Well, of course I wanna know!
Who's got Emi making such risky choices? What kind of guy is he?
Ohh? A nice place.
Uhh...
ding dong
ding dooong

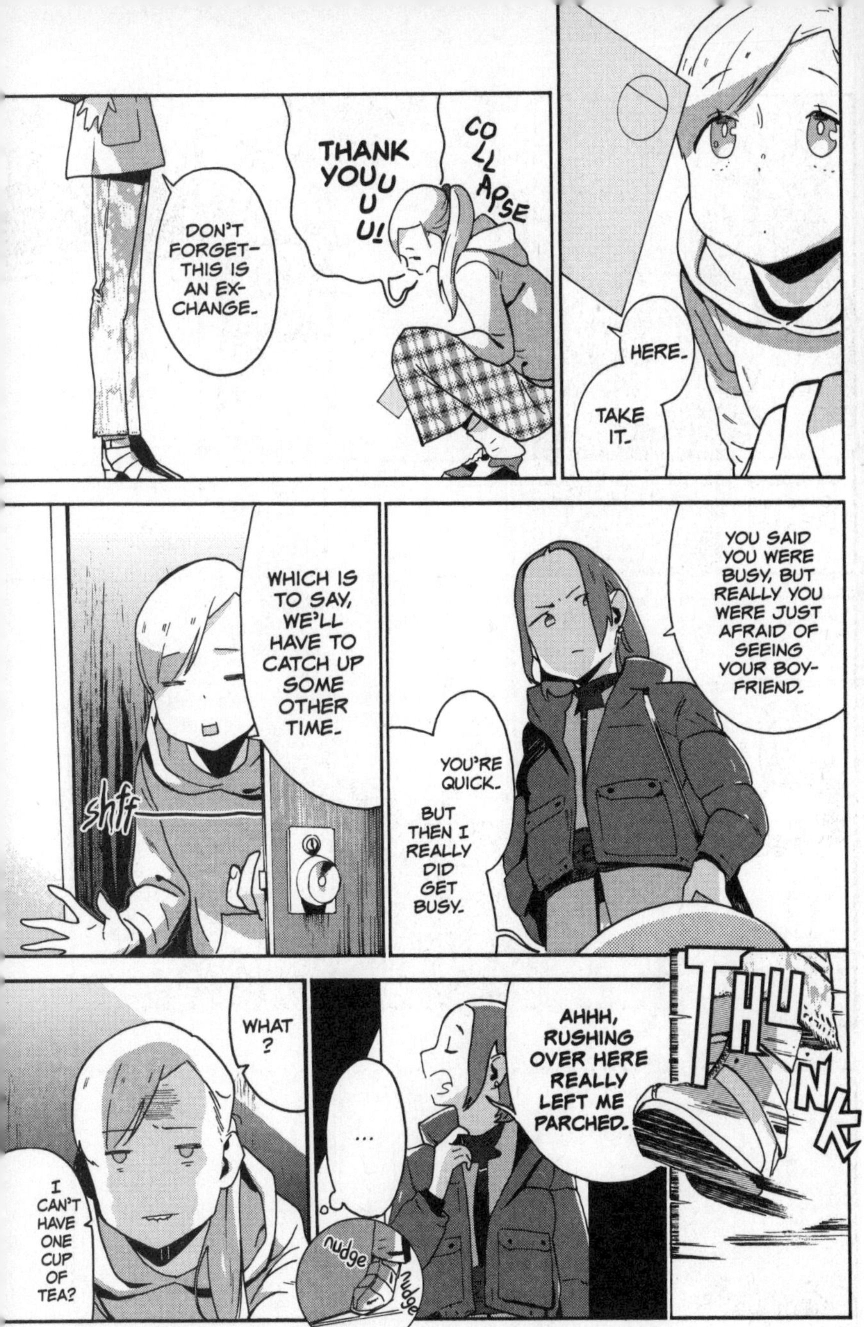
HERE.
TAKE IT.
COLLAPSE
THANK YOUUUU!
DON'T FORGET-THIS IS AN EXCHANGE.
YOU SAID YOU WERE BUSY, BUT REALLY YOU WERE JUST AFRAID OF SEEING YOUR BOYFRIEND.
YOU'RE QUICK.
BUT THEN I REALLY DID GET BUSY.
WHICH IS TO SAY, WE'LL HAVE TO CATCH UP SOME OTHER TIME.
shff
THUNK
AHHH, RUSHING OVER HERE REALLY LEFT ME PARCHED.
...
nudge
nudge
WHAT?
I CAN'T HAVE ONE CUP OF TEA?

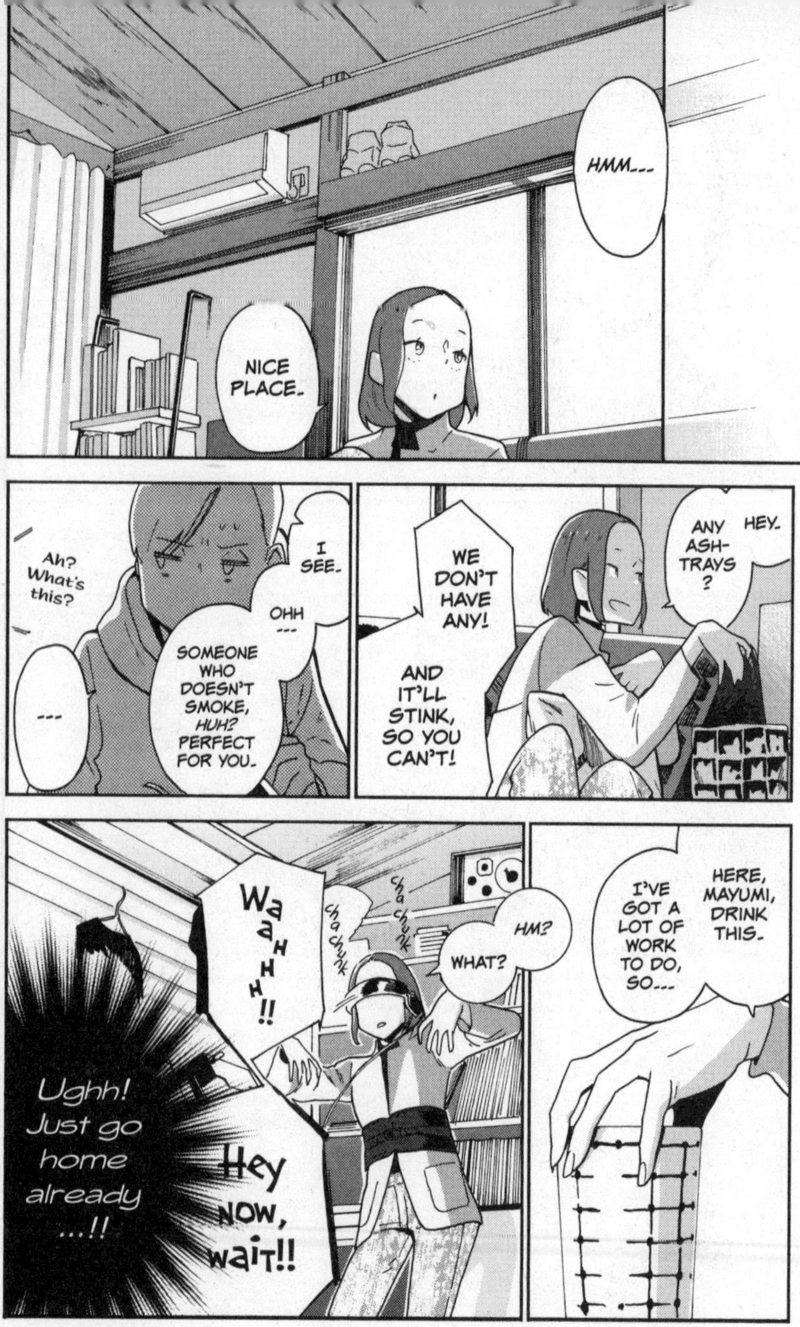
HMM...
NICE PLACE.
HEY.
ANY ASHTRAYS?
WE DON'T HAVE ANY!
AND IT'LL STINK, SO YOU CAN'T!
I SEE.
OHH...
SOMEONE WHO DOESN'T SMOKE, HUH? PERFECT FOR YOU.
Ah? What's this?
...
HERE, MAYUMI, DRINK THIS.
I'VE GOT A LOT OF WORK TO DO, SO...
HM?
WHAT?
cha chunk
cha chunk
WaAHHH!!
Hey NOW, waIT!!
Ughh! Just go home already...!!

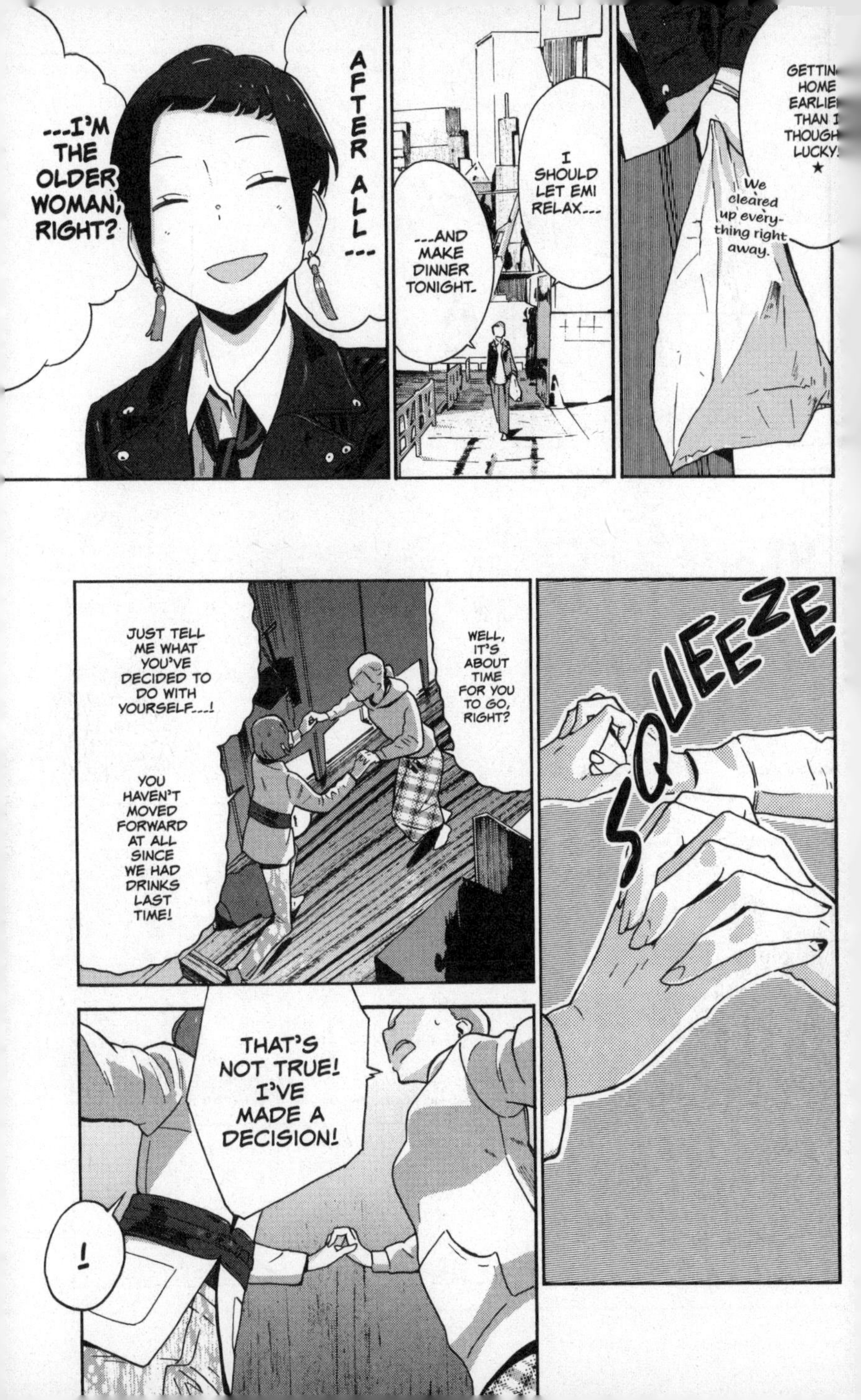
GETTIN HOME EARLIE THAN I THOUGH LUCKY! ★
We cleared up everything right away.
I SHOULD LET EMI RELAX...
...AND MAKE DINNER TONIGHT.
AFTER ALL---
---I'M THE OLDER WOMAN, RIGHT?
SQUEEZE
WELL, IT'S ABOUT TIME FOR YOU TO GO, RIGHT?
JUST TELL ME WHAT YOU'VE DECIDED TO DO WITH YOURSELF...!
YOU HAVEN'T MOVED FORWARD AT ALL SINCE WE HAD DRINKS LAST TIME!
THAT'S NOT TRUE! I'VE MADE A DECISION!
!

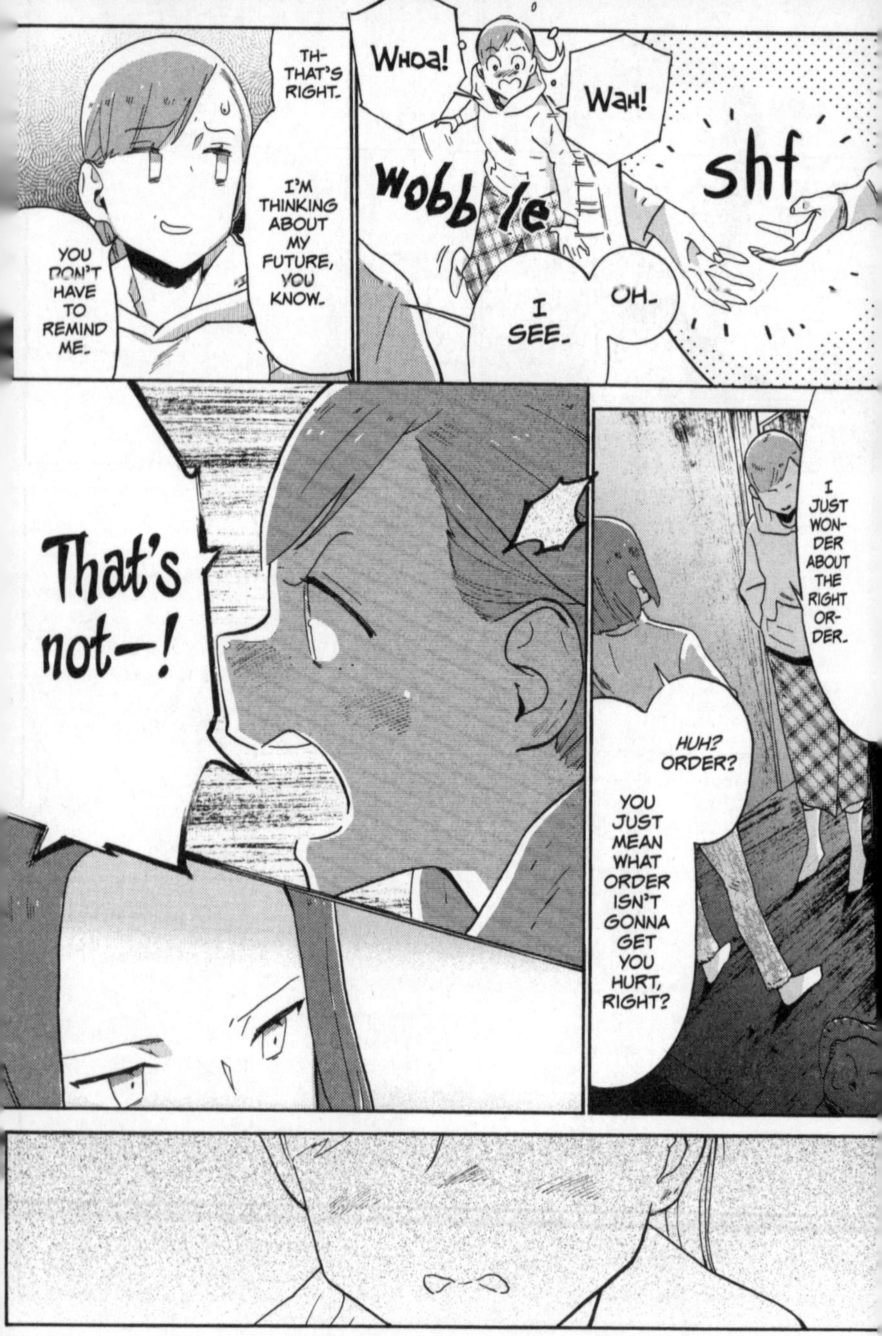
Whoa!
Wah!
wobble
shf
OH.
I SEE.
TH-THAT'S RIGHT.
I'M THINKING ABOUT MY FUTURE, YOU KNOW.
YOU DON'T HAVE TO REMIND ME.
I JUST WONDER ABOUT THE RIGHT ORDER.
HUH? ORDER?
YOU JUST MEAN WHAT ORDER ISN'T GONNA GET YOU HURT, RIGHT?
That's not—!

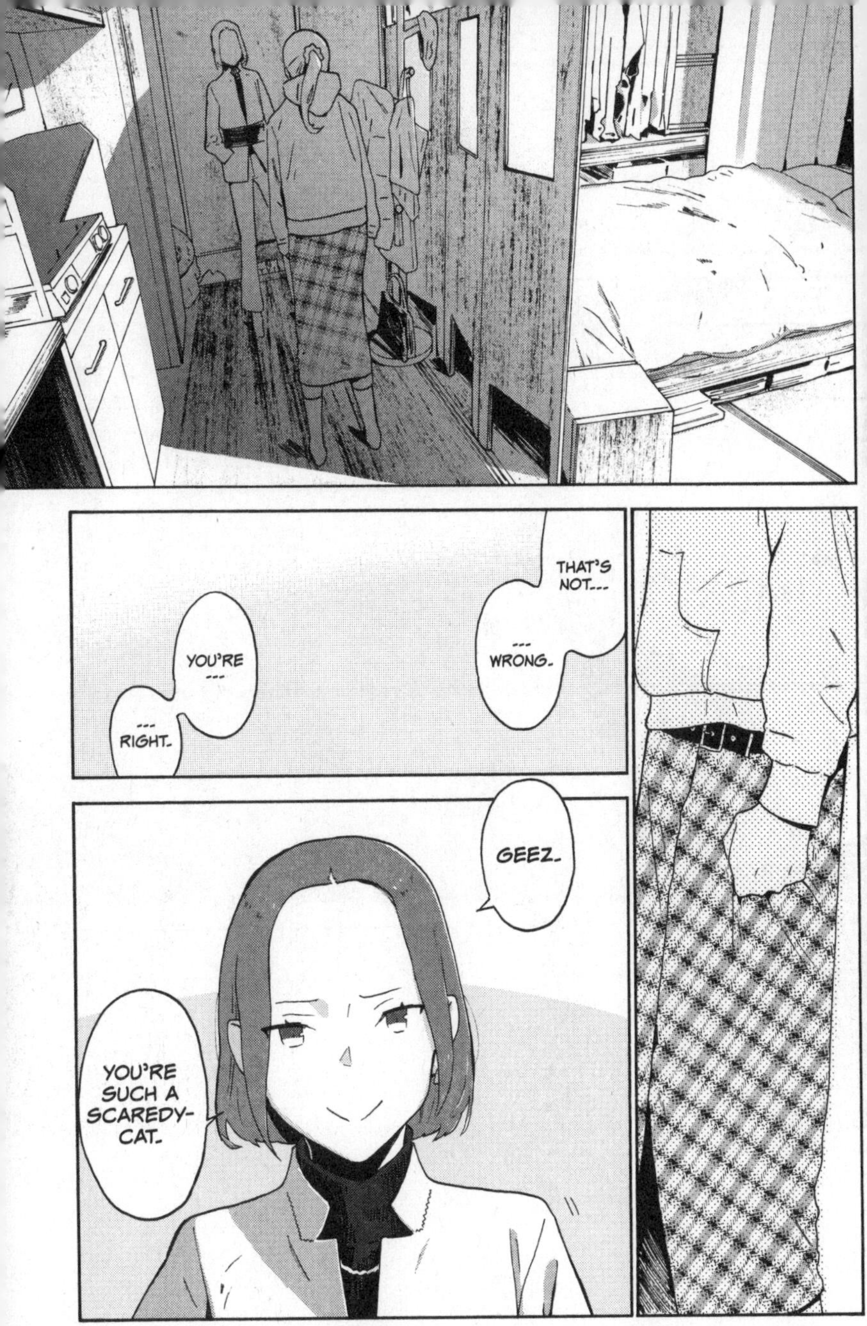
THAT'S NOT... ...WRONG.
YOU'RE ... ...RIGHT.
GEEZ.
YOU'RE SUCH A SCAREDY-CAT.

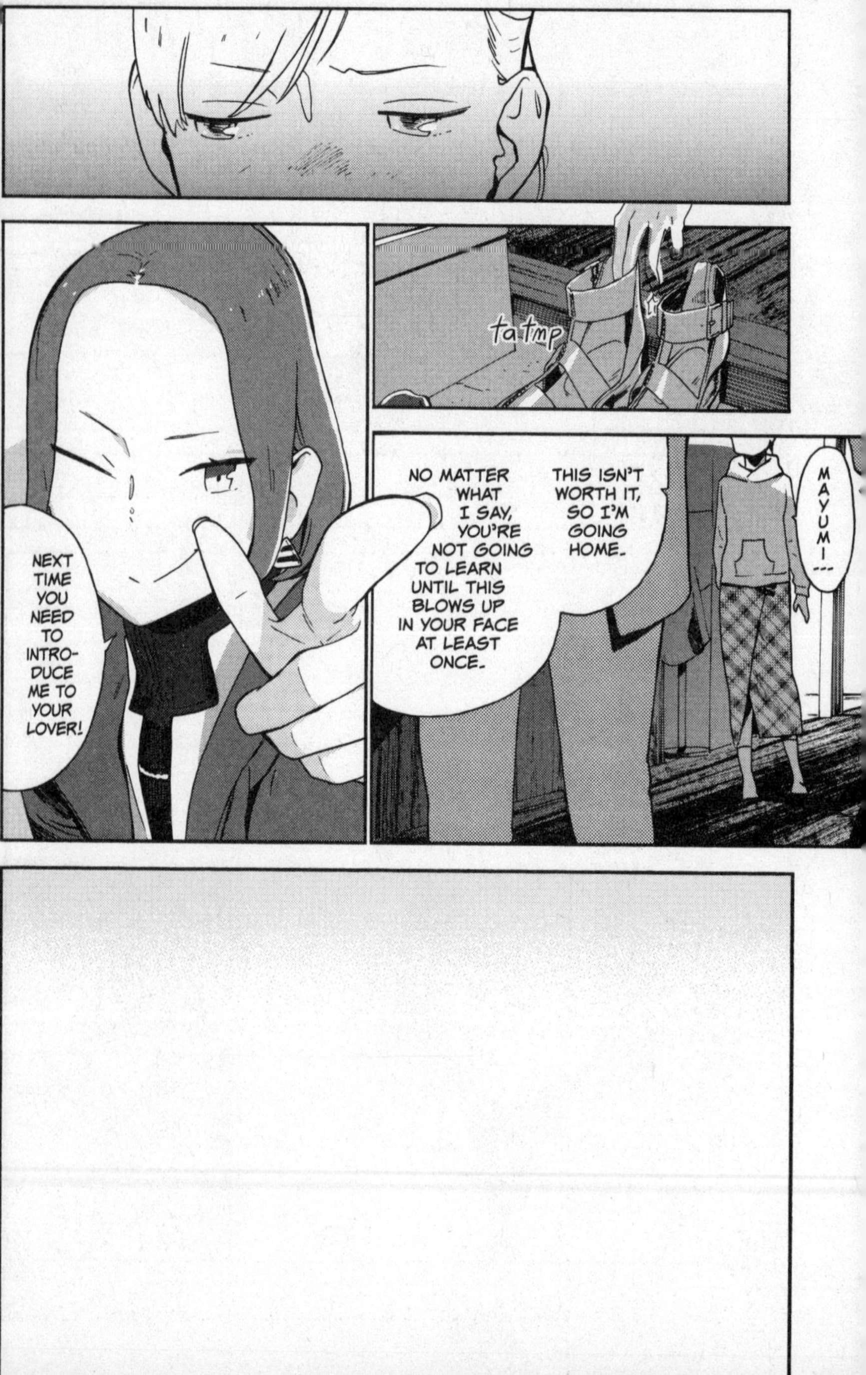
ta tmp
MAYUMI---
THIS ISN'T WORTH IT, SO I'M GOING HOME.
NO MATTER WHAT I SAY, YOU'RE NOT GOING TO LEARN UNTIL THIS BLOWS UP IN YOUR FACE AT LEAST ONCE.
NEXT TIME YOU NEED TO INTRO-DUCE ME TO YOUR LOVER!

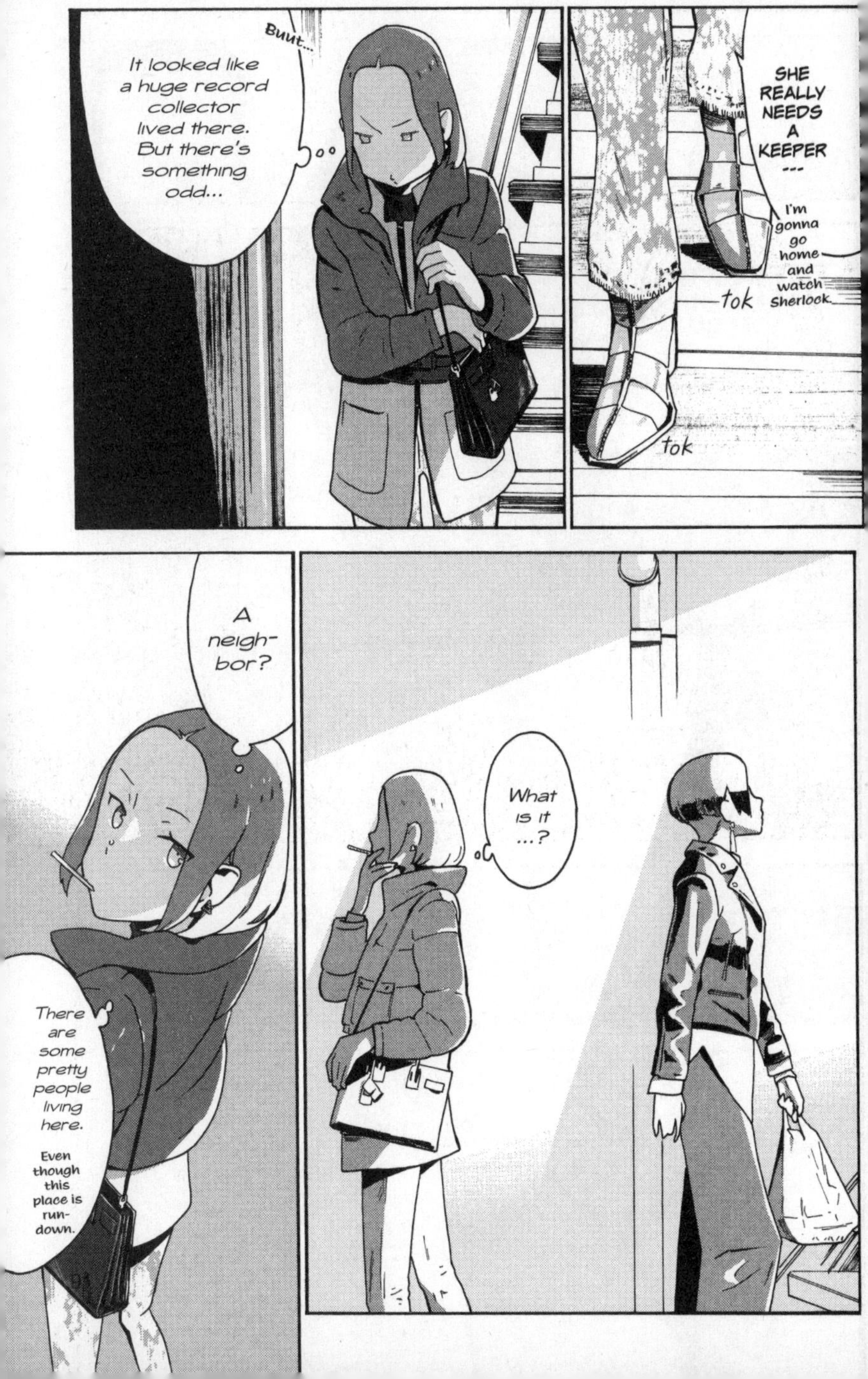
SHE REALLY NEEDS A KEEPER---
I'm gonna go home and watch Sherlock.
tok
tok
Buut...
It looked like a huge record collector lived there. But there's something odd...
What is it ...?
A neighbor?
There are some pretty people living here.
Even though this place is run-down.

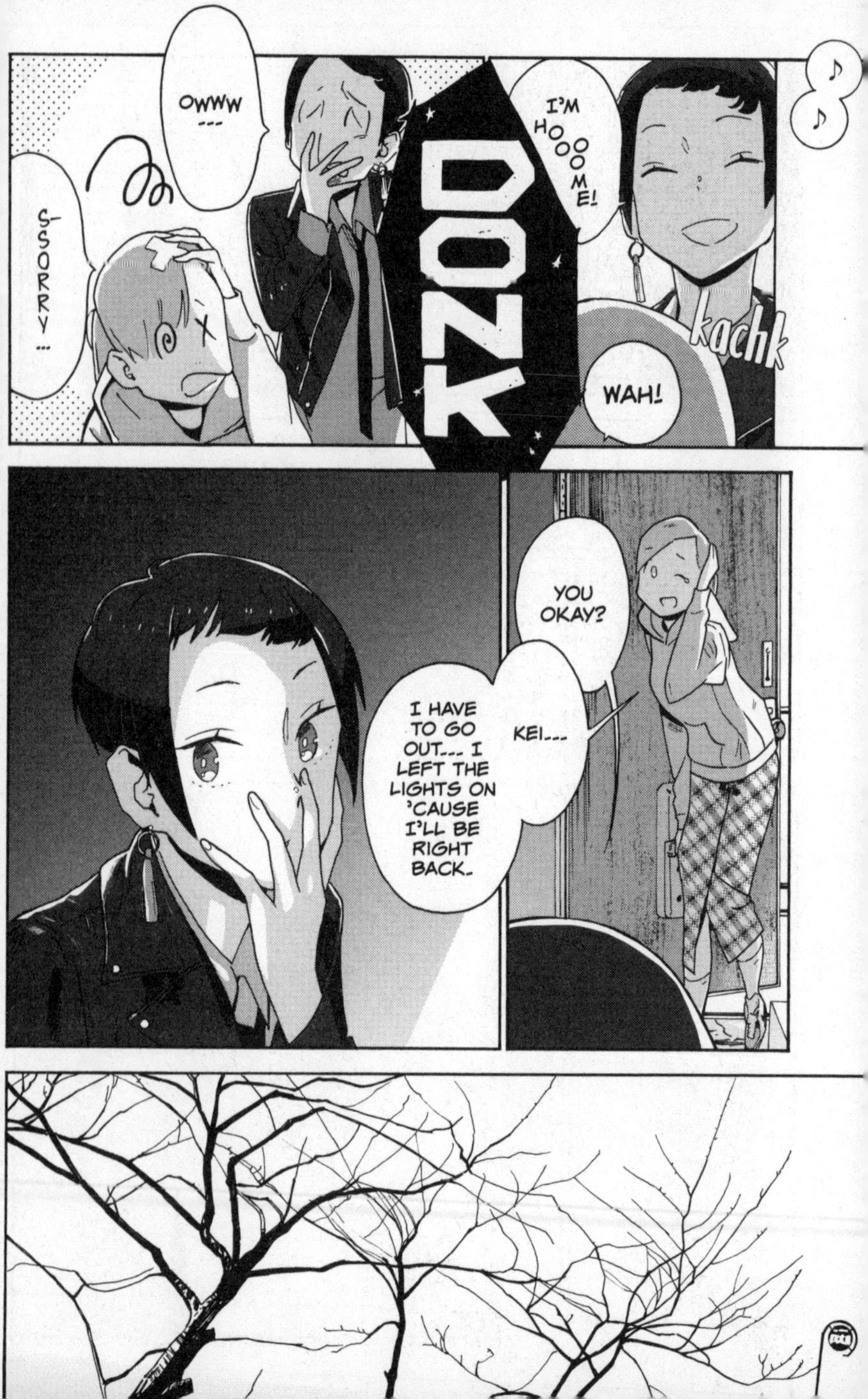
I'M HOOOOOME!
kachk
WAH!
DONK
OWWW...
S-SORRY...
YOU OKAY?
KEI...
I HAVE TO GO OUT... I LEFT THE LIGHTS ON 'CAUSE I'LL BE RIGHT BACK.

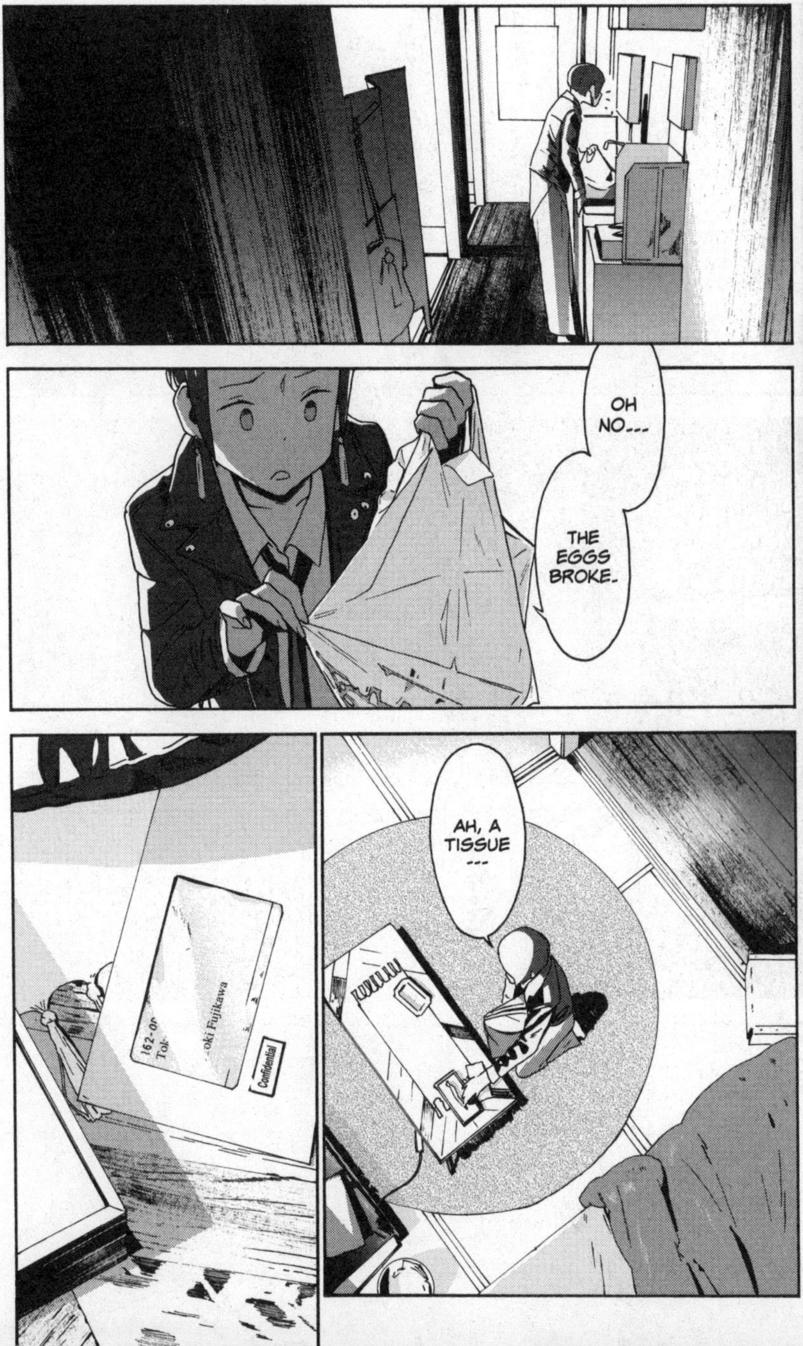
OH NO...
THE EGGS BROKE.
AH, A TISSUE...
Confidential

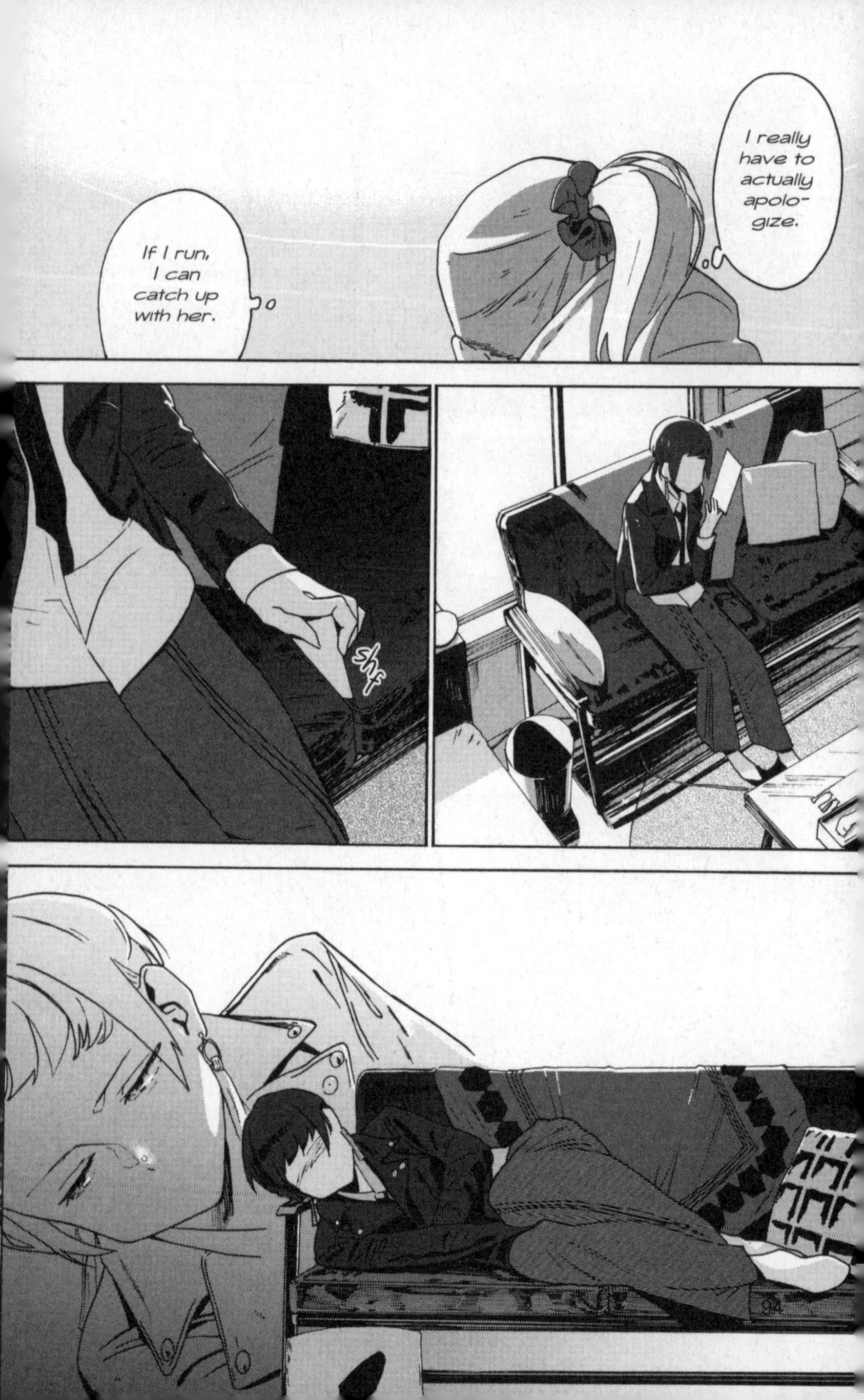
I really have to actually apolo-gize.
If I run, I can catch up with her.
shf

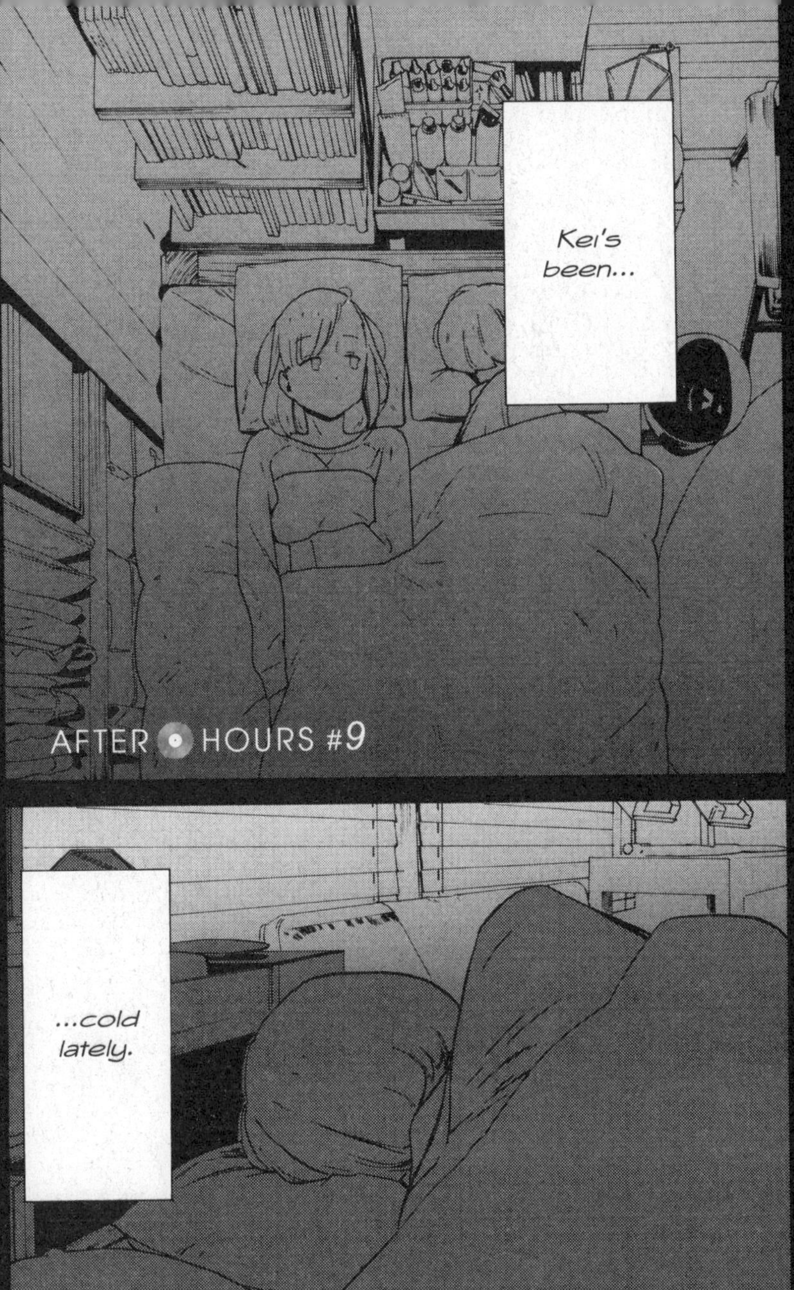
Kei's been...
AFTER HOURS #9
...cold lately.

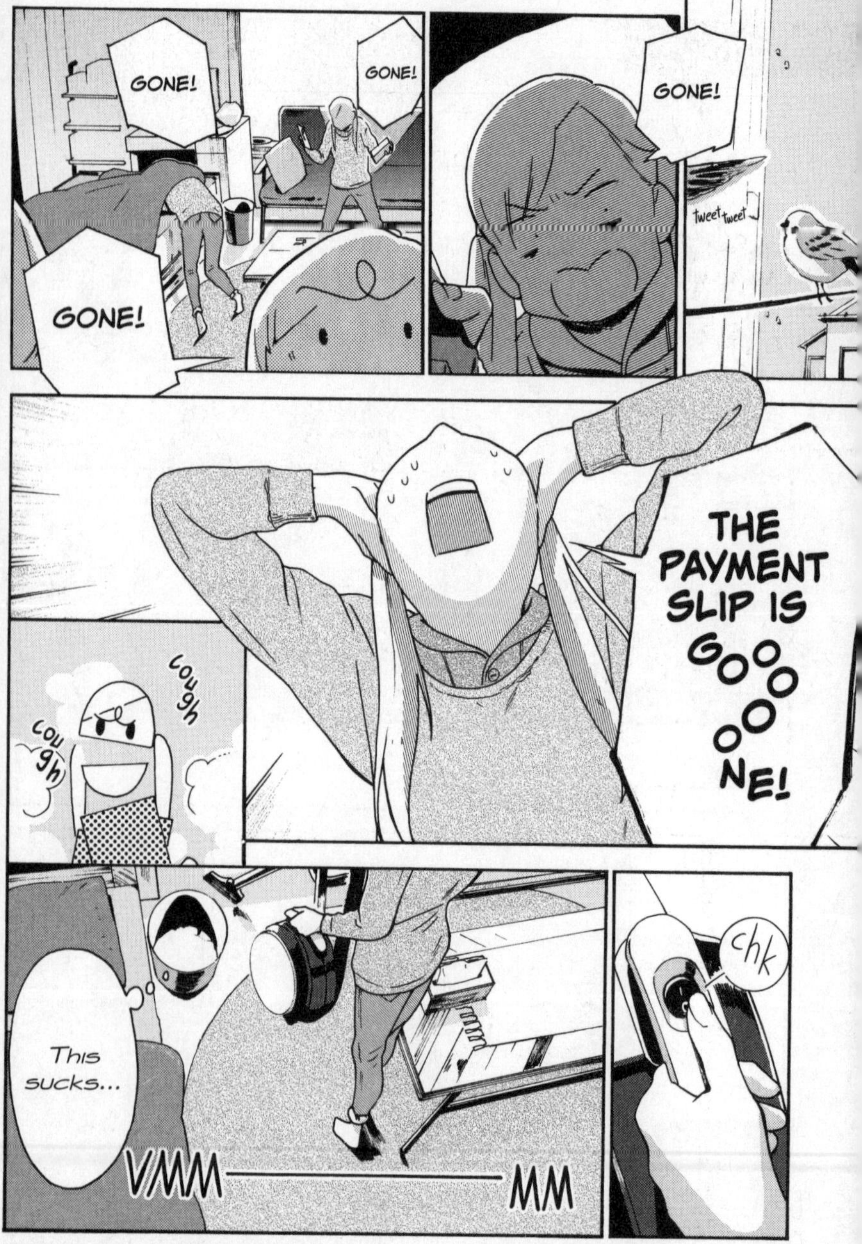
GONE!
tweet tweet
GONE!
GONE!
GONE!
THE PAYMENT SLIP IS GOOOOOONE!
cough
cough
chk
This sucks...
VMM———MM

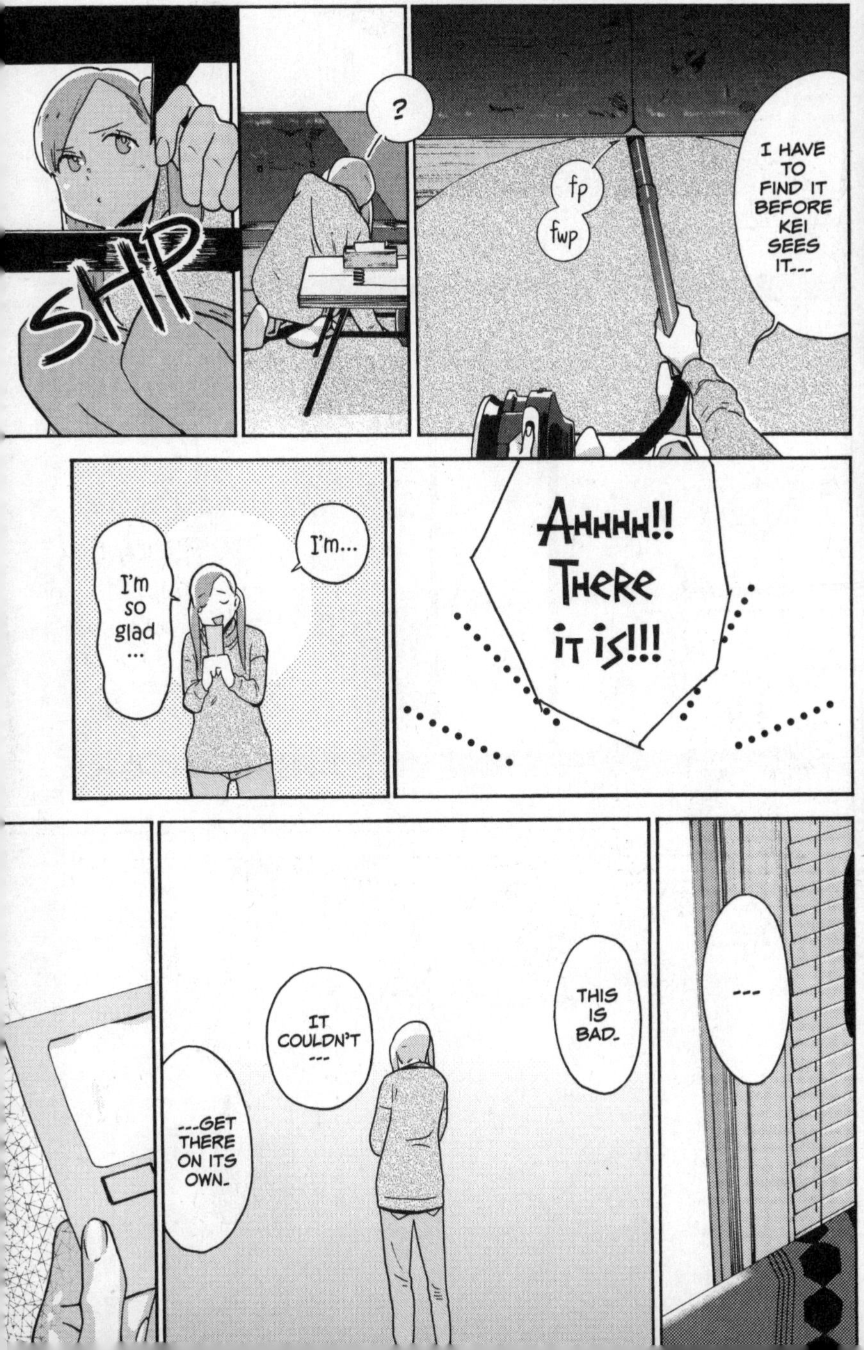
I HAVE TO FIND IT BEFORE KEI SEES IT...
fp
fwp
?
SHP
AHHHH!! THERE IT IS!!!
I'm...
I'm so glad...
...
THIS IS BAD.
IT COULDN'T...
...GET THERE ON ITS OWN.

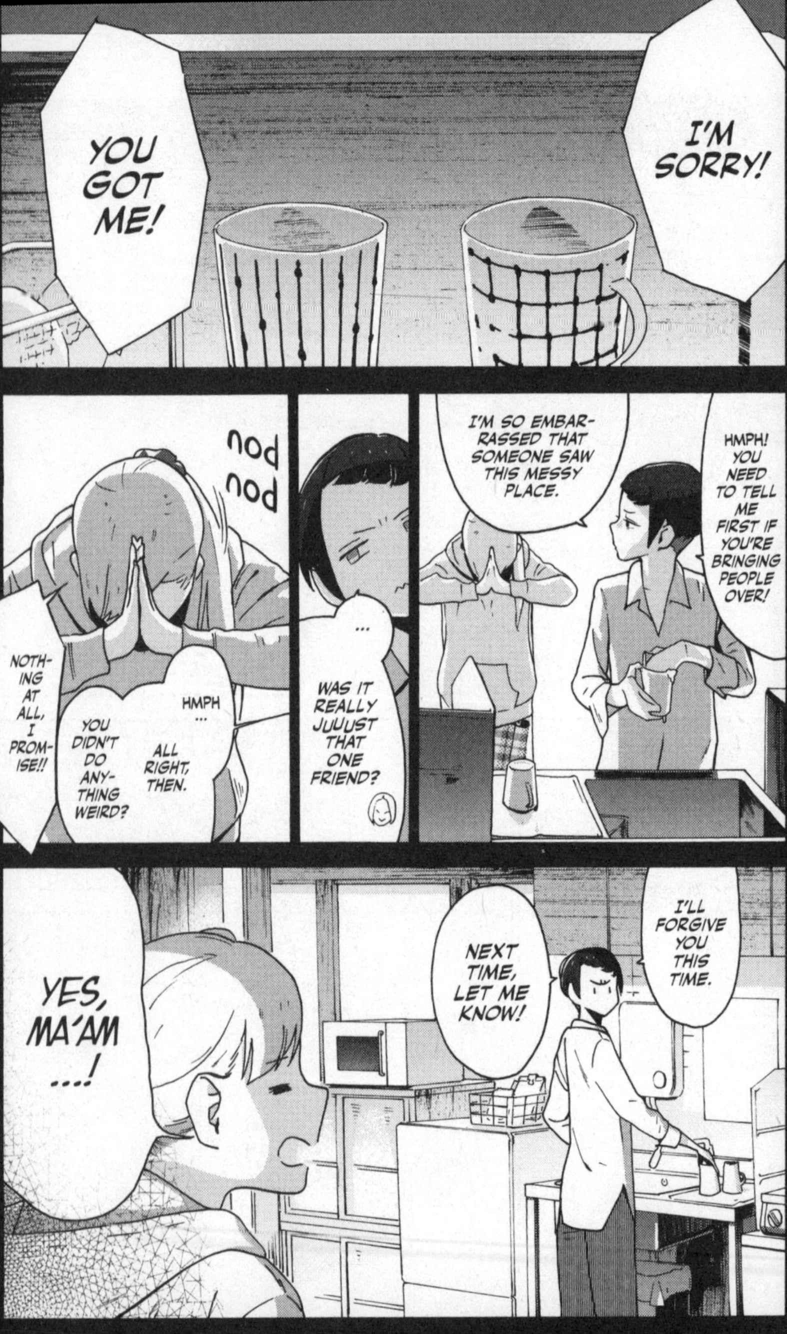
I'M SORRY!
YOU GOT ME!
HMPH! YOU NEED TO TELL ME FIRST IF YOU'RE BRINGING PEOPLE OVER!
I'M SO EMBARRASSED THAT SOMEONE SAW THIS MESSY PLACE.
...
WAS IT REALLY JUUUST THAT ONE FRIEND?
nod nod
HMPH ...
ALL RIGHT, THEN.
YOU DIDN'T DO ANYTHING WEIRD?
NOTHING AT ALL, I PROMISE!!
I'LL FORGIVE YOU THIS TIME.
NEXT TIME, LET ME KNOW!
YES, MA'AM ...!

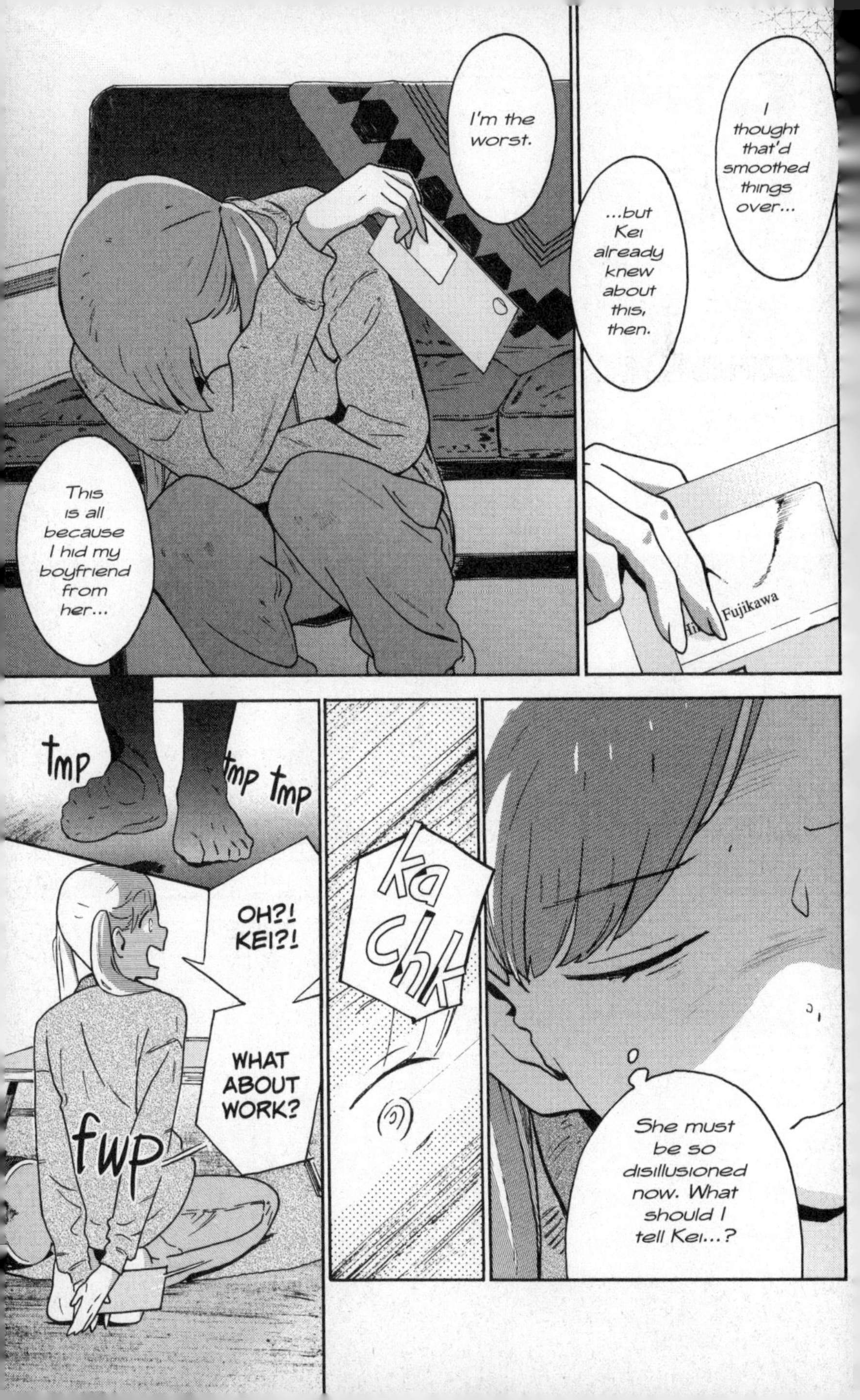
I thought that'd smoothed things over...
...but Kei already knew about this, then.
Fujikawa
I'm the worst.
This is all because I hid my boyfriend from her...
She must be so disillusioned now. What should I tell Kei...?
ka chk
tmp
tmp tmp
OH?! KEI?!
WHAT ABOUT WORK?
fwp

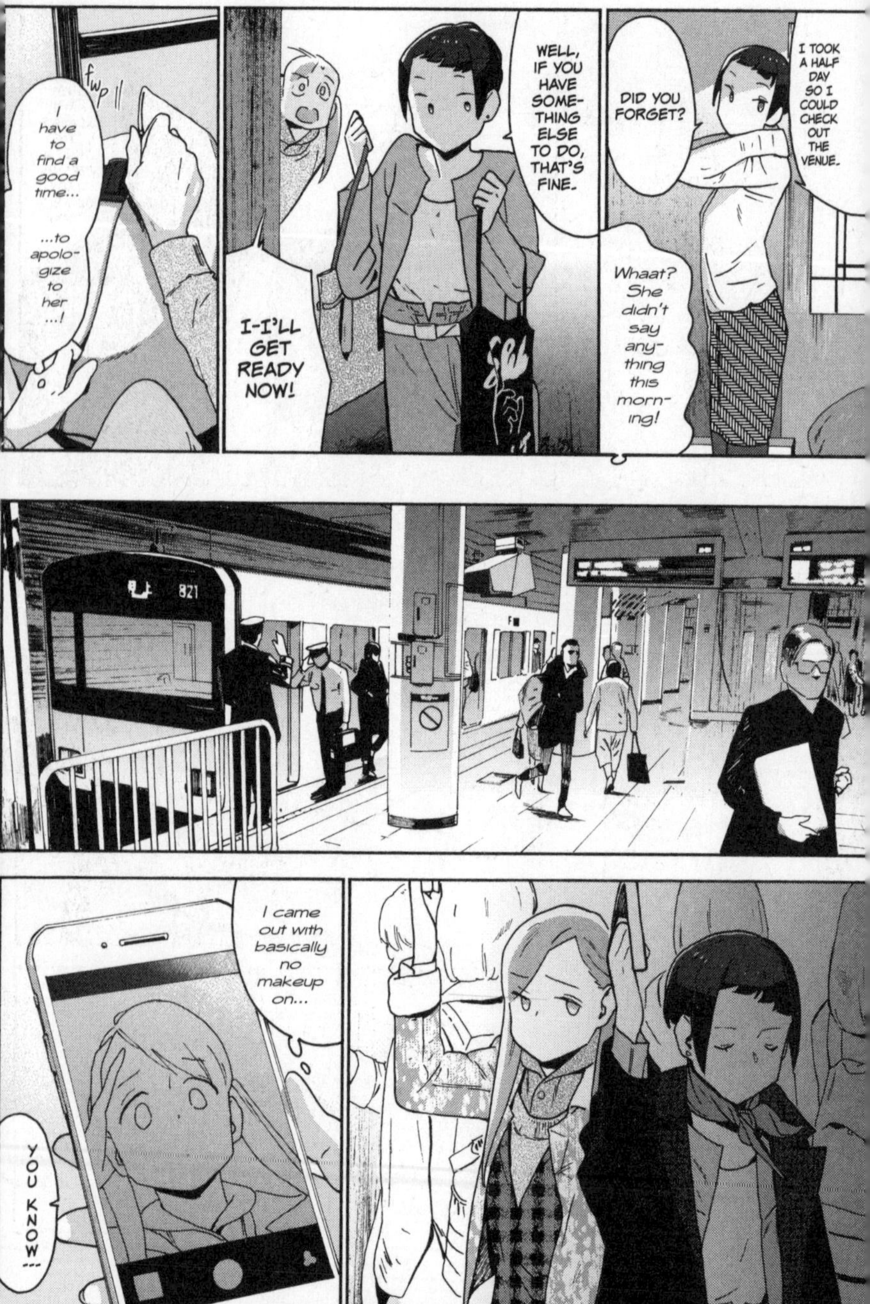
I TOOK A HALF DAY SO I COULD CHECK OUT THE VENUE.
DID YOU FORGET?
Whaat? She didn't say anything this morning!
WELL, IF YOU HAVE SOMETHING ELSE TO DO, THAT'S FINE.
I-I'LL GET READY NOW!
fwp
I have to find a good time...
...to apologize to her...!
821
I came out with basically no makeup on...
YOU KNOW...

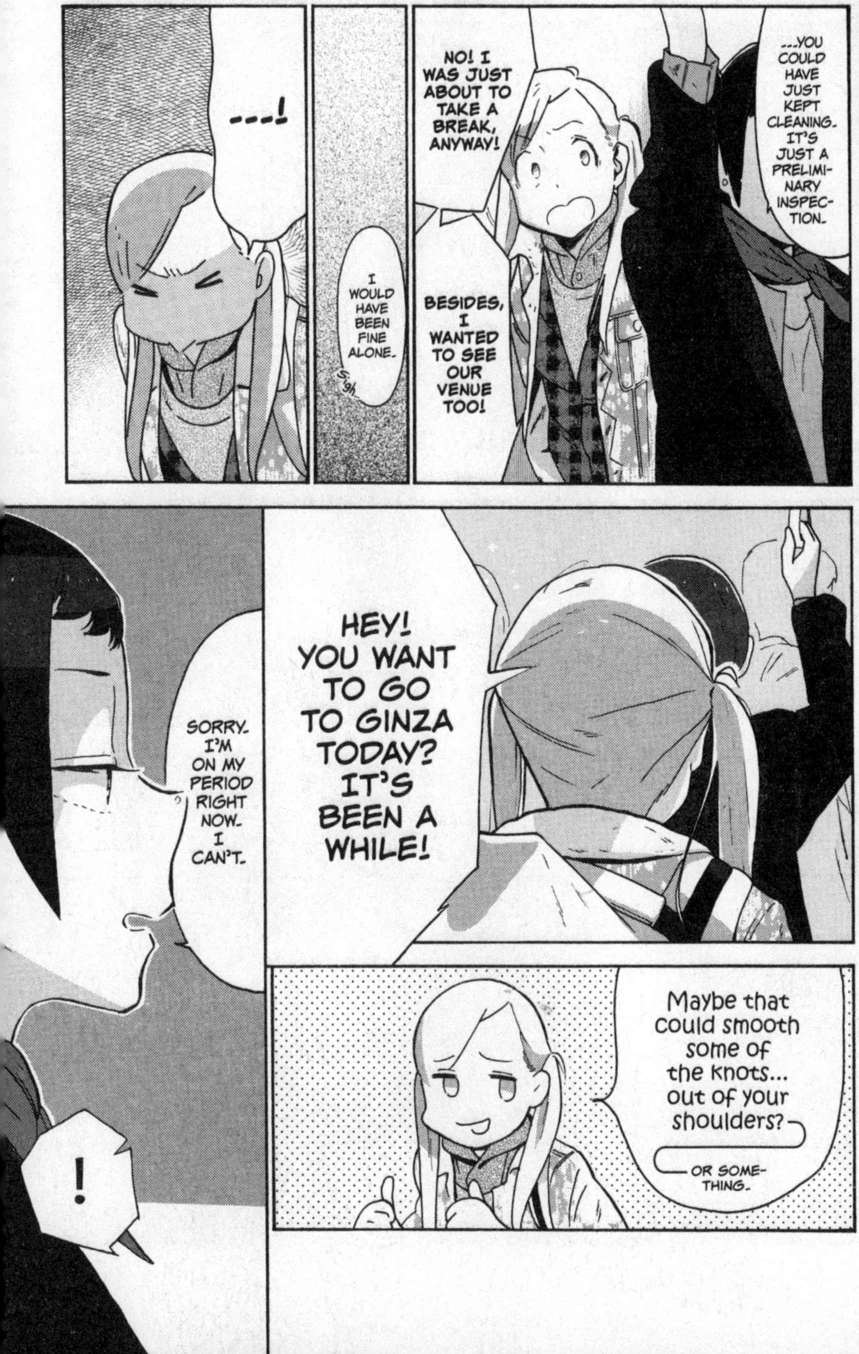
...YOU COULD HAVE JUST KEPT CLEANING. IT'S JUST A PRELIMINARY INSPECTION.
NO! I WAS JUST ABOUT TO TAKE A BREAK, ANYWAY!
BESIDES, I WANTED TO SEE OUR VENUE TOO!
I WOULD HAVE BEEN FINE ALONE.
Sigh...
...!
HEY! YOU WANT TO GO TO GINZA TODAY? IT'S BEEN A WHILE!
Maybe that could smooth some of the knots... out of your shoulders?
OR SOMETHING.
SORRY. I'M ON MY PERIOD RIGHT NOW. I CAN'T.
!

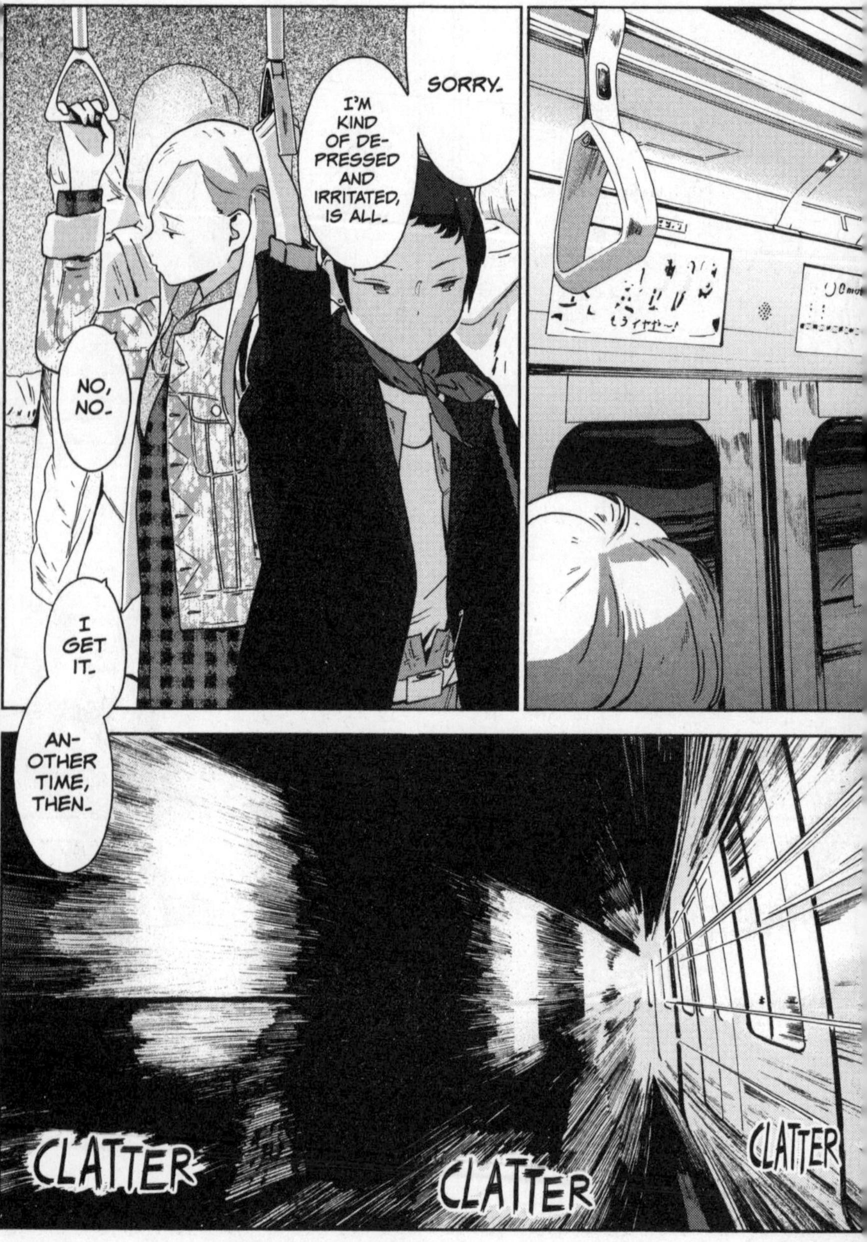
SORRY.
I'M KIND OF DE-PRESSED AND IRRITATED, IS ALL.
NO, NO.
I GET IT.
AN-OTHER TIME, THEN.
CLATTER
CLATTER
CLATTER

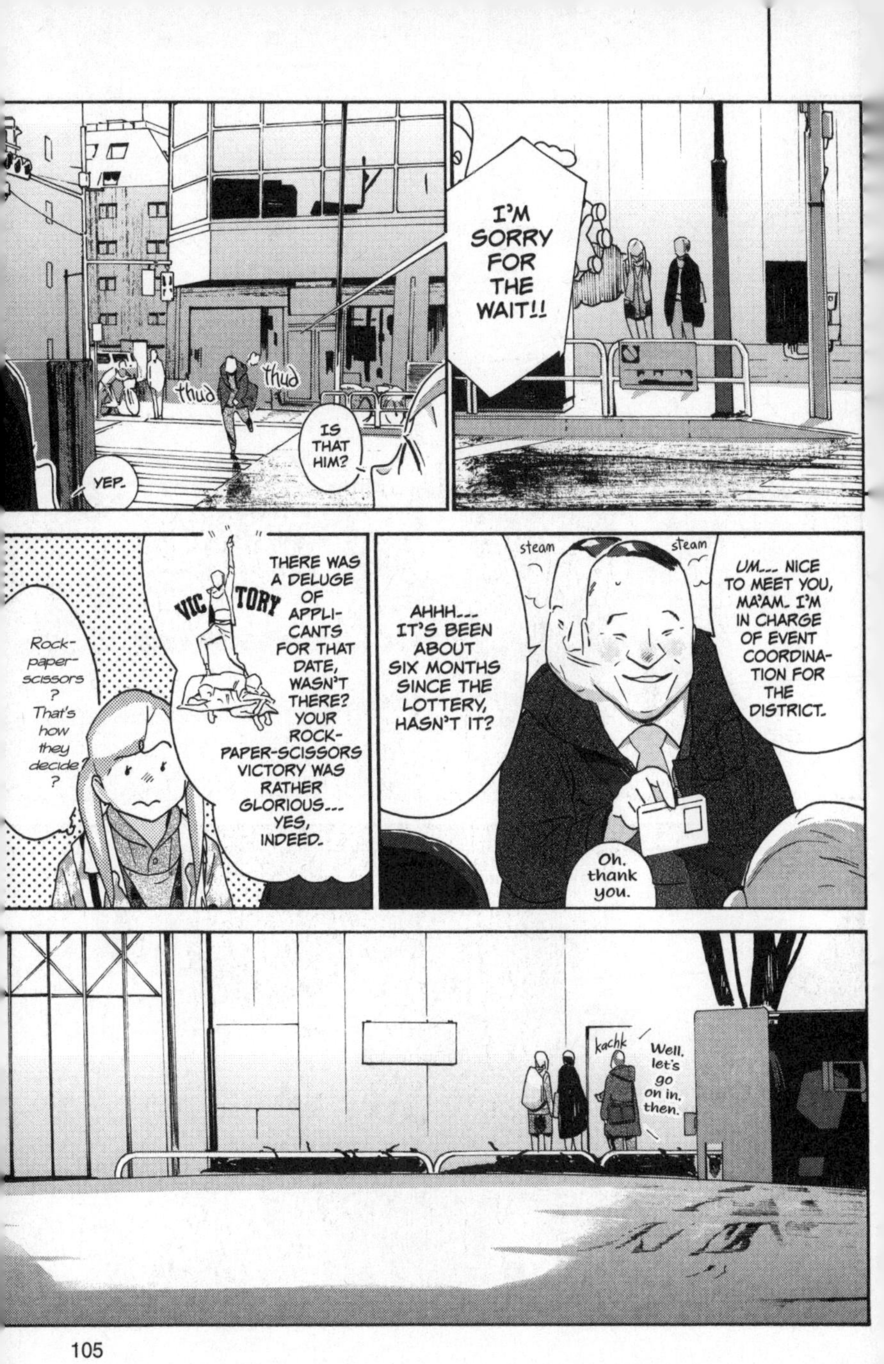
I'M SORRY FOR THE WAIT!!
thud
thud
IS THAT HIM?
YEP.
steam
steam
UM... NICE TO MEET YOU, MA'AM. I'M IN CHARGE OF EVENT COORDINATION FOR THE DISTRICT.
AHHH... IT'S BEEN ABOUT SIX MONTHS SINCE THE LOTTERY, HASN'T IT?
Oh, thank you.
THERE WAS A DELUGE OF APPLI-CANTS FOR THAT DATE, WASN'T THERE? YOUR ROCK-PAPER-SCISSORS VICTORY WAS RATHER GLORIOUS... YES, INDEED.
VICTORY
Rock-paper-scissors? That's how they decide?
Well, let's go on in, then.
kachk

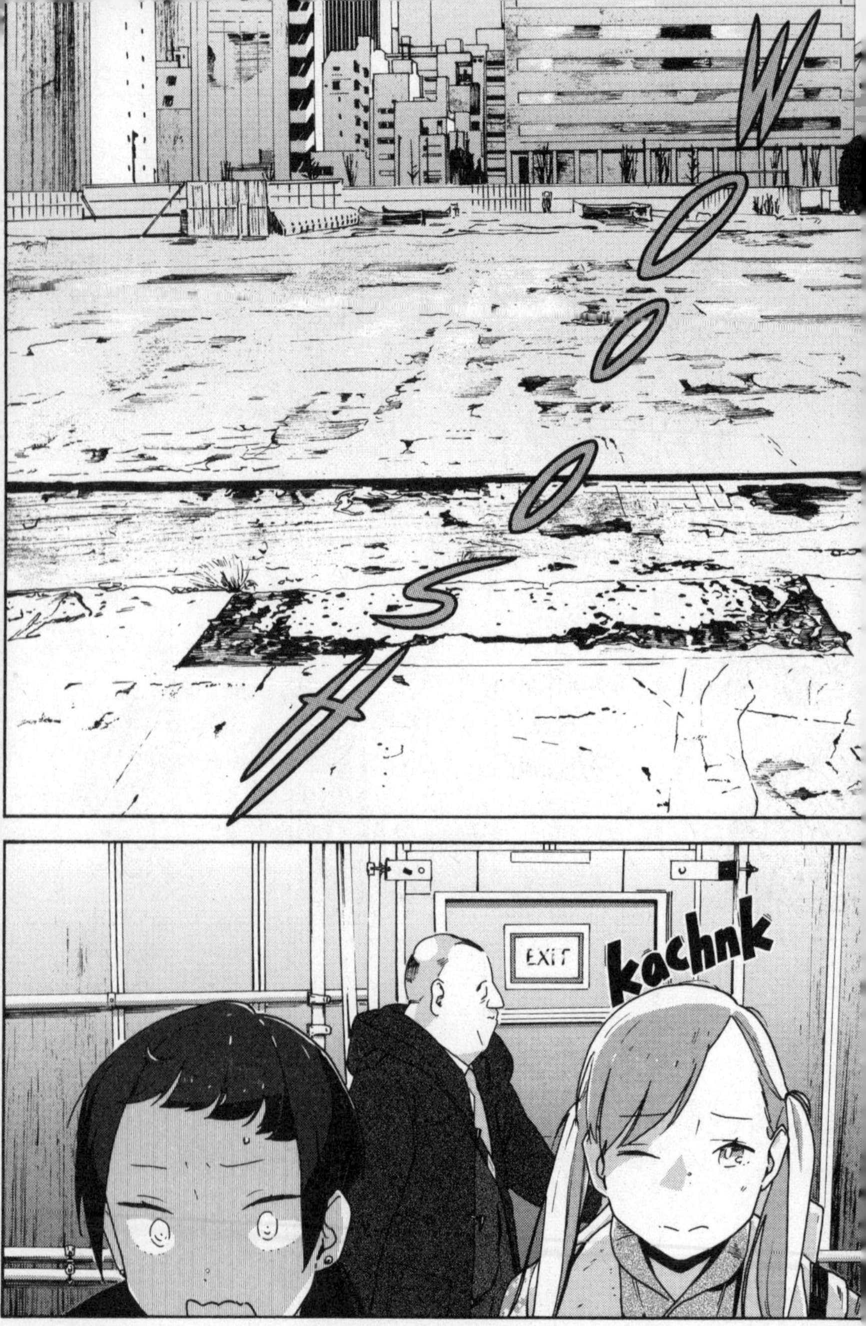
WOOOSH
EXIT
kachnk

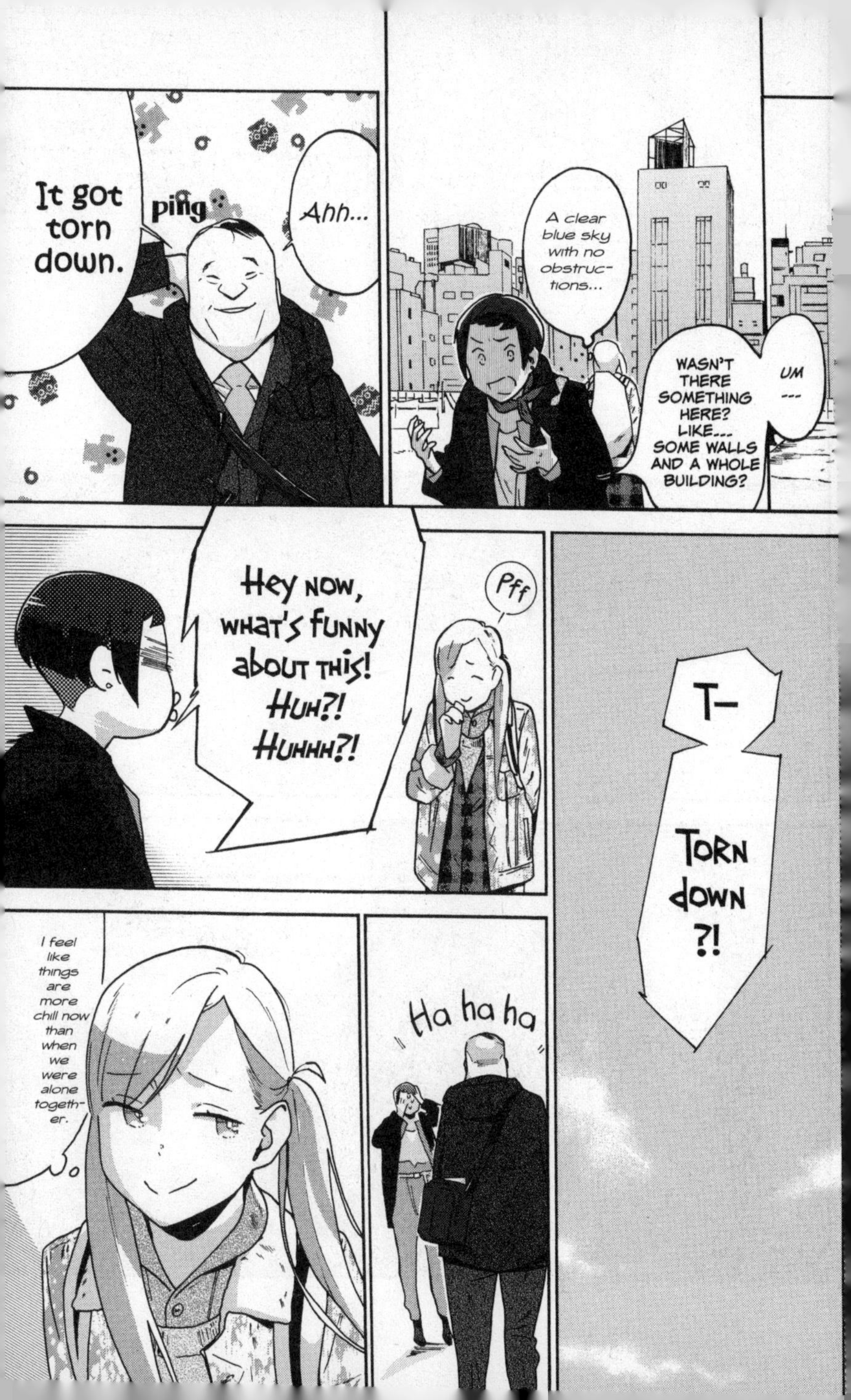
A clear blue sky with no obstructions...
UM ---
WASN'T THERE SOMETHING HERE? LIKE... SOME WALLS AND A WHOLE BUILDING?
Ahh...
ping
It got torn down.
T— TORN DOWN?!
Pff
Hey now, what's funny about this! Huh?! Huhhh?!
Ha ha ha
I feel like things are more chill now than when we were alone together.

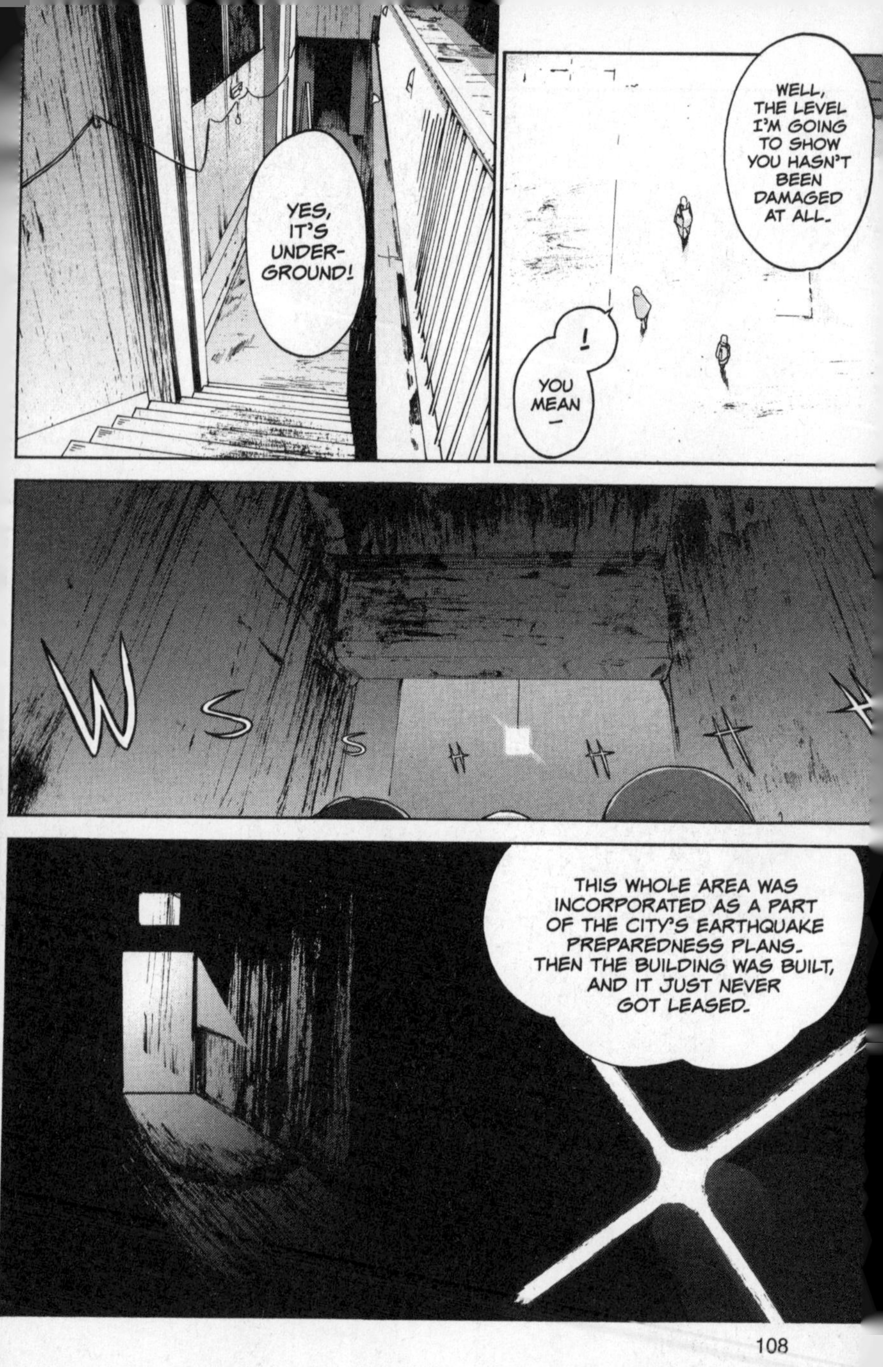
WELL, THE LEVEL I'M GOING TO SHOW YOU HASN'T BEEN DAMAGED AT ALL.
! YOU MEAN—
YES, IT'S UNDER-GROUND!
WSSHHHH
THIS WHOLE AREA WAS INCORPORATED AS A PART OF THE CITY'S EARTHQUAKE PREPAREDNESS PLANS. THEN THE BUILDING WAS BUILT, AND IT JUST NEVER GOT LEASED.

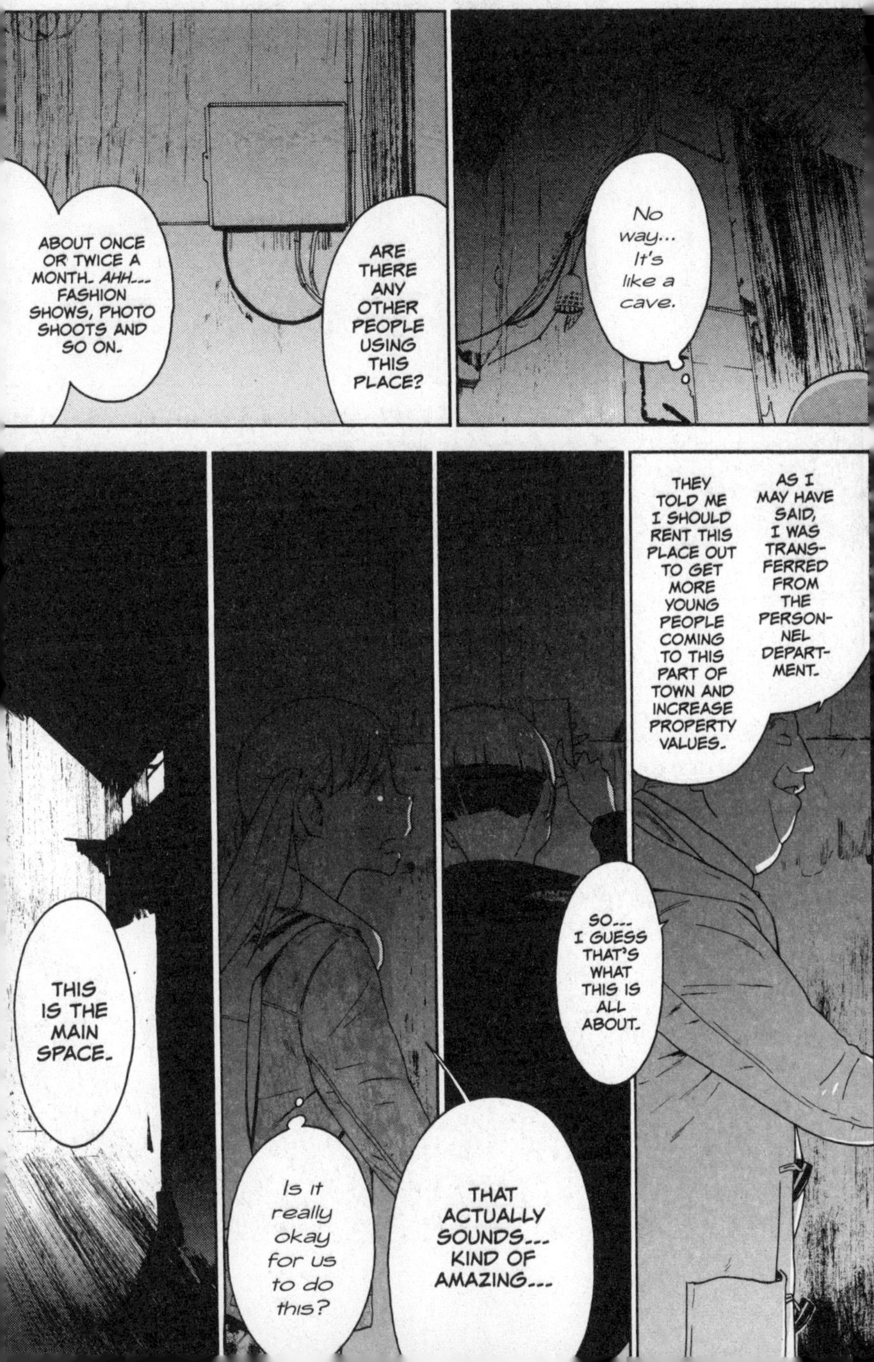
No way... It's like a cave.
ARE THERE ANY OTHER PEOPLE USING THIS PLACE?
ABOUT ONCE OR TWICE A MONTH. *AHH...* FASHION SHOWS, PHOTO SHOOTS AND SO ON.
AS I MAY HAVE SAID, I WAS TRANS-FERRED FROM THE PERSON-NEL DEPART-MENT.
THEY TOLD ME I SHOULD RENT THIS PLACE OUT TO GET MORE YOUNG PEOPLE COMING TO THIS PART OF TOWN AND INCREASE PROPERTY VALUES.
SO... I GUESS THAT'S WHAT THIS IS ALL ABOUT.
THAT ACTUALLY SOUNDS... KIND OF AMAZING...
Is it really okay for us to do this?
THIS IS THE MAIN SPACE.

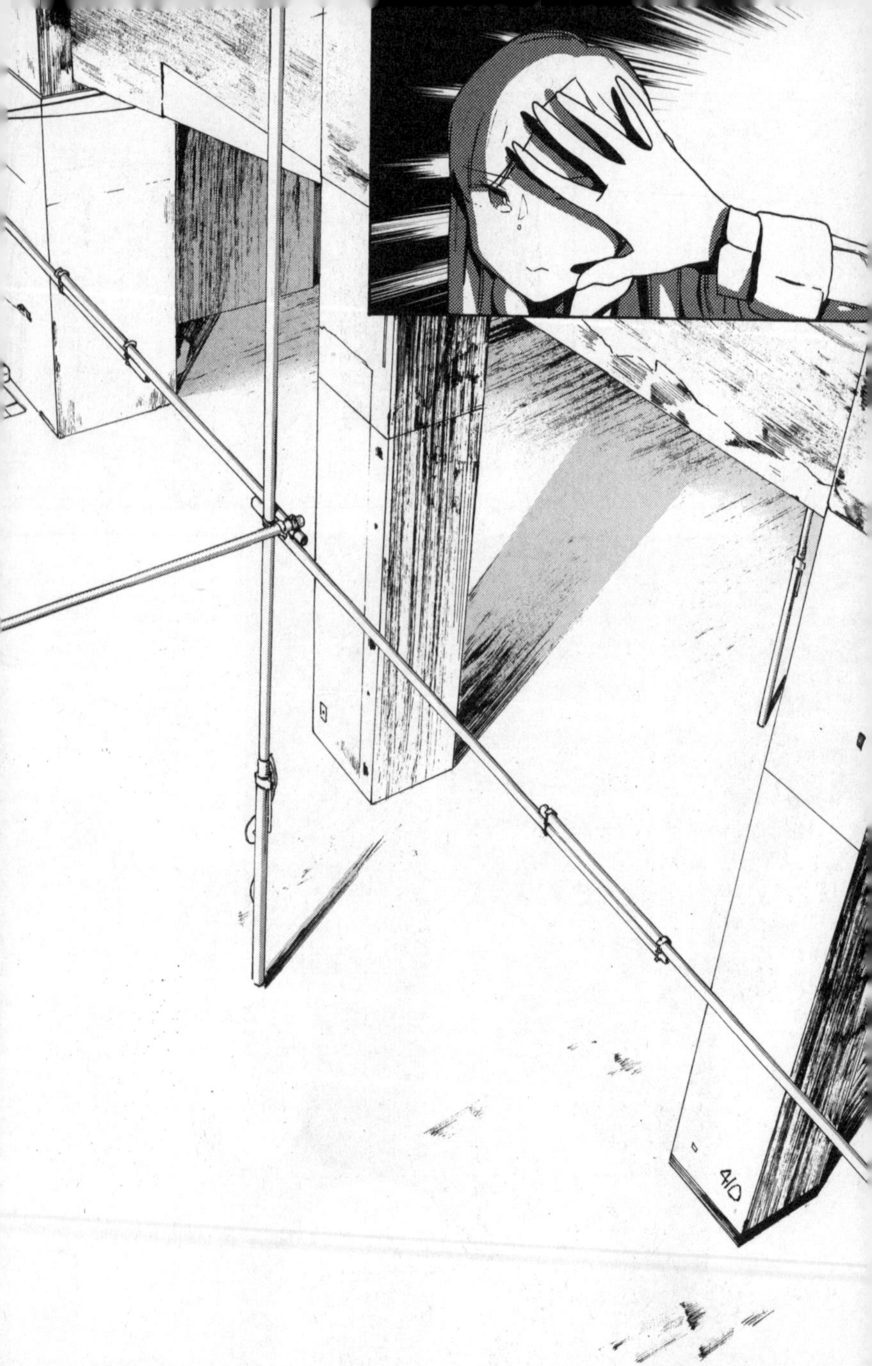
410

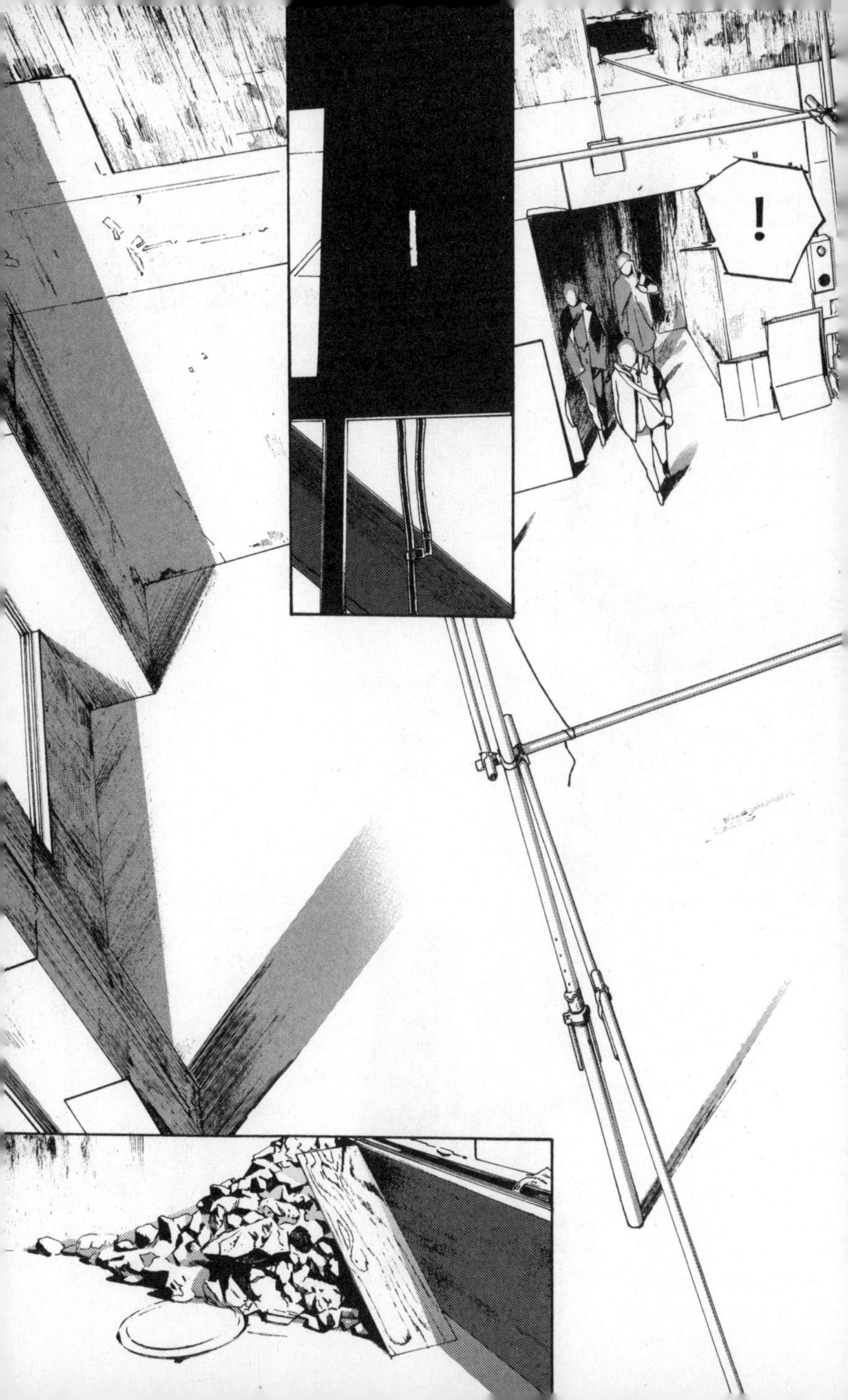
!

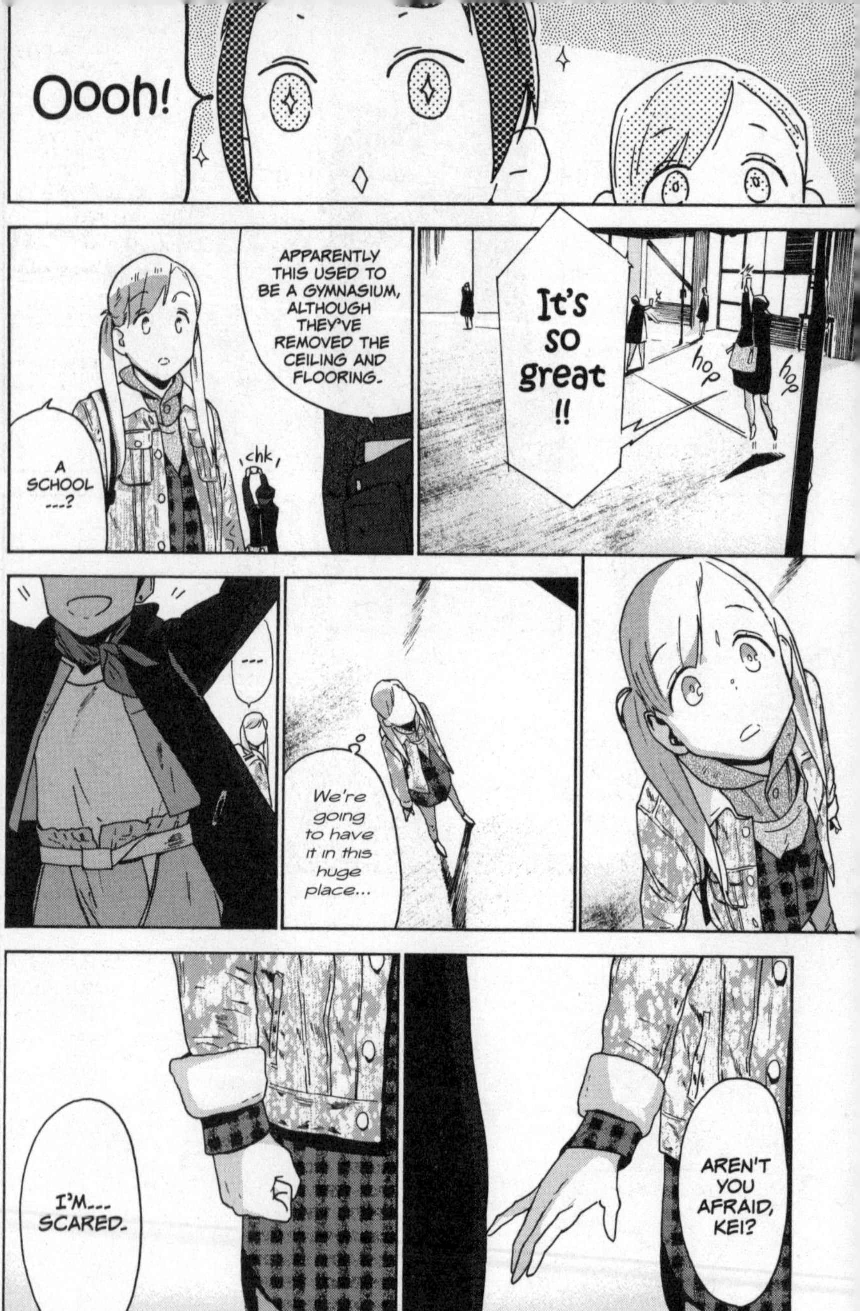
Oooh!
It's so great!!
hop hop
APPARENTLY THIS USED TO BE A GYMNASIUM, ALTHOUGH THEY'VE REMOVED THE CEILING AND FLOORING.
chk
A SCHOOL...?
We're going to have it in this huge place...
...
AREN'T YOU AFRAID, KEI?
I'M... SCARED.

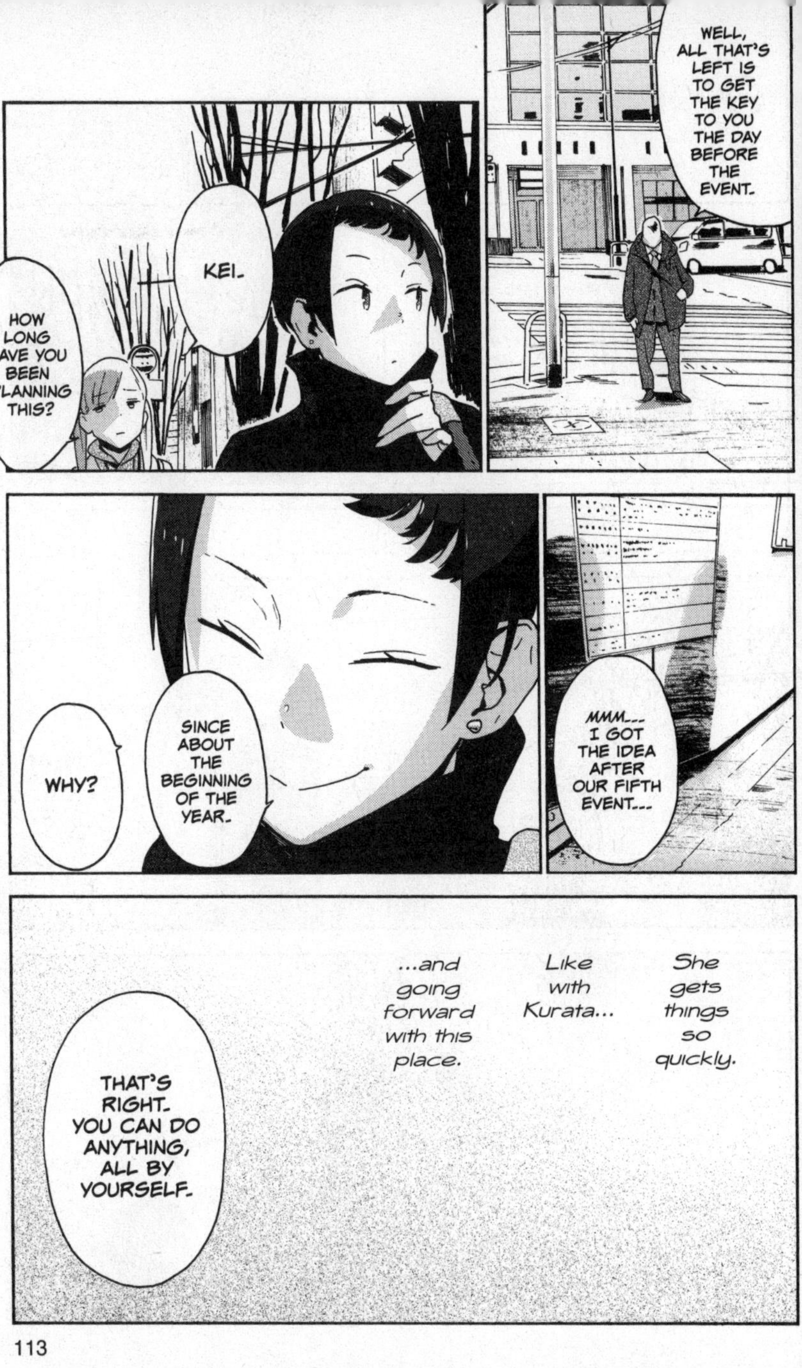
WELL, ALL THAT'S LEFT IS TO GET THE KEY TO YOU THE DAY BEFORE THE EVENT.
KEI.
HOW LONG HAVE YOU BEEN PLANNING THIS?
MMM... I GOT THE IDEA AFTER OUR FIFTH EVENT...
SINCE ABOUT THE BEGINNING OF THE YEAR.
WHY?
She gets things so quickly.
Like with Kurata...
...and going forward with this place.
THAT'S RIGHT. YOU CAN DO ANYTHING, ALL BY YOURSELF.

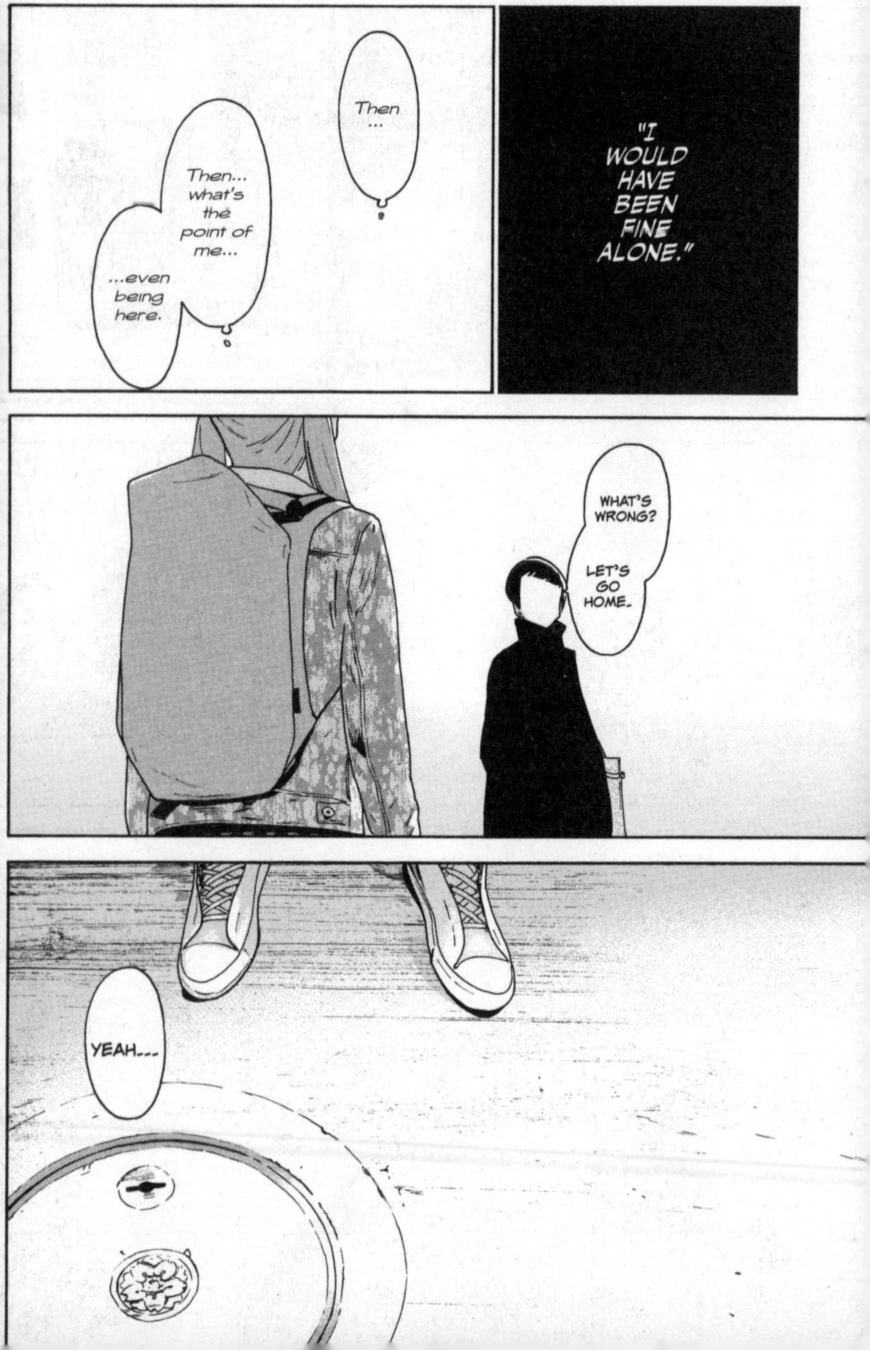
"I WOULD HAVE BEEN FINE ALONE."
Then ...
Then... what's the point of me...
...even being here.
WHAT'S WRONG?
LET'S GO HOME.
YEAH...

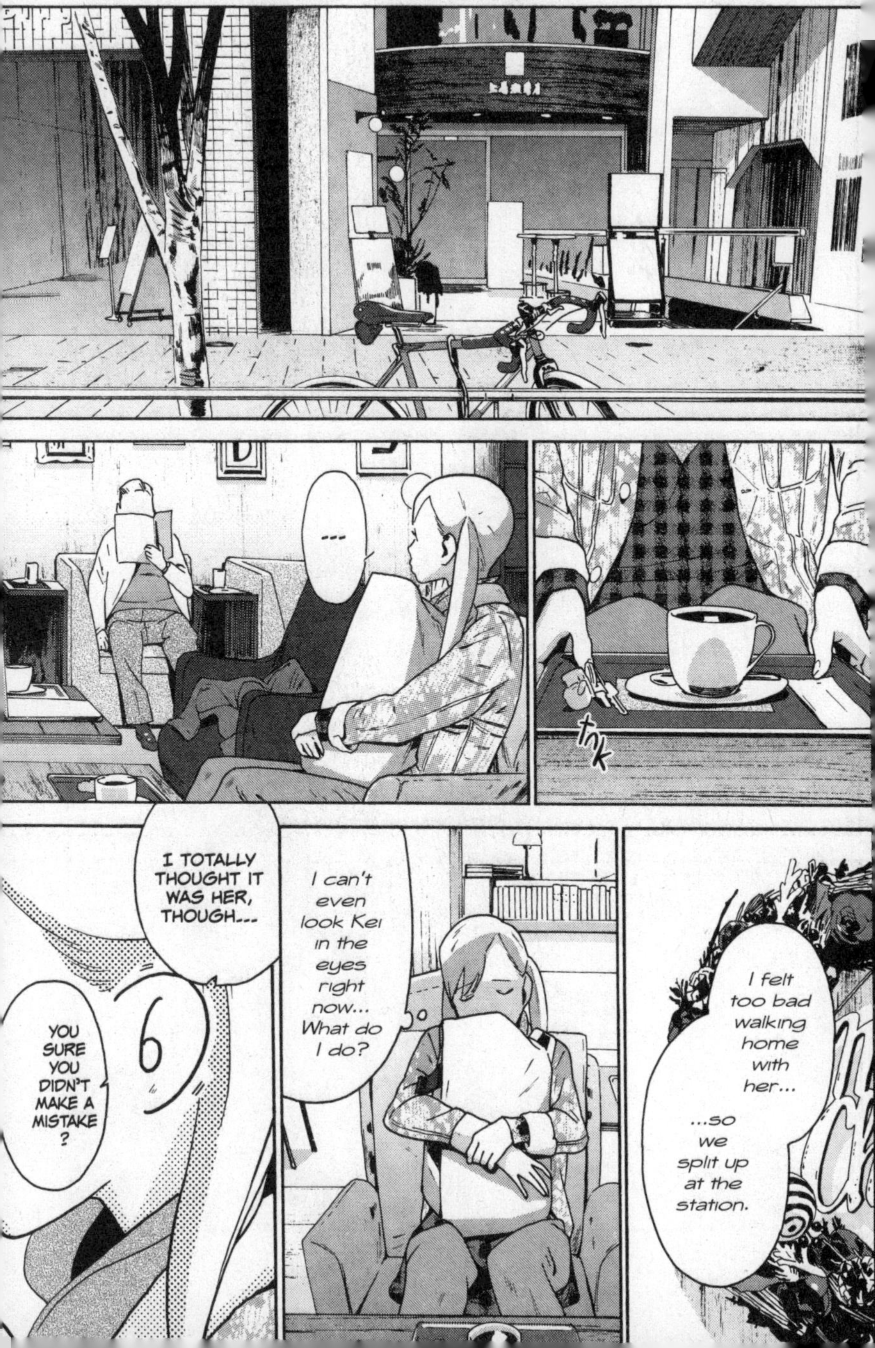
tnk
...
I felt too bad walking home with her...
...so we split up at the station.
I can't even look Kei in the eyes right now... What do I do?
I TOTALLY THOUGHT IT WAS HER, THOUGH...
YOU SURE YOU DIDN'T MAKE A MISTAKE?

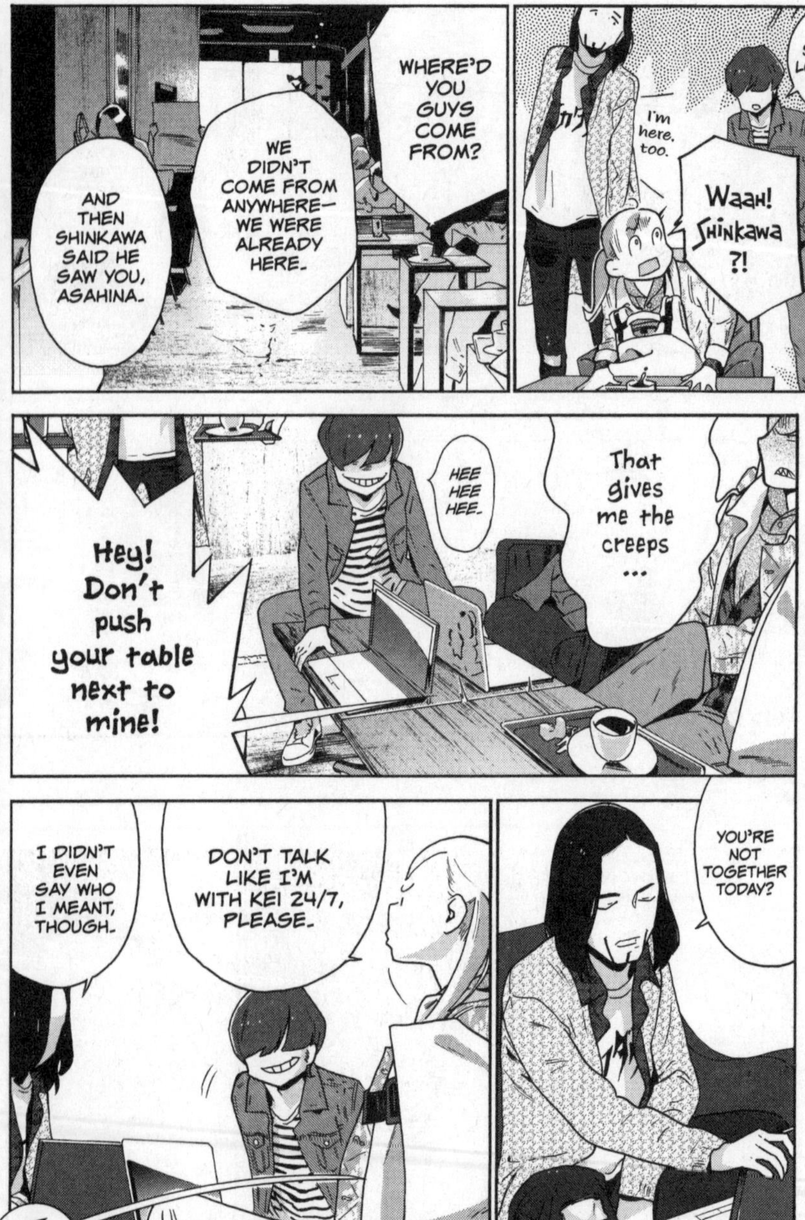

SEE, LOOK.
Waah! Shinkawa?!
I'm here, too.
WHERE'D YOU GUYS COME FROM?
WE DIDN'T COME FROM ANYWHERE— WE WERE ALREADY HERE.
AND THEN SHINKAWA SAID HE SAW YOU, ASAHINA.
That gives me the creeps...
HEE HEE HEE.
Hey! Don't push your table next to mine!
YOU'RE NOT TOGETHER TODAY?
DON'T TALK LIKE I'M WITH KEI 24/7, PLEASE.
I DIDN'T EVEN SAY WHO I MEANT, THOUGH.

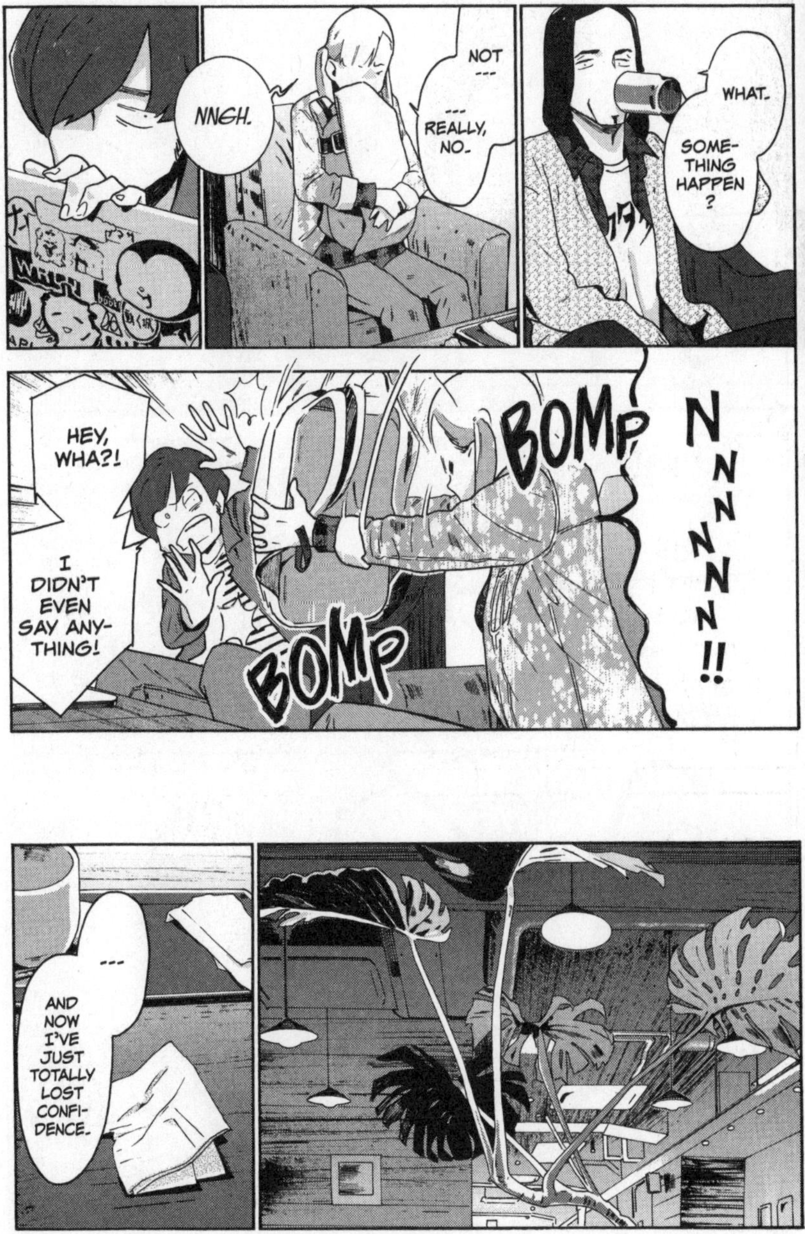
WHAT.
SOME-THING HAPPEN?
NOT --- --- REALLY, NO.
NNGH.
NNNNNN!!
BOMP
HEY, WHA?!
I DIDN'T EVEN SAY ANY-THING!
BOMP
--- AND NOW I'VE JUST TOTALLY LOST CONFI-DENCE.

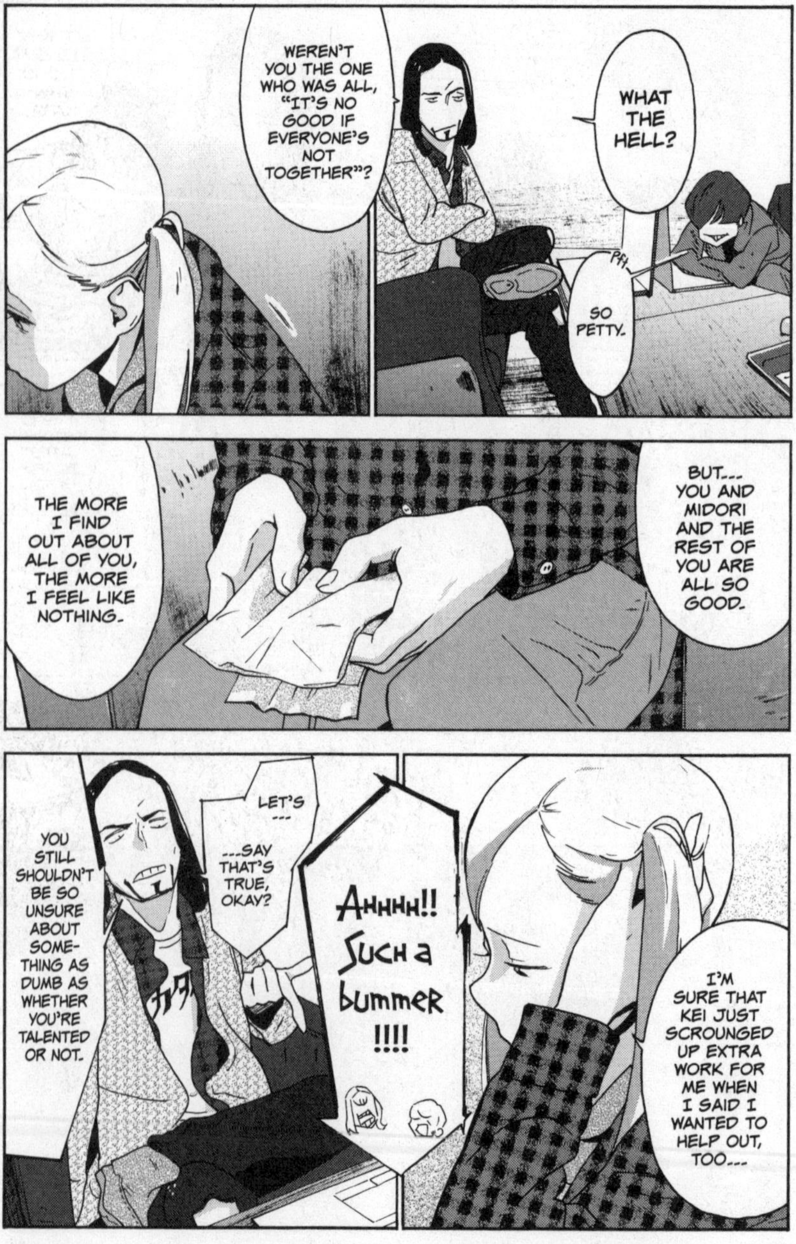
WHAT THE HELL?
WEREN'T YOU THE ONE WHO WAS ALL, "IT'S NO GOOD IF EVERYONE'S NOT TOGETHER"?
Pft
SO PETTY.
BUT... YOU AND MIDORI AND THE REST OF YOU ARE ALL SO GOOD.
THE MORE I FIND OUT ABOUT ALL OF YOU, THE MORE I FEEL LIKE NOTHING.
I'M SURE THAT KEI JUST SCROUNGED UP EXTRA WORK FOR ME WHEN I SAID I WANTED TO HELP OUT, TOO...
AHHHH!! SUCH A BUMMER !!!!
LET'S...
...SAY THAT'S TRUE, OKAY?
YOU STILL SHOULDN'T BE SO UNSURE ABOUT SOME-THING AS DUMB AS WHETHER YOU'RE TALENTED OR NOT.

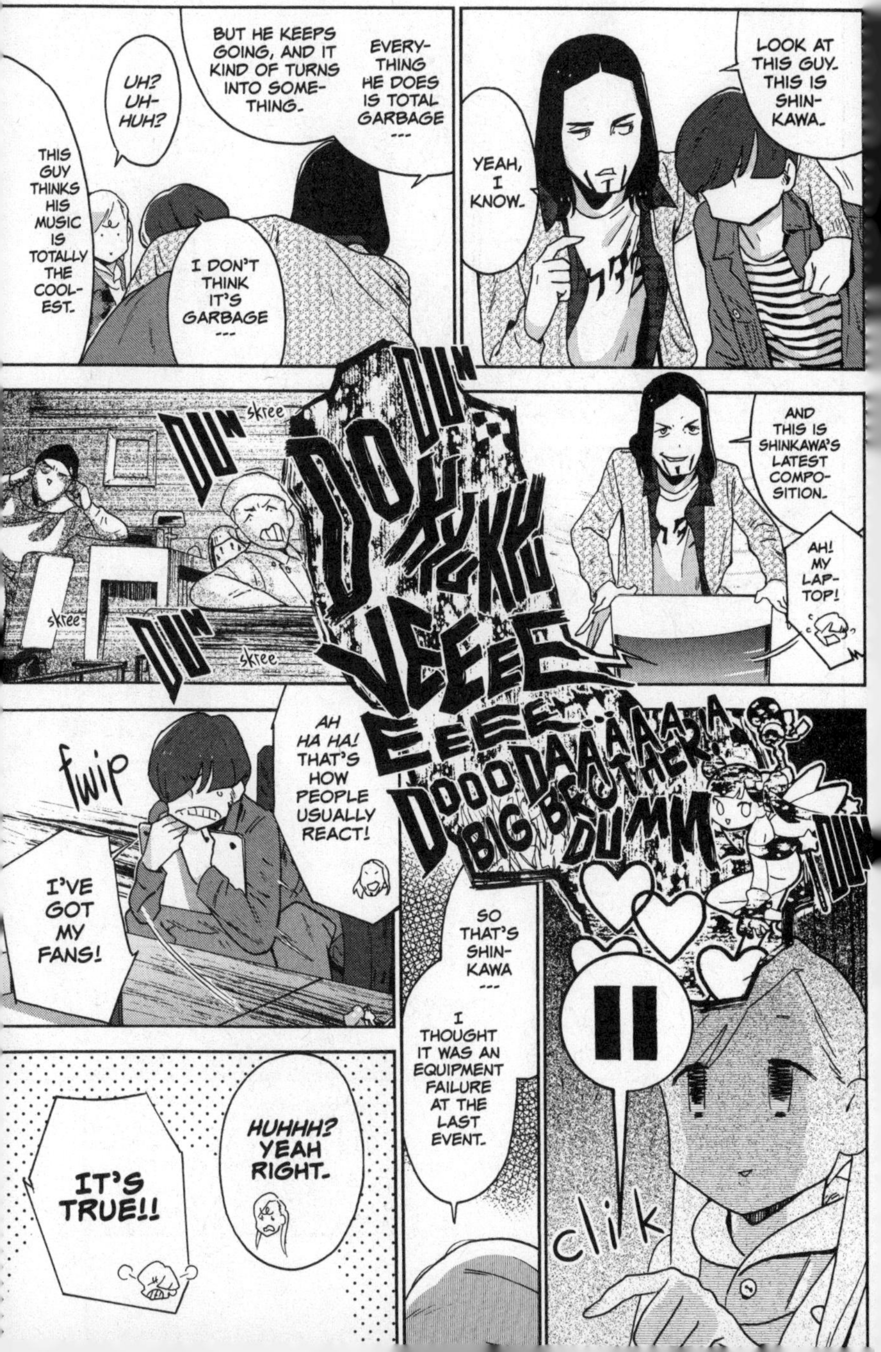
LOOK AT THIS GUY. THIS IS SHINKAWA.
YEAH, I KNOW.
EVERYTHING HE DOES IS TOTAL GARBAGE ---
BUT HE KEEPS GOING, AND IT KIND OF TURNS INTO SOMETHING.
UH? UH-HUH?
THIS GUY THINKS HIS MUSIC IS TOTALLY THE COOLEST.
I DON'T THINK IT'S GARBAGE ---
AND THIS IS SHINKAWA'S LATEST COMPOSITION.
AH! MY LAPTOP!
DUN
skree
DUN
skree
skree
VEEEEEE
BIG BROTHER!
DUMM
DUN
clik
SO THAT'S SHINKAWA ---
I THOUGHT IT WAS AN EQUIPMENT FAILURE AT THE LAST EVENT.
AH HA HA! THAT'S HOW PEOPLE USUALLY REACT!
fwip
I'VE GOT MY FANS!
HUHHH? YEAH RIGHT.
IT'S TRUE!!

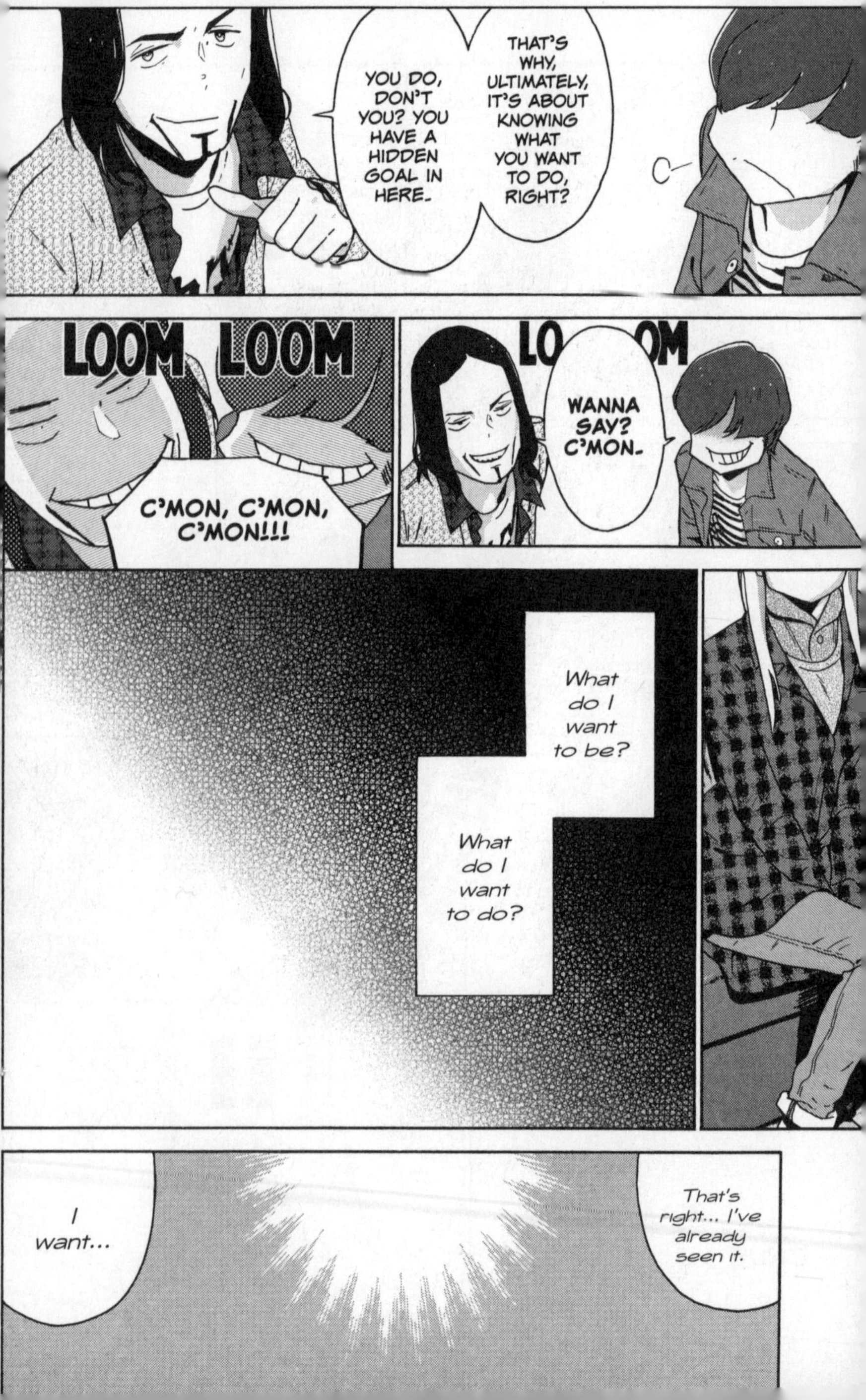
C—
THAT'S WHY, ULTIMATELY, IT'S ABOUT KNOWING WHAT YOU WANT TO DO, RIGHT?
YOU DO, DON'T YOU? YOU HAVE A HIDDEN GOAL IN HERE.
LO OM
WANNA SAY? C'MON.
LOOM LOOM
C'MON, C'MON, C'MON!!!
What do I want to be?
What do I want to do?
That's right... I've already seen it.
I want...

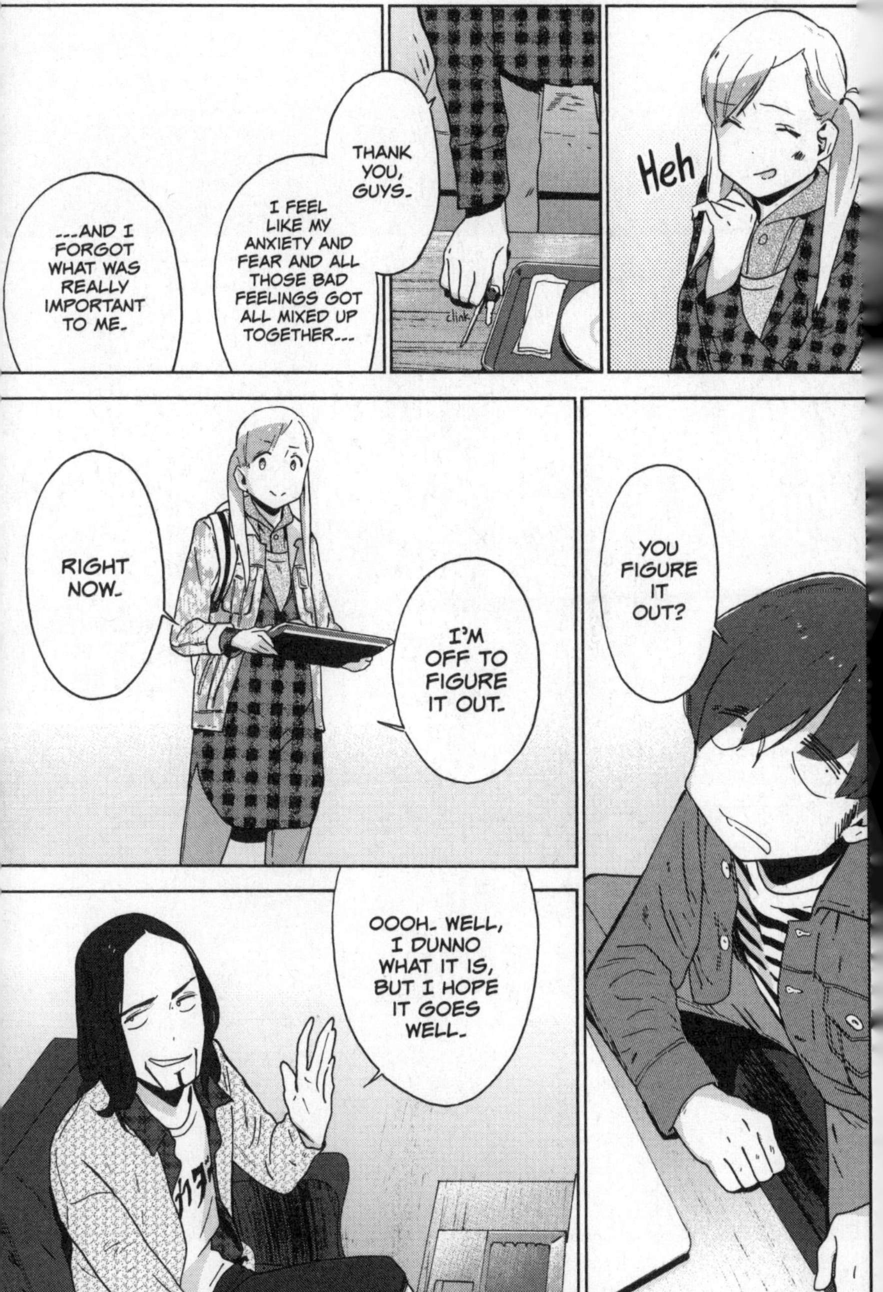
Heh
clink
THANK YOU, GUYS.
I FEEL LIKE MY ANXIETY AND FEAR AND ALL THOSE BAD FEELINGS GOT ALL MIXED UP TOGETHER...
...AND I FORGOT WHAT WAS REALLY IMPORTANT TO ME.
YOU FIGURE IT OUT?
I'M OFF TO FIGURE IT OUT.
RIGHT NOW.
OOOH. WELL, I DUNNO WHAT IT IS, BUT I HOPE IT GOES WELL.

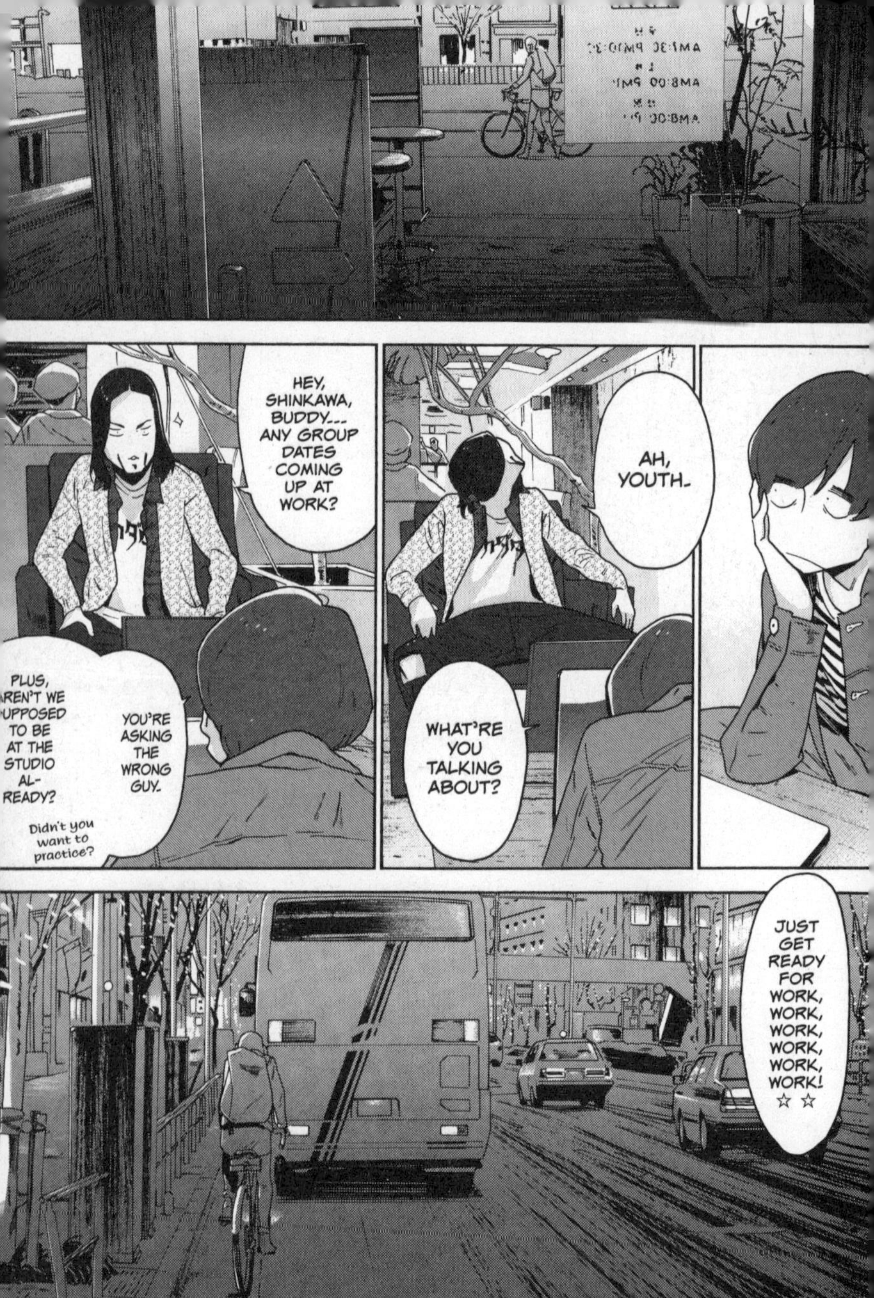
AH, YOUTH.
WHAT'RE YOU TALKING ABOUT?
HEY, SHINKAWA, BUDDY... ANY GROUP DATES COMING UP AT WORK?
YOU'RE ASKING THE WRONG GUY.
PLUS, REN'T WE UPPOSED TO BE AT THE STUDIO AL-READY?
Didn't you want to practice?
JUST GET READY FOR WORK, WORK, WORK, WORK, WORK, WORK! ☆ ☆

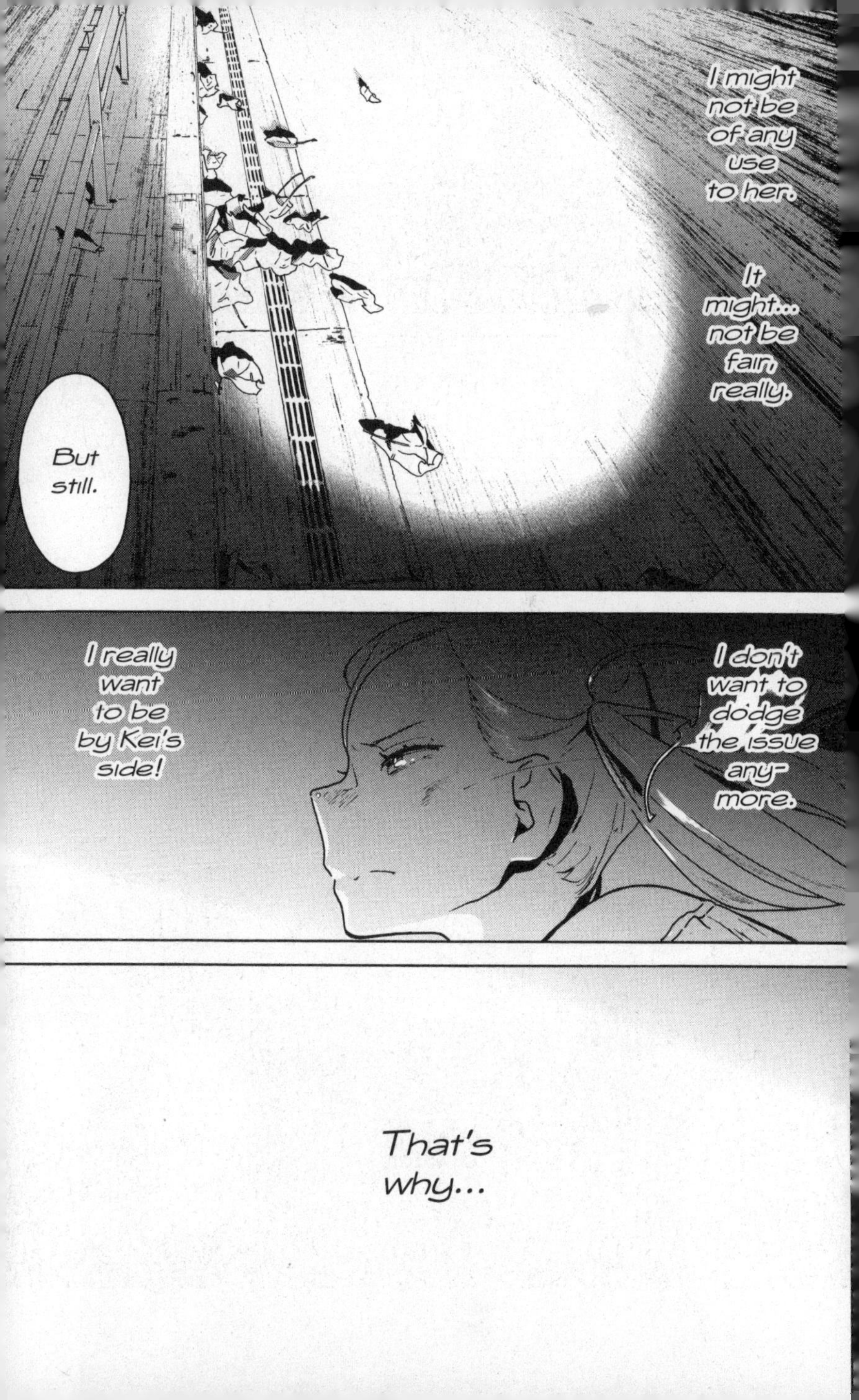
I might not be of any use to her.
It might... not be fair, really.
But still.
I don't want to dodge the issue any-more.
I really want to be by Kei's side!
That's why...

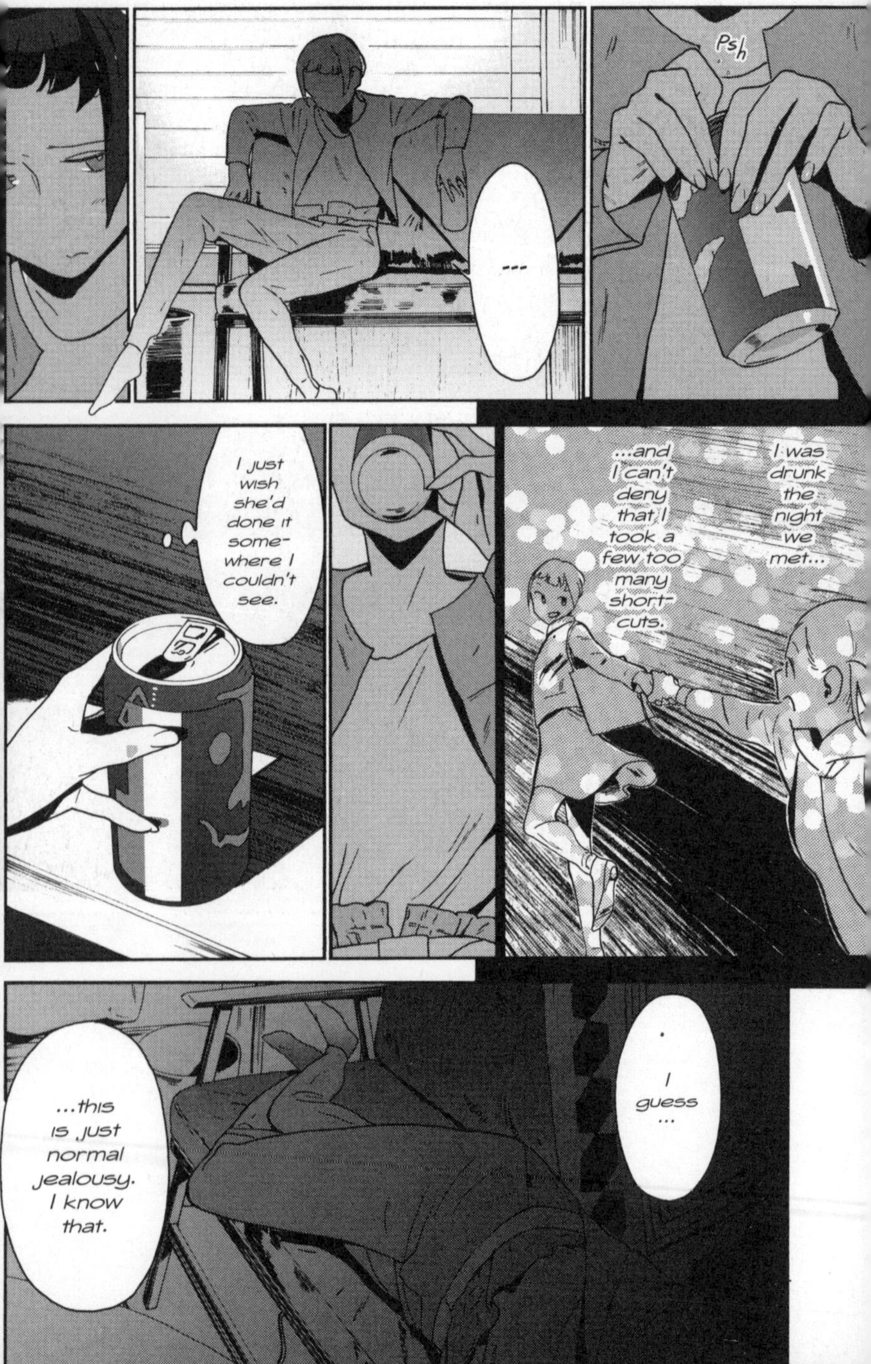
Psh

I was drunk the night we met...
...and I can't deny that I took a few too many short-cuts.
I just wish she'd done it somewhere I couldn't see.
I guess...
...this is just normal jealousy. I know that.

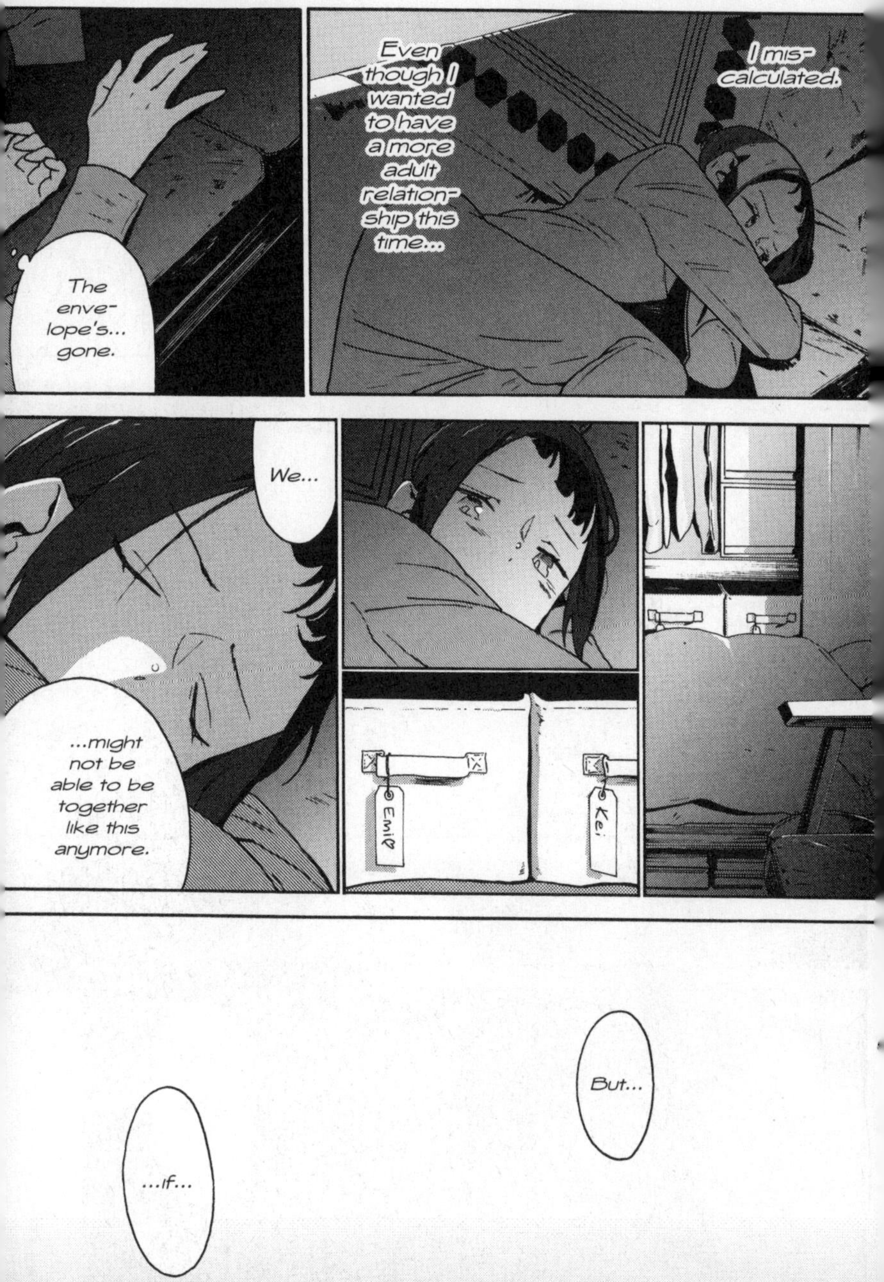
I mis-calculated.
Even though I wanted to have a more adult relation-ship this time...
The enve-lope's... gone.
Kei
We...
...might not be able to be together like this anymore.
But...
...if...

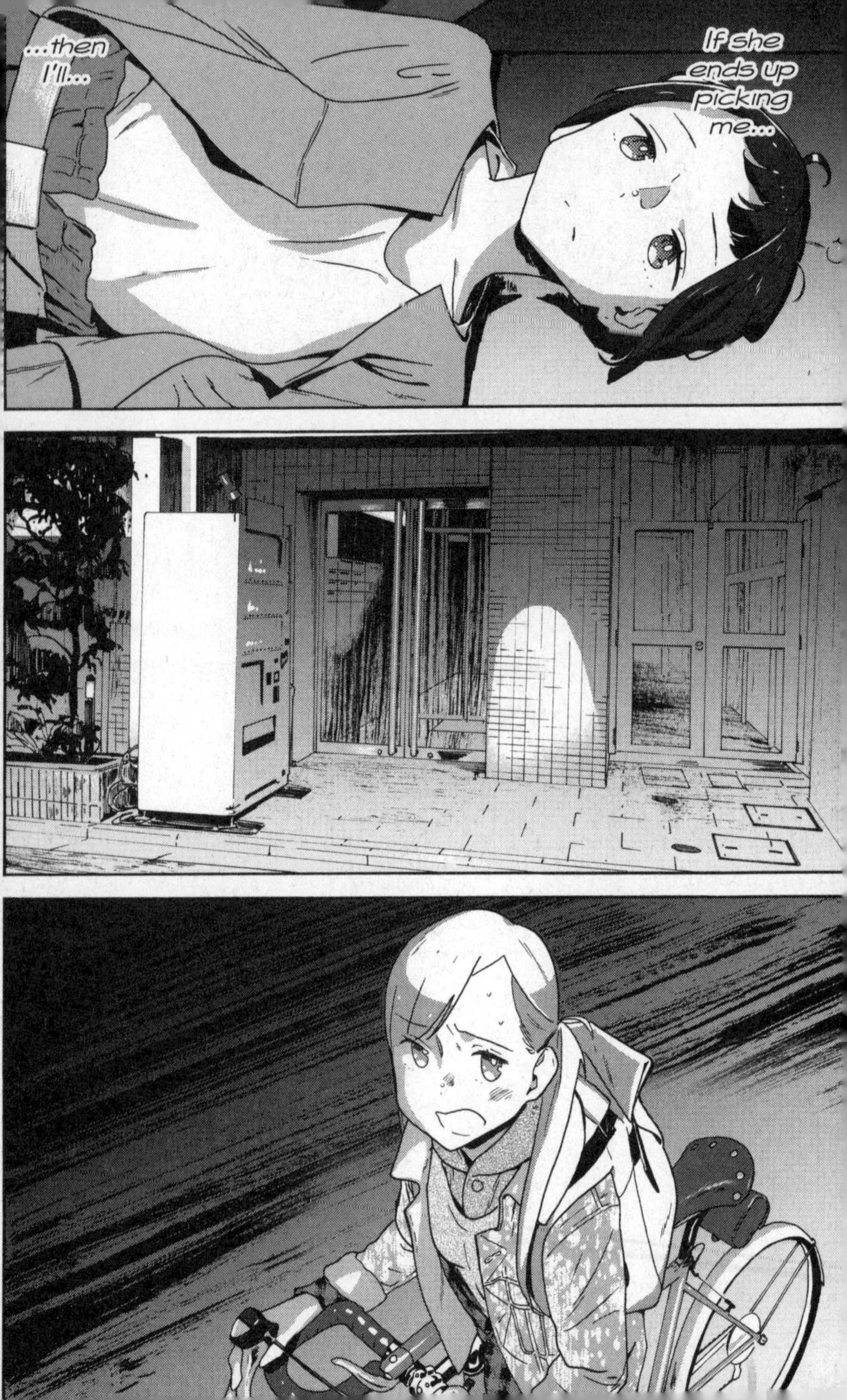
If she ends up picking me...
...then I'll...

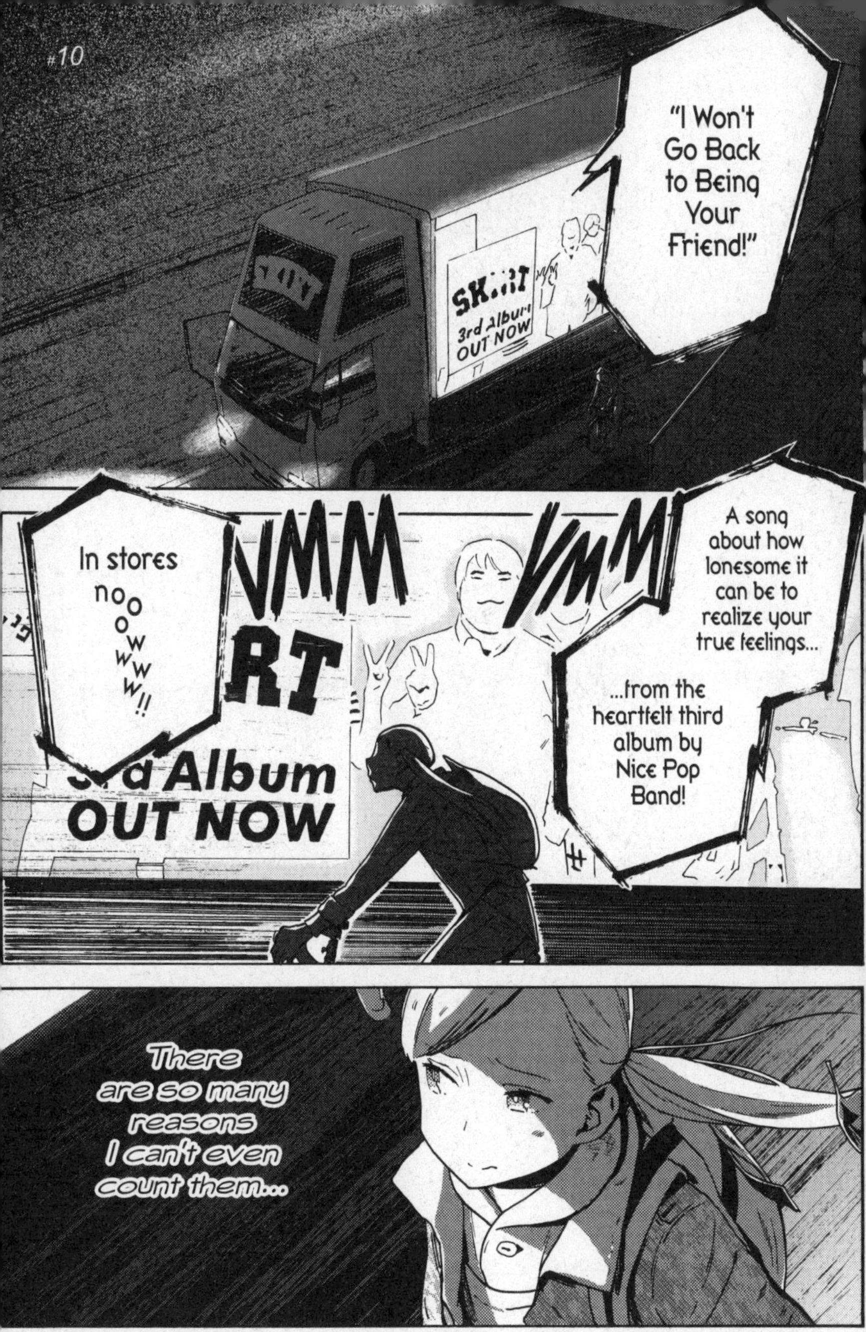
"I Won't Go Back to Being Your Friend!"
3rd Album OUT NOW
A song about how lonesome it can be to realize your true feelings...
...from the heartfelt third album by Nice Pop Band!
VMM
VMM
In stores noooowwww!!
Album OUT NOW
There are so many reasons I can't even count them...

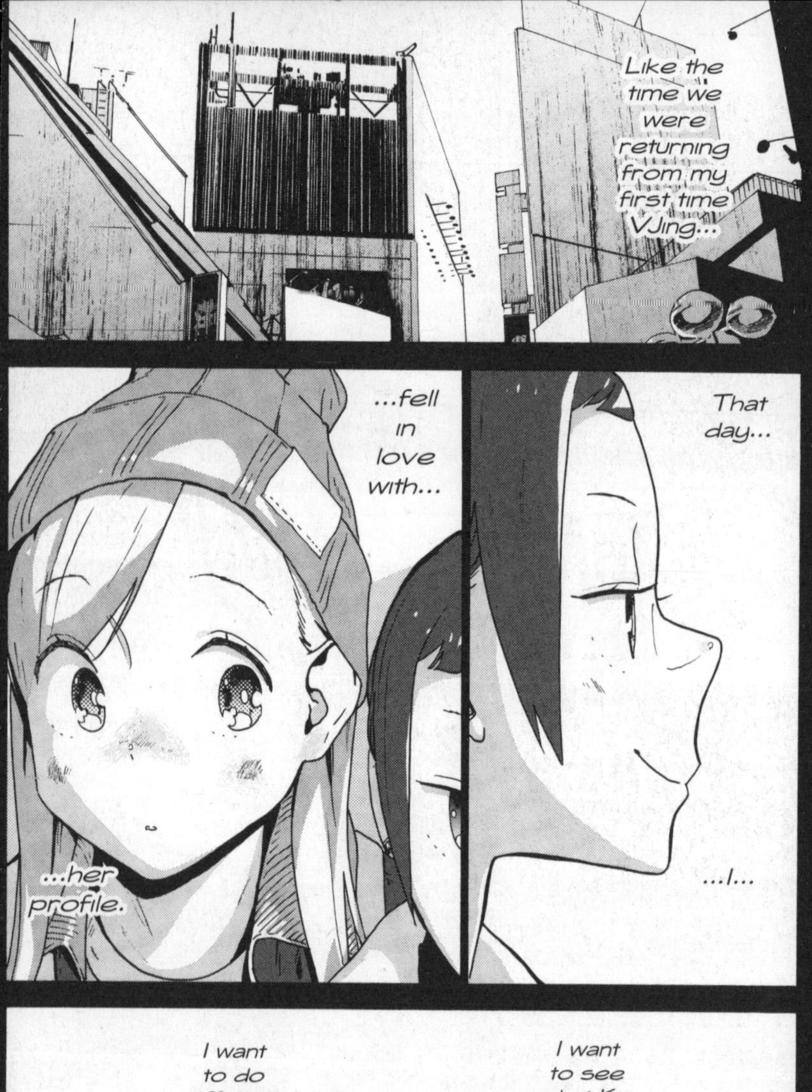
Like the time we were returning from my first time VJing...
That day...
...I...
...fell in love with...
...her profile.
I want to see what Kei sees, by her side.
I want to do different fun things with her and see that expression on her face again.

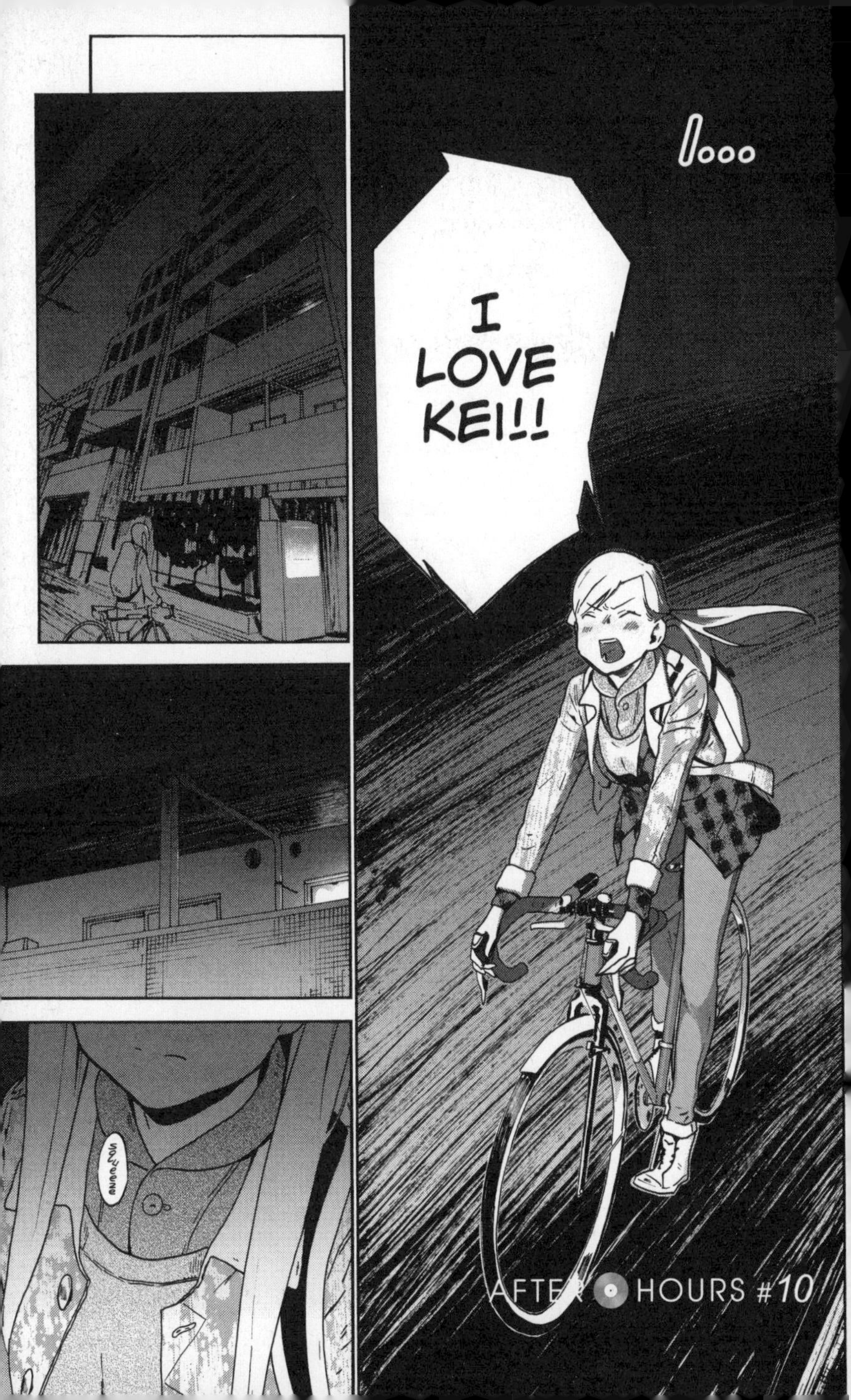
looo
I LOVE KEI!!
AFTER HOURS #10
squeeze

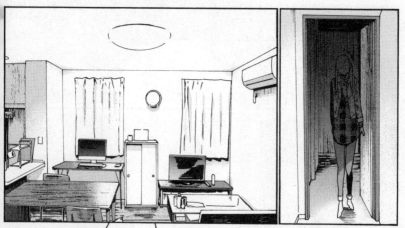

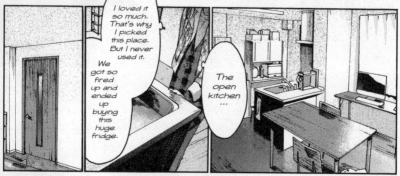

The open kitchen ...
I loved it so much. That's why I picked this place. But I never used it.
We got so fired up and ended up buying this huge fridge.
knock
...

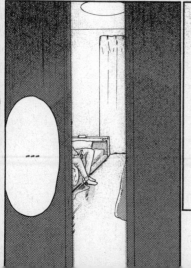

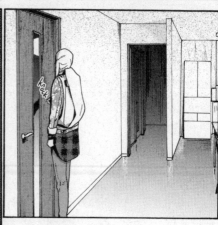

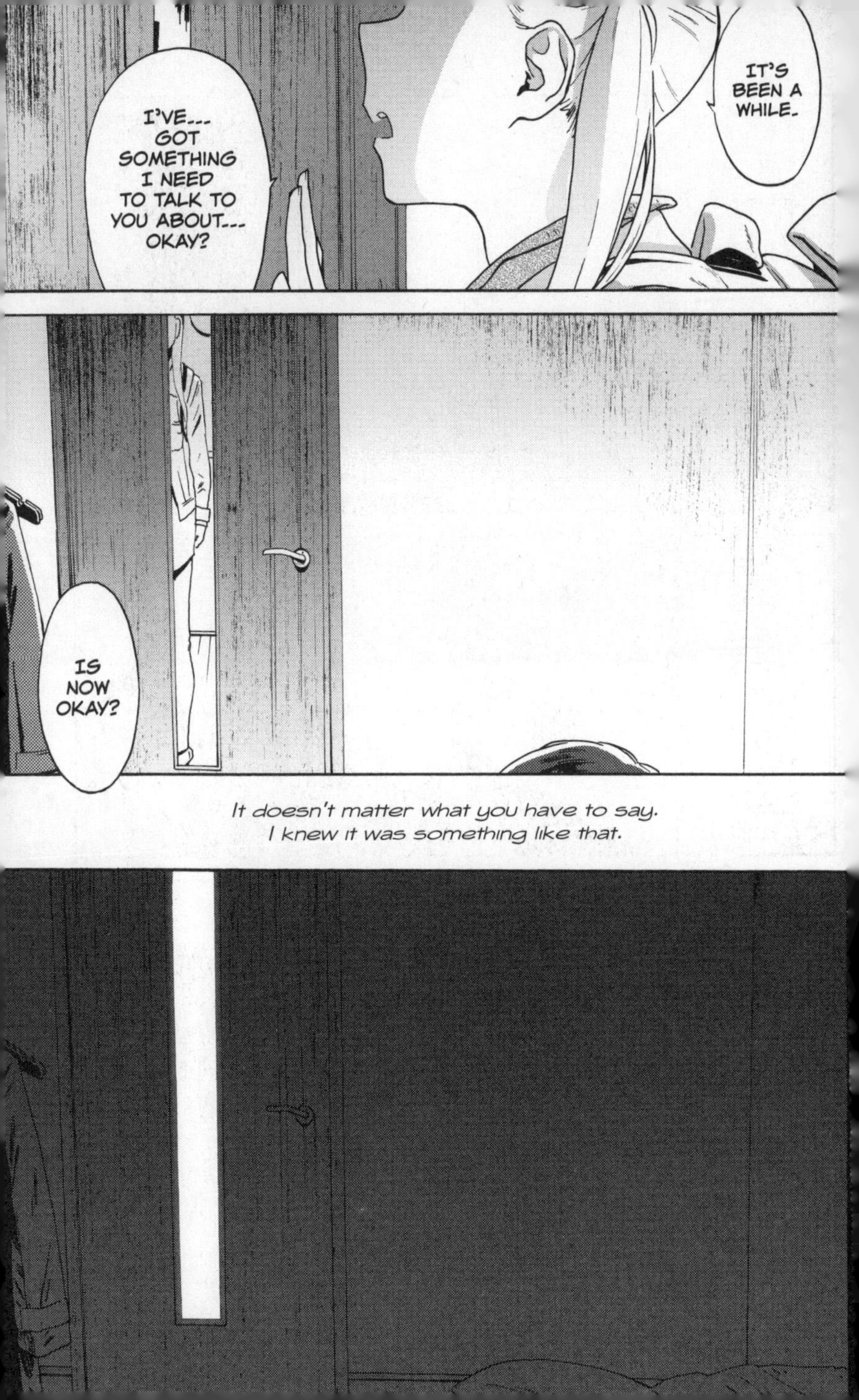
IT'S BEEN A WHILE.
I'VE... GOT SOMETHING I NEED TO TALK TO YOU ABOUT... OKAY?
IS NOW OKAY?
It doesn't matter what you have to say. I knew it was something like that.

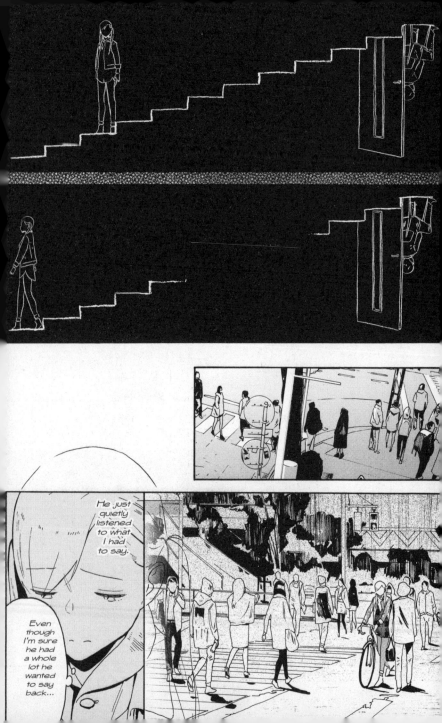

He just quietly listened to what I had to say.

Even though I'm sure he had a whole lot he wanted to say back...

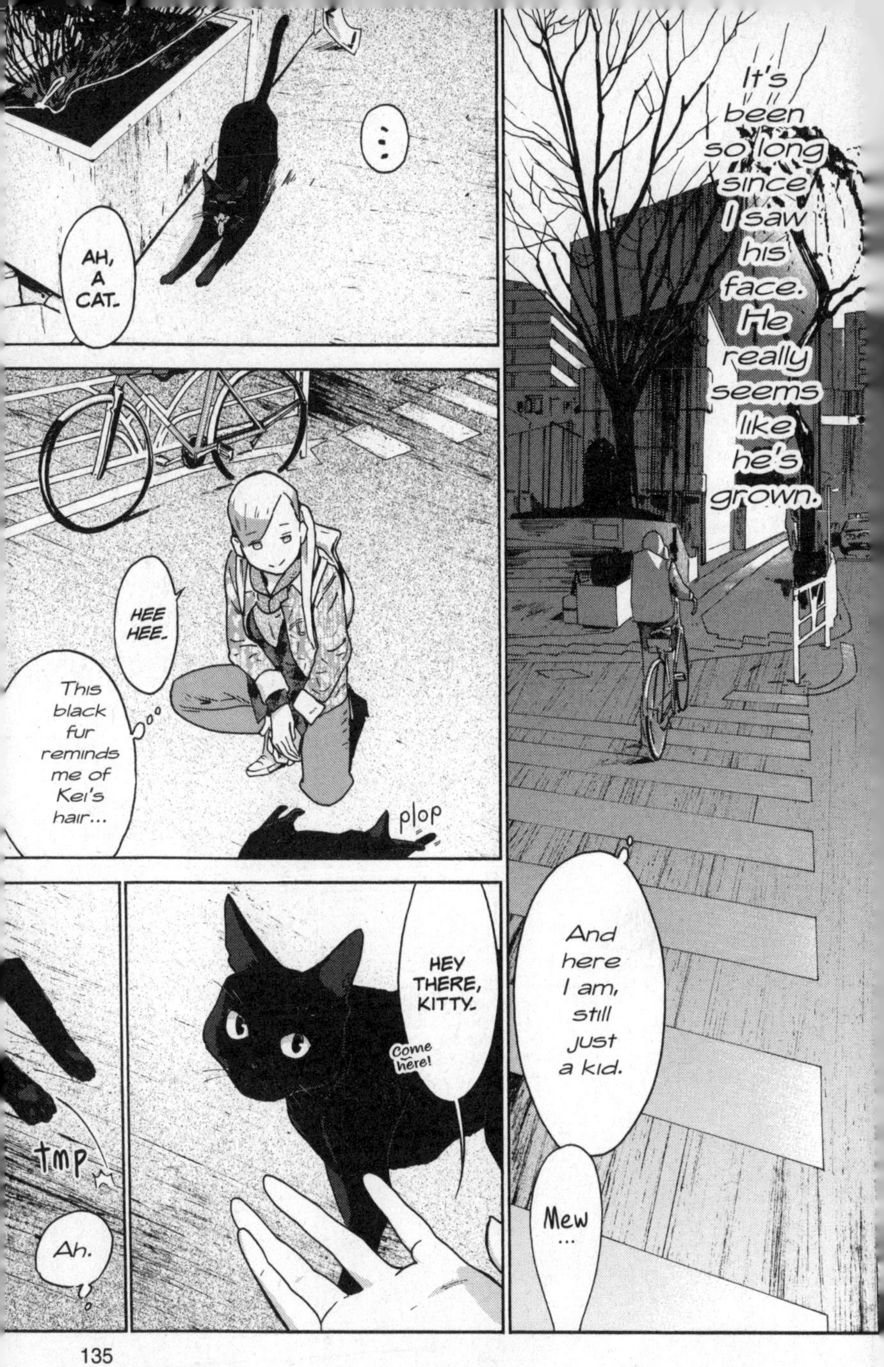

It's been so long since I saw his face. He really seems like he's grown.
And here I am, still just a kid.
Mew ...
...
AH, A CAT.
HEE HEE.
This black fur reminds me of Kei's hair...
plop
HEY THERE, KITTY.
Come here!
tmp
Ah.

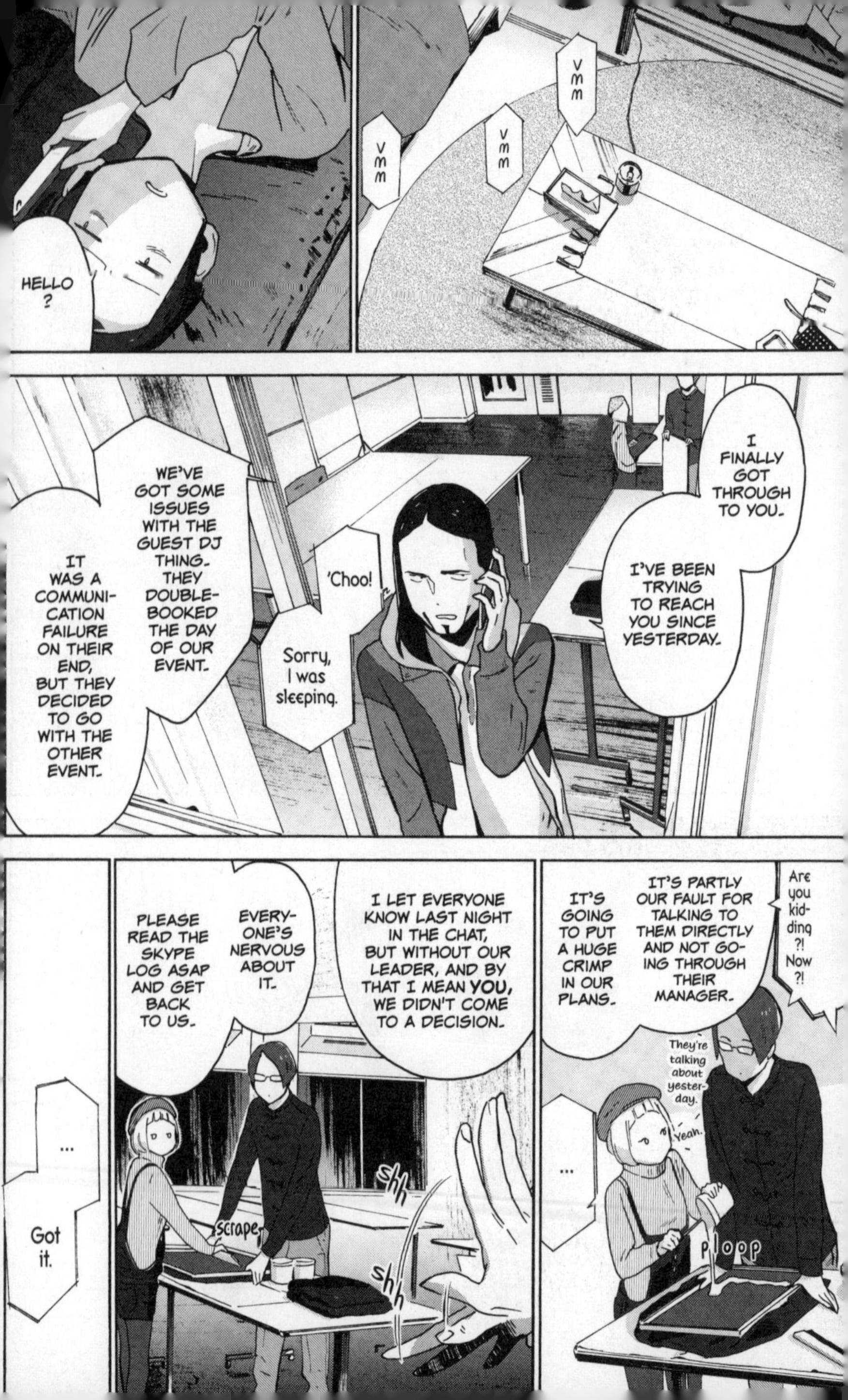
VMM
VMM
VMM
HELLO?
I FINALLY GOT THROUGH TO YOU.
I'VE BEEN TRYING TO REACH YOU SINCE YESTERDAY.
'Choo!
Sorry, I was sleeping.
WE'VE GOT SOME ISSUES WITH THE GUEST DJ THING. THEY DOUBLE-BOOKED THE DAY OF OUR EVENT.
IT WAS A COMMUNICATION FAILURE ON THEIR END, BUT THEY DECIDED TO GO WITH THE OTHER EVENT.
Are you kidding?! Now?!
IT'S PARTLY OUR FAULT FOR TALKING TO THEM DIRECTLY AND NOT GOING THROUGH THEIR MANAGER.
IT'S GOING TO PUT A HUGE CRIMP IN OUR PLANS.
They're talking about yesterday.
Yeah.
...
plopp
I LET EVERYONE KNOW LAST NIGHT IN THE CHAT, BUT WITHOUT OUR LEADER, AND BY THAT I MEAN YOU, WE DIDN'T COME TO A DECISION.
EVERYONE'S NERVOUS ABOUT IT.
PLEASE READ THE SKYPE LOG ASAP AND GET BACK TO US.
shh
shh
scrape
...
Got it.

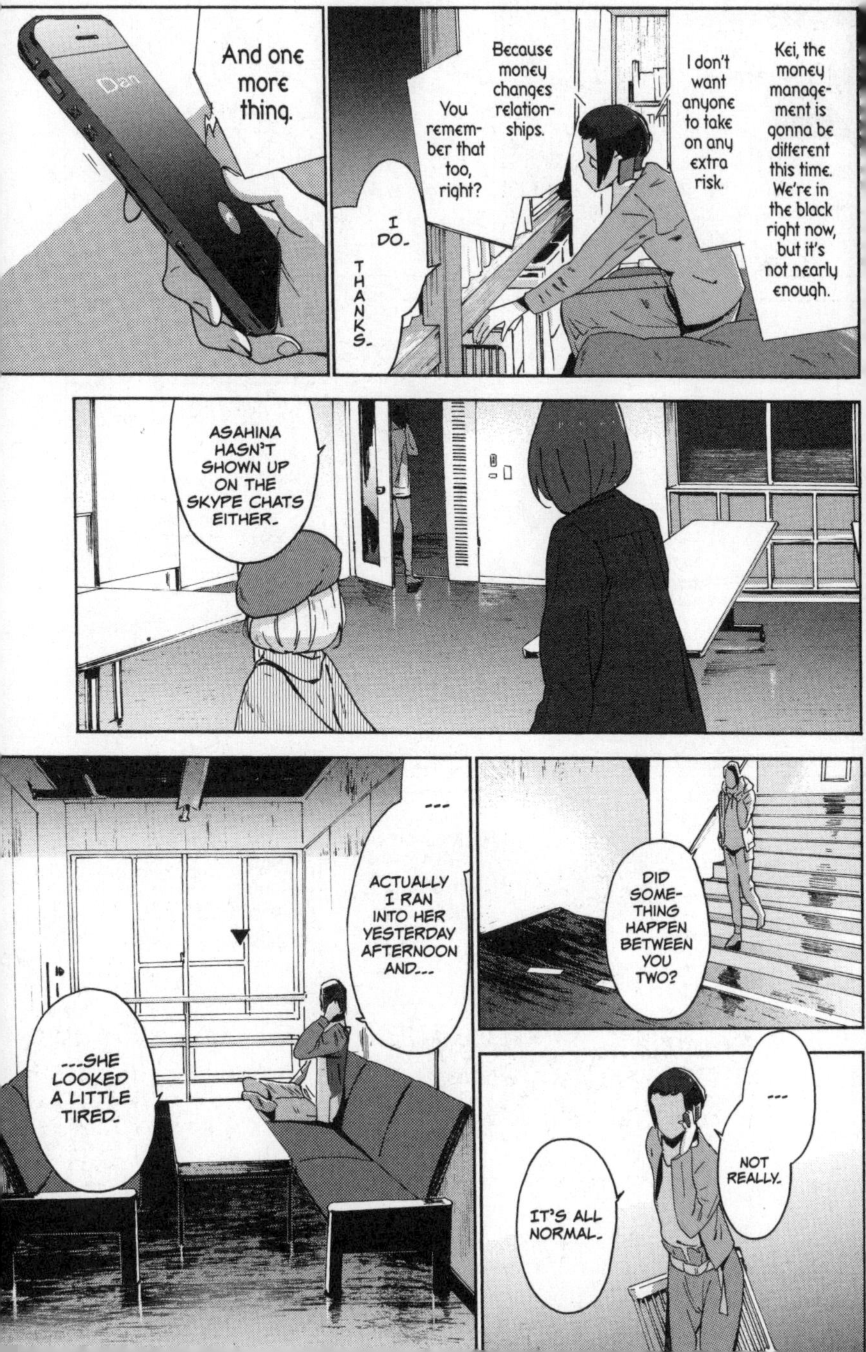
Kei, the money management is gonna be different this time. We're in the black right now, but it's not nearly enough.
I don't want anyone to take on any extra risk.
Because money changes relationships.
You remember that too, right?
I DO.
THANKS.
And one more thing.
ASAHINA HASN'T SHOWN UP ON THE SKYPE CHATS EITHER.
DID SOMETHING HAPPEN BETWEEN YOU TWO?
...
NOT REALLY.
IT'S ALL NORMAL.
...
ACTUALLY I RAN INTO HER YESTERDAY AFTERNOON AND...
...SHE LOOKED A LITTLE TIRED.

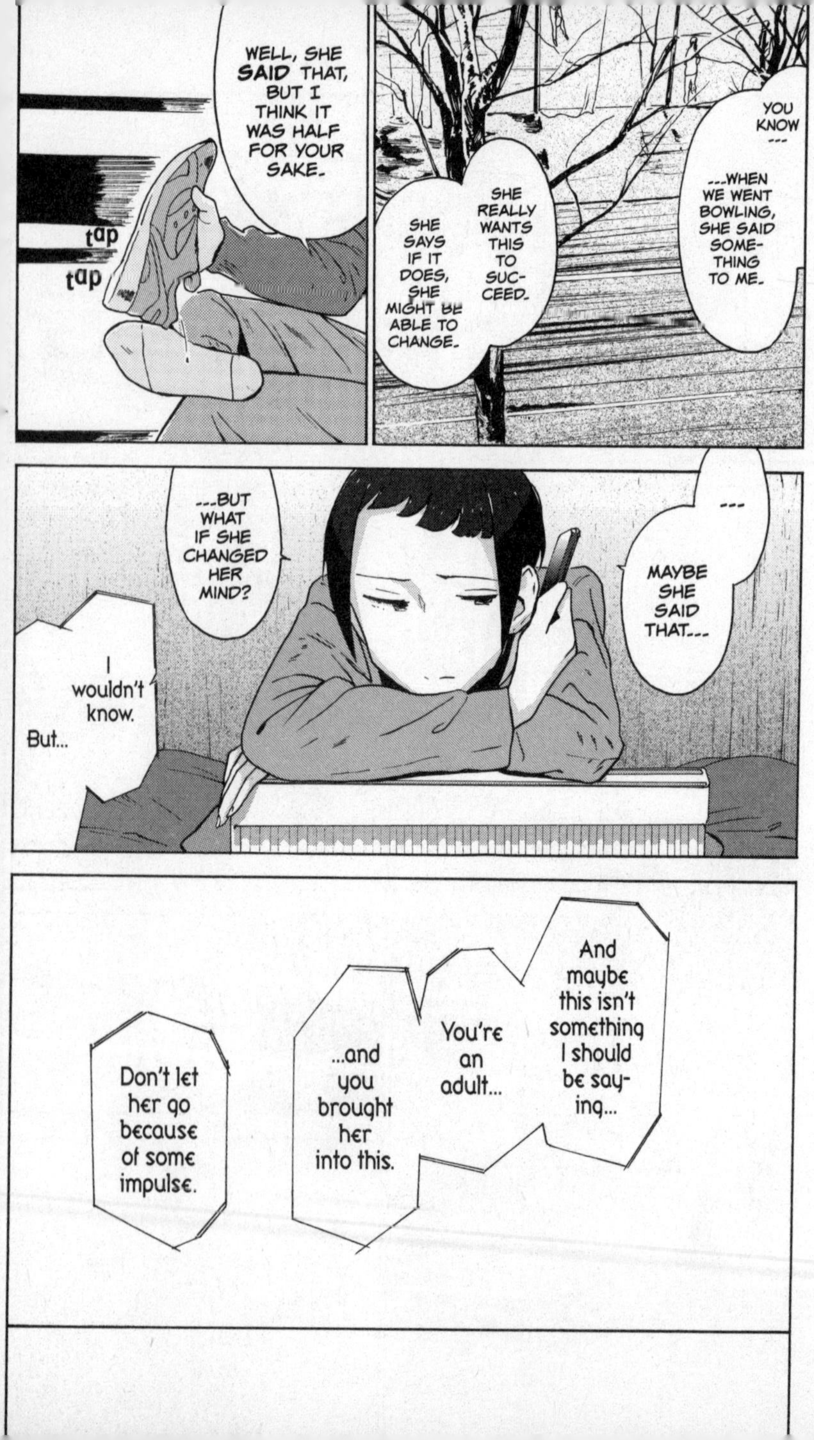
YOU KNOW ---
---WHEN WE WENT BOWLING, SHE SAID SOMETHING TO ME.
SHE REALLY WANTS THIS TO SUCCEED.
SHE SAYS IF IT DOES, SHE MIGHT BE ABLE TO CHANGE.
WELL, SHE SAID THAT, BUT I THINK IT WAS HALF FOR YOUR SAKE.
tap
tap

MAYBE SHE SAID THAT...
...BUT WHAT IF SHE CHANGED HER MIND?
I wouldn't know.
But...
And maybe this isn't something I should be saying...
You're an adult...
...and you brought her into this.
Don't let her go because of some impulse.

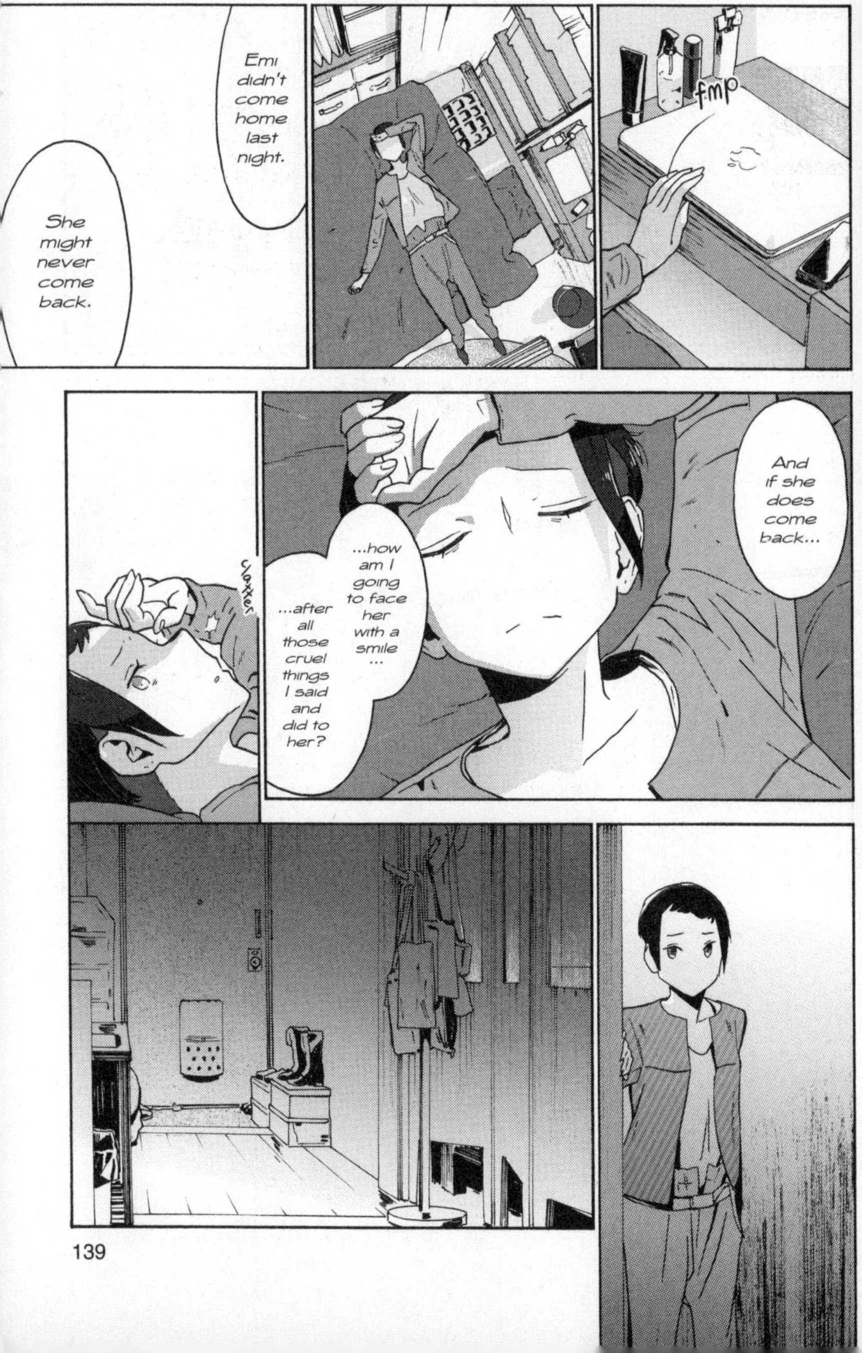
fmp
Emi didn't come home last night.
She might never come back.
And if she does come back...
...how am I going to face her with a smile...
...after all those cruel things I said and did to her?
clatter

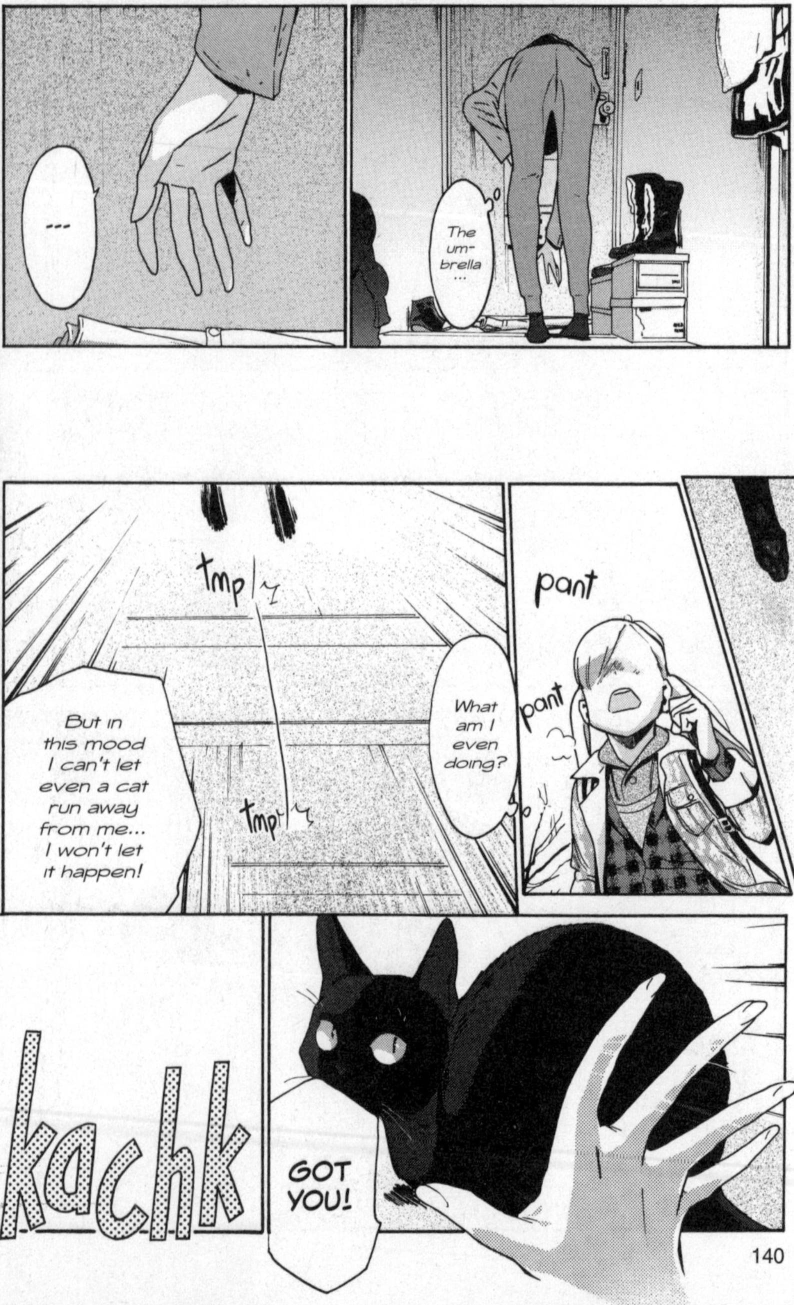

The um-brella...
...
...
pant
pant
What am I even doing?
tmp
tmp
But in this mood I can't let even a cat run away from me... I won't let it happen!
GOT YOU!
kachk

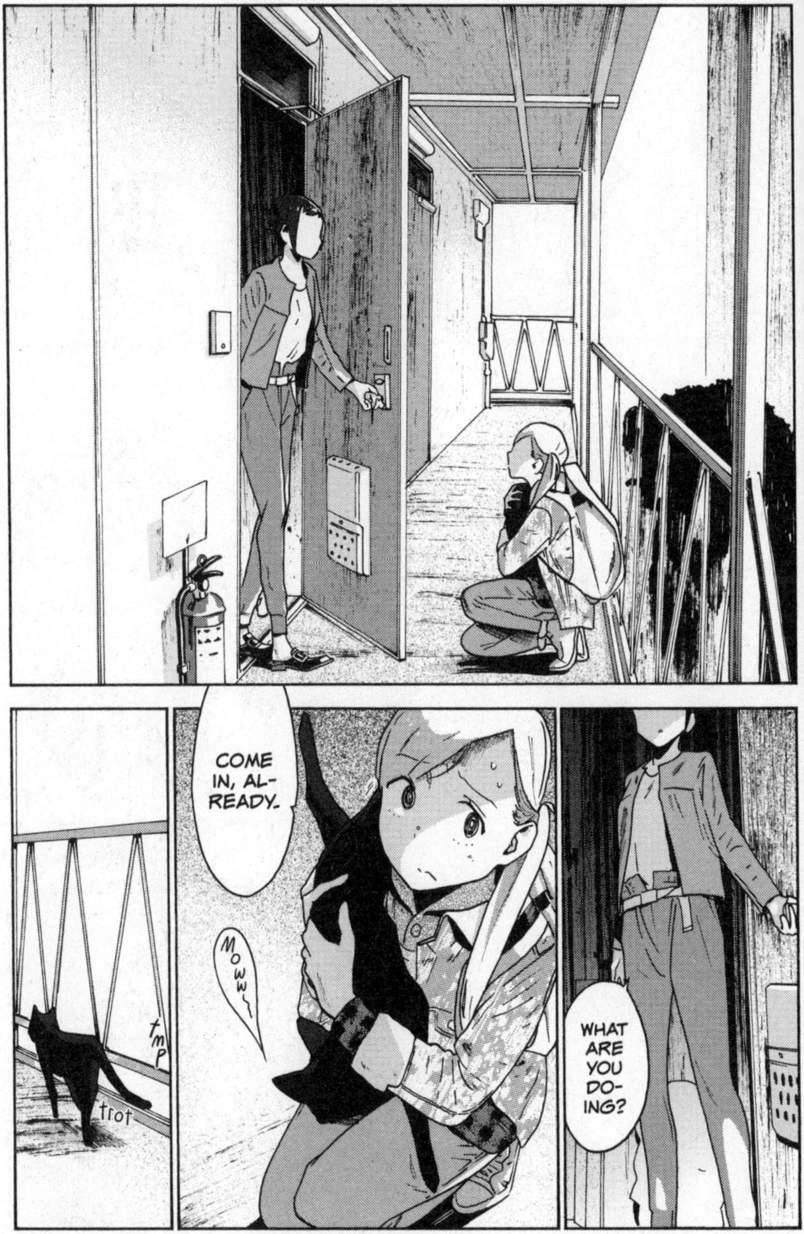
WHAT ARE YOU DOING?
COME IN, ALREADY…
MOWW~
tmp
trot

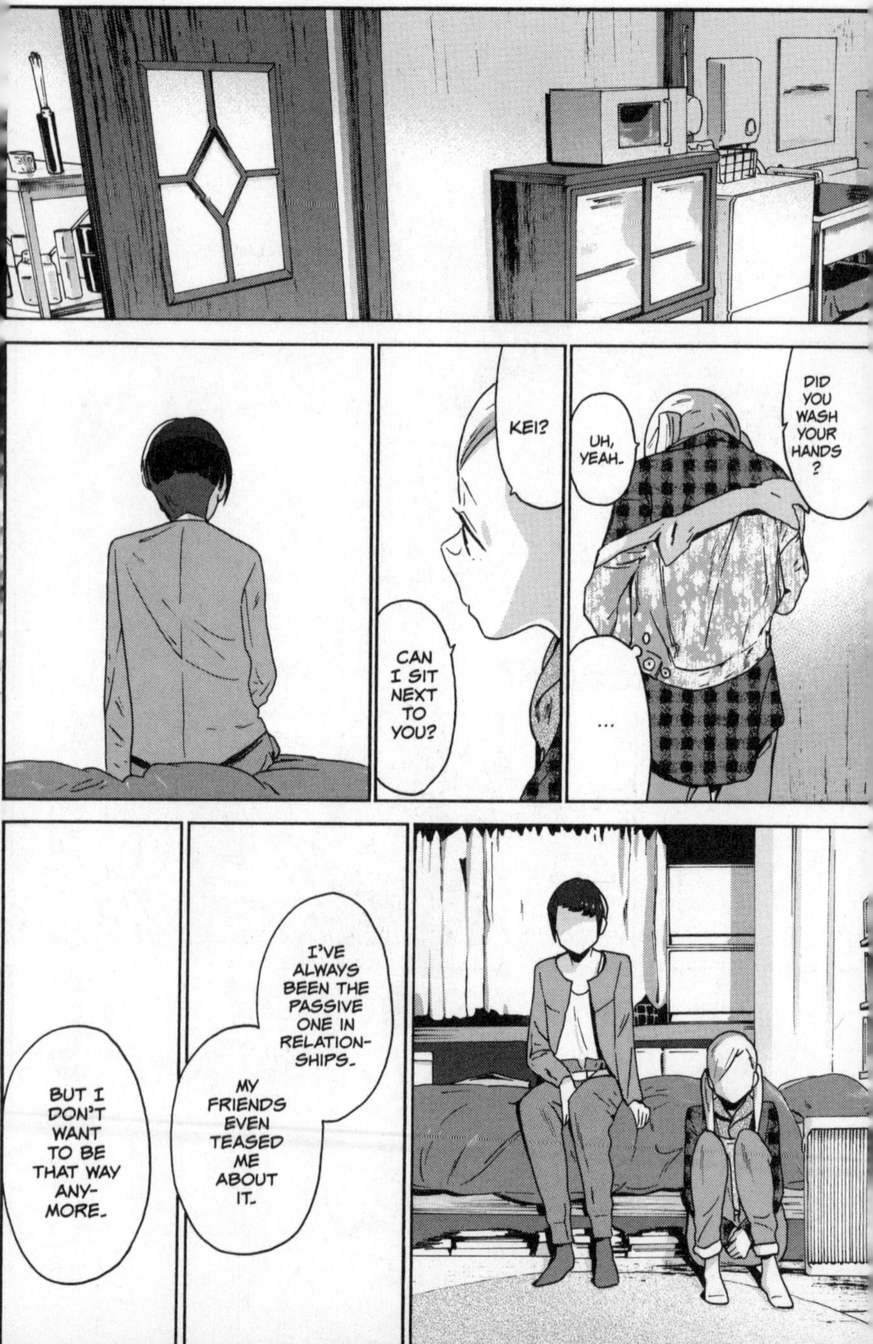
DID YOU WASH YOUR HANDS?
UH, YEAH.
...
KEI?
CAN I SIT NEXT TO YOU?
I'VE ALWAYS BEEN THE PASSIVE ONE IN RELATION-SHIPS.
MY FRIENDS EVEN TEASED ME ABOUT IT.
BUT I DON'T WANT TO BE THAT WAY ANY-MORE.

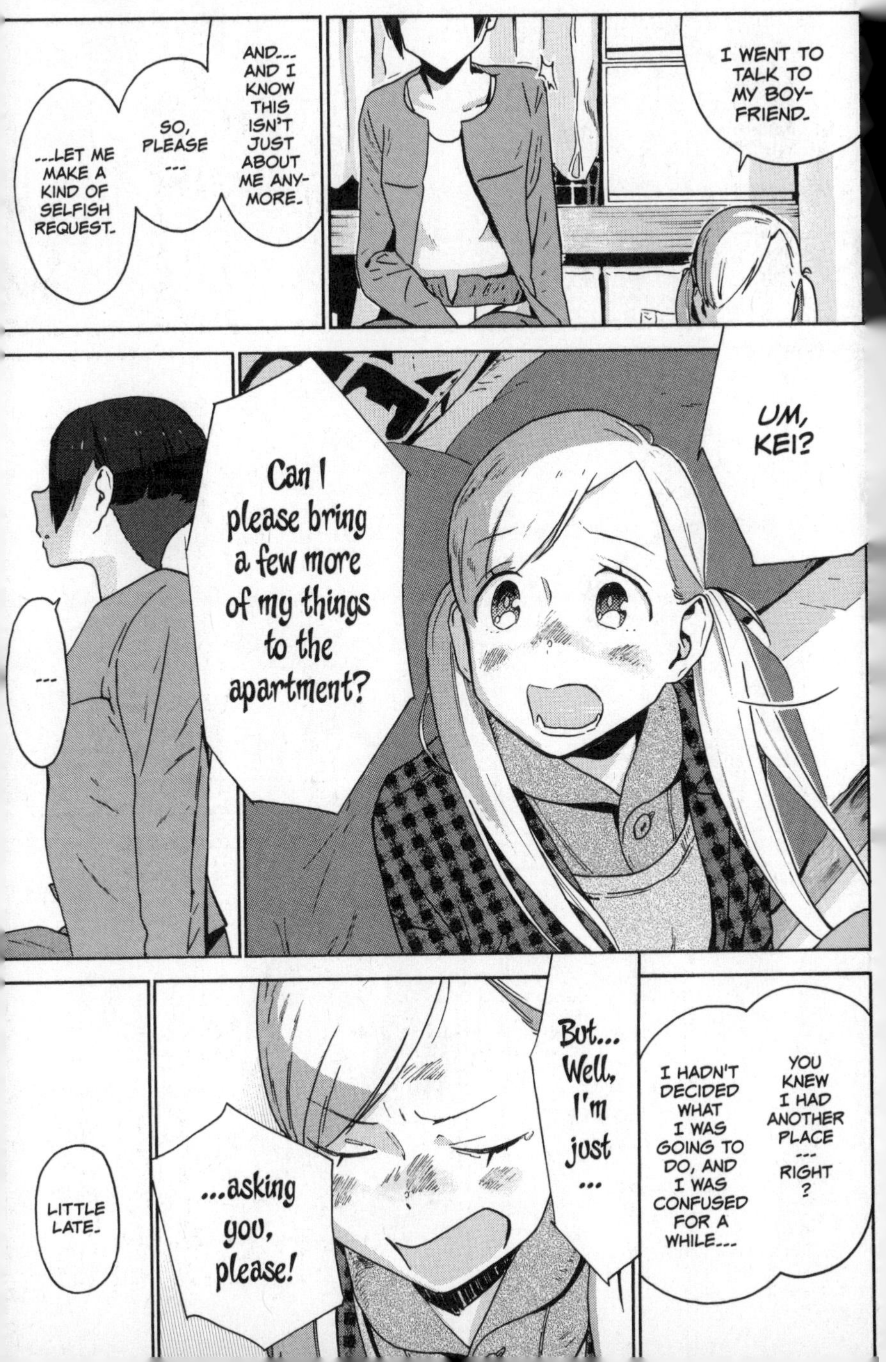
I WENT TO TALK TO MY BOY-FRIEND.
AND... AND I KNOW THIS ISN'T JUST ABOUT ME ANY-MORE.
SO, PLEASE ...
...LET ME MAKE A KIND OF SELFISH REQUEST.
UM, KEI?
Can I please bring a few more of my things to the apartment?
...
YOU KNEW I HAD ANOTHER PLACE ... RIGHT?
I HADN'T DECIDED WHAT I WAS GOING TO DO, AND I WAS CONFUSED FOR A WHILE...
But... Well, I'm just ...
...asking you, please!
LITTLE LATE.

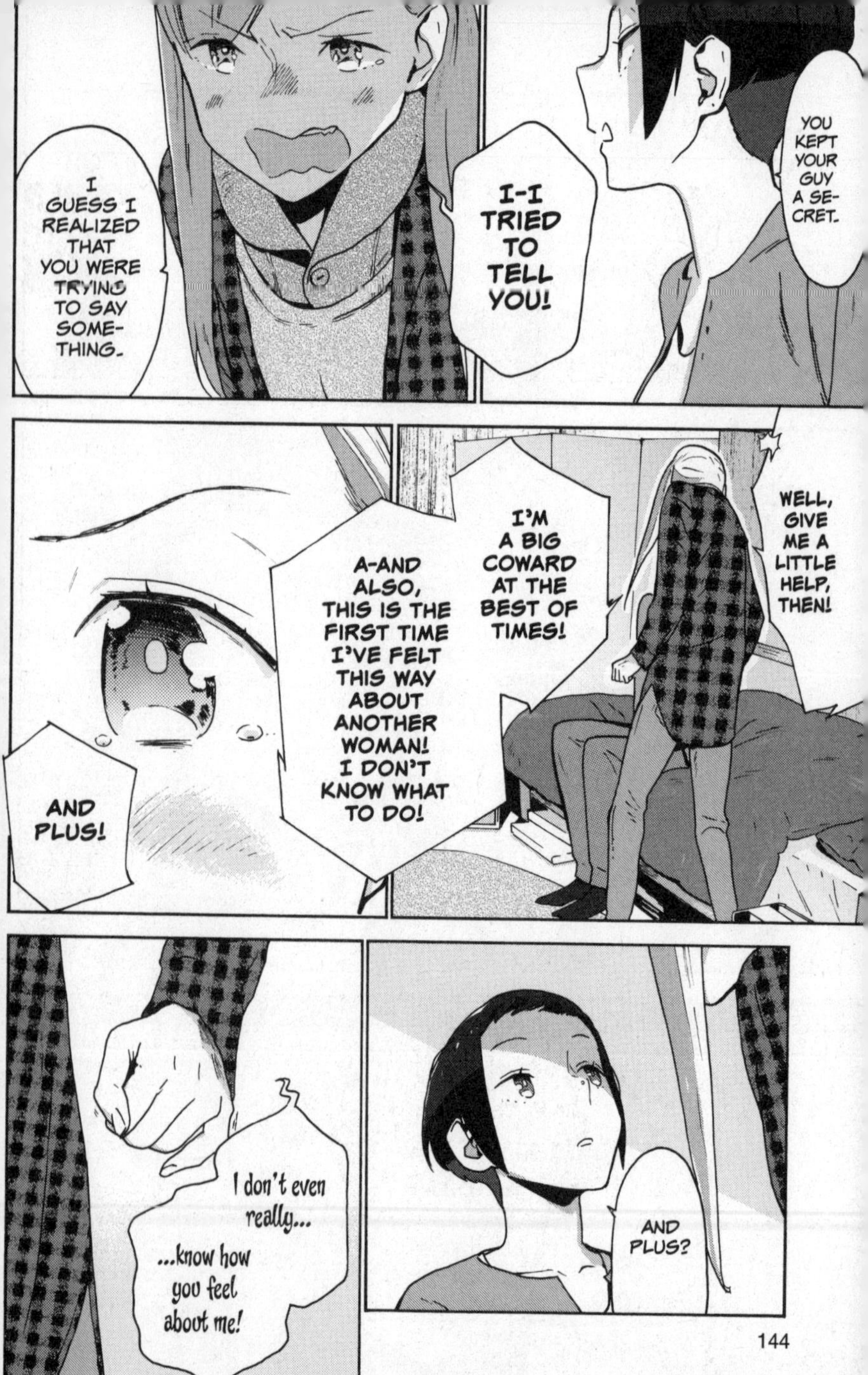
YOU KEPT YOUR GUY A SECRET.
I-I TRIED TO TELL YOU!
I GUESS I REALIZED THAT YOU WERE TRYING TO SAY SOMETHING.
WELL, GIVE ME A LITTLE HELP, THEN!
I'M A BIG COWARD AT THE BEST OF TIMES!
A-AND ALSO, THIS IS THE FIRST TIME I'VE FELT THIS WAY ABOUT ANOTHER WOMAN! I DON'T KNOW WHAT TO DO!
AND PLUS!
AND PLUS?
I don't even really...
...know how you feel about me!

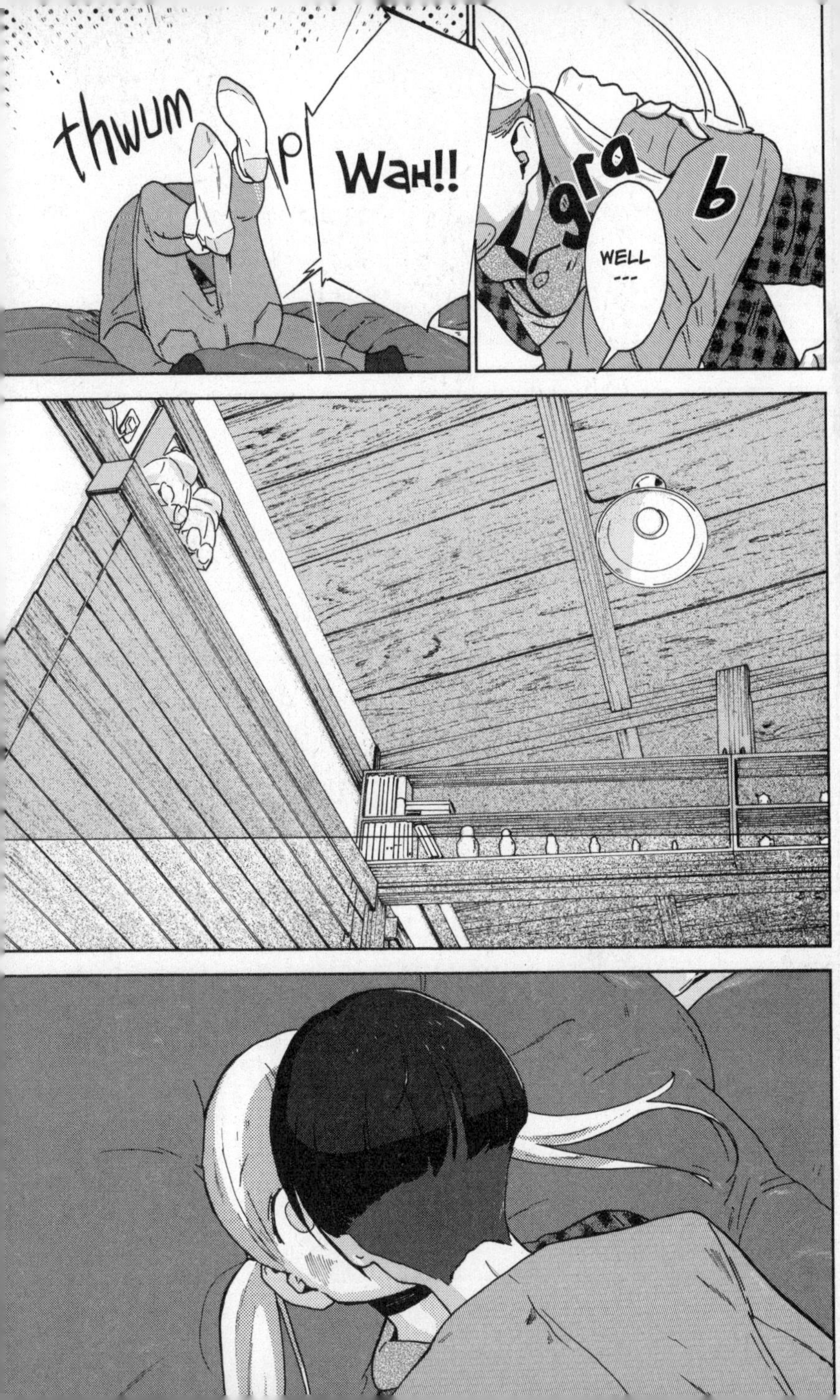
grab
WELL ---
Wah!!
thwump

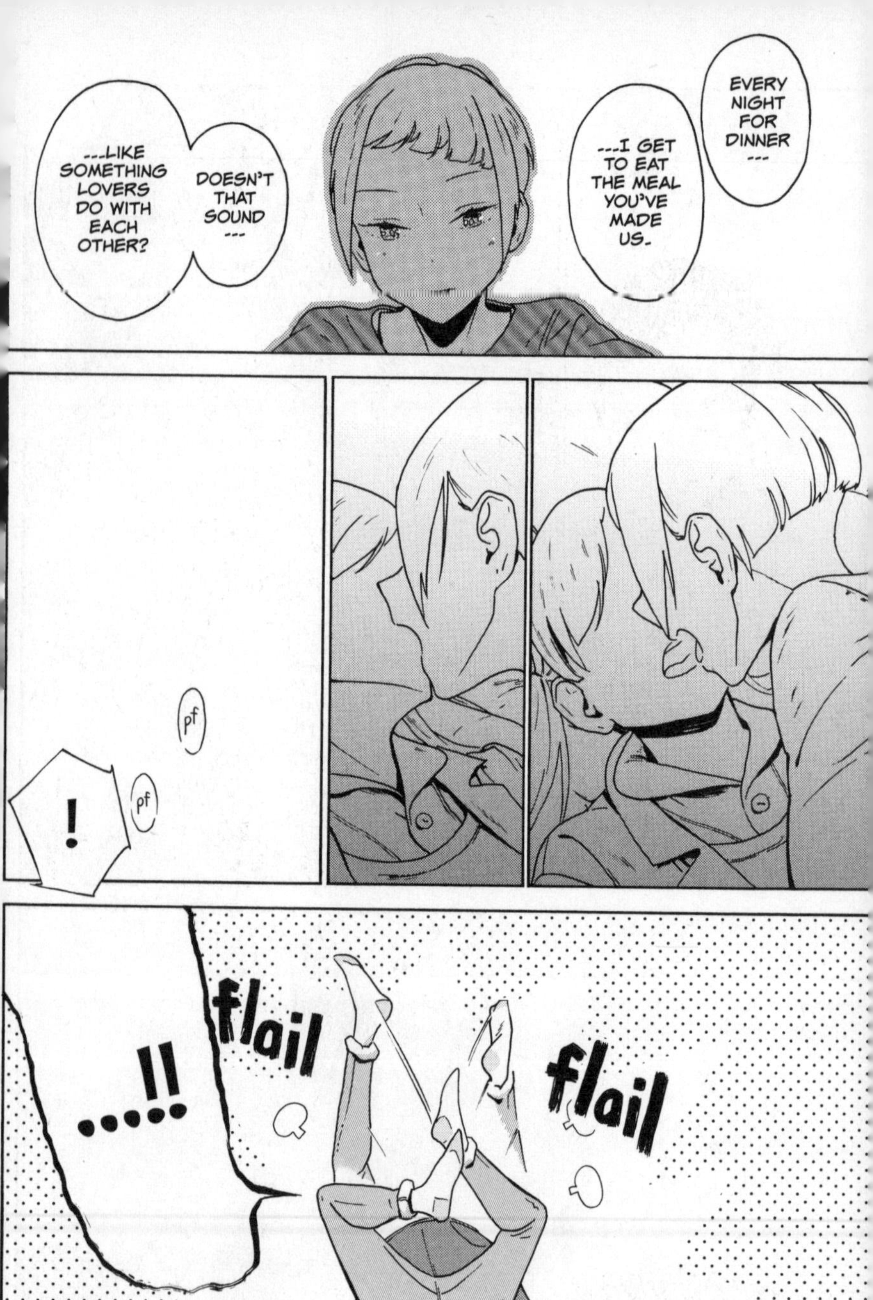
EVERY NIGHT FOR DINNER ---
---I GET TO EAT THE MEAL YOU'VE MADE US.
DOESN'T THAT SOUND ---
---LIKE SOMETHING LOVERS DO WITH EACH OTHER?
pf
pf
!
flail
flail
...!!

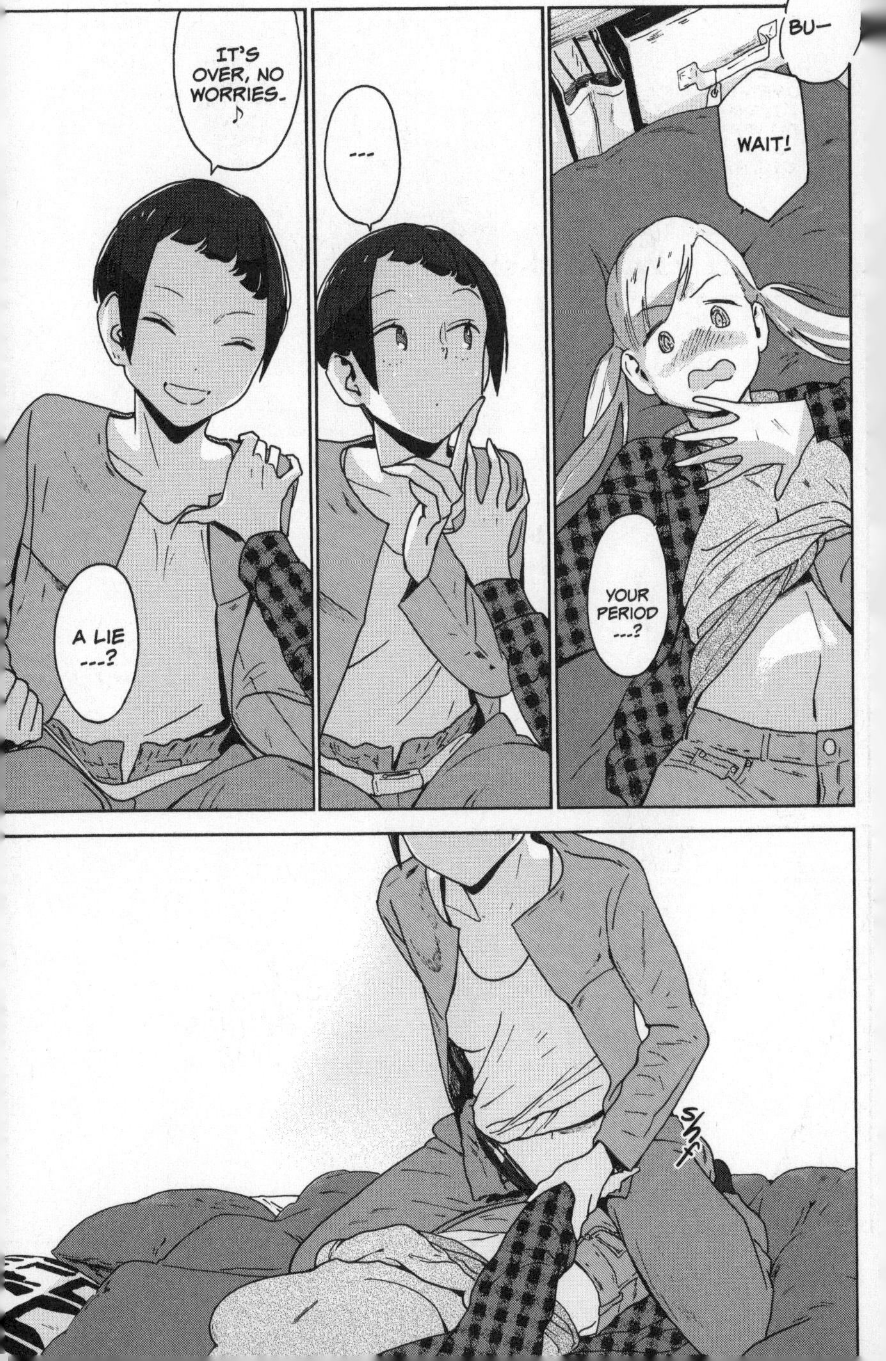
BU—
WAIT!
YOUR PERIOD ---?

IT'S OVER, NO WORRIES.♪
A LIE ---?
SHF

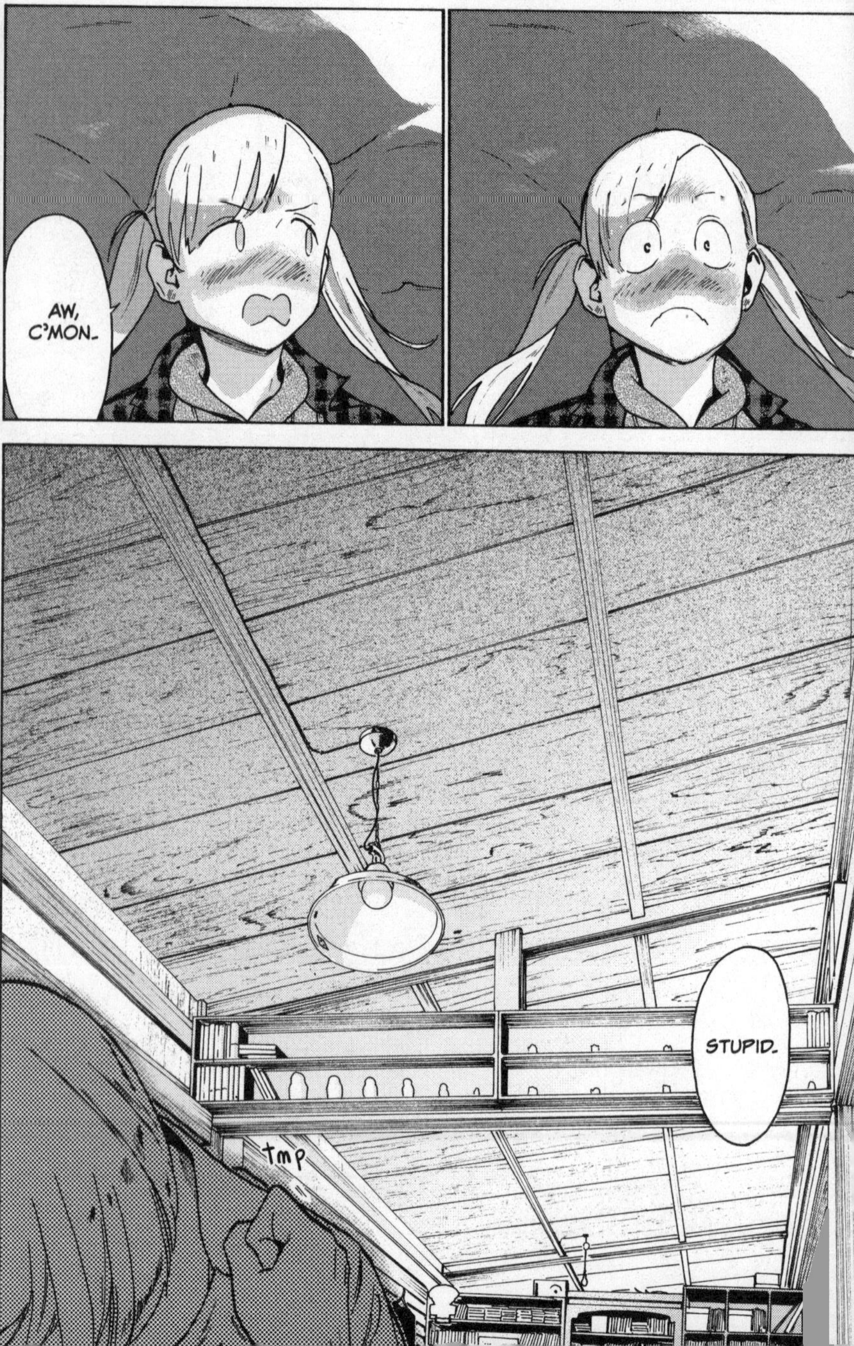
AW, C'MON.
STUPID.
tmp

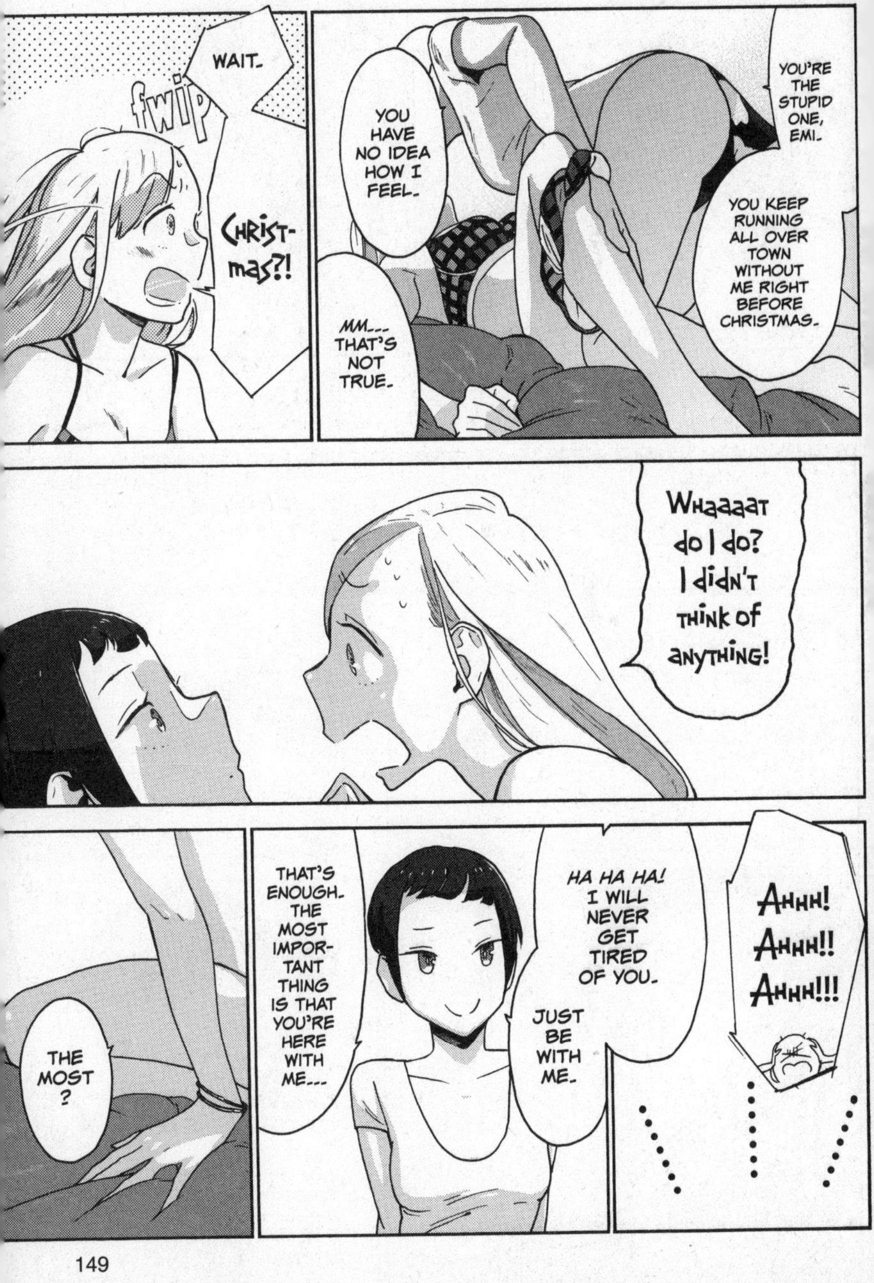
YOU'RE THE STUPID ONE, EMI.
YOU KEEP RUNNING ALL OVER TOWN WITHOUT ME RIGHT BEFORE CHRISTMAS.
YOU HAVE NO IDEA HOW I FEEL.
MM... THAT'S NOT TRUE.
WAIT.
fwip
CHRIST-mas?!
Whaaaat do I do? I didn't think of anything!
Ahhh! Ahhh!! Ahhh!!!
HA HA HA! I WILL NEVER GET TIRED OF YOU.
JUST BE WITH ME.
THAT'S ENOUGH. THE MOST IMPORTANT THING IS THAT YOU'RE HERE WITH ME...
THE MOST?

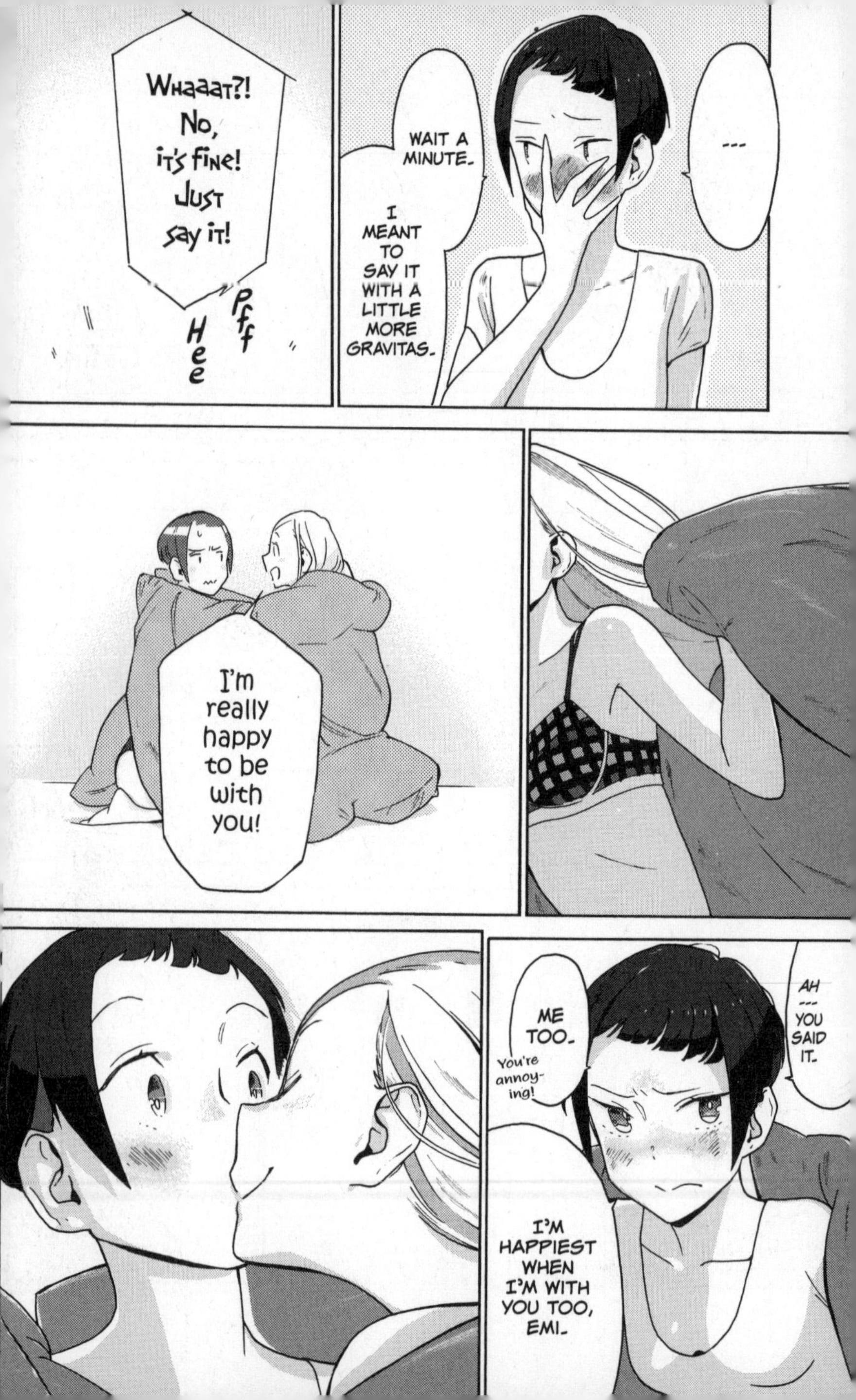
...
WAIT A MINUTE.
I MEANT TO SAY IT WITH A LITTLE MORE GRAVITAS.
Whaaat?! No, it's fine! Just say it!
Pfff
Hee
I'm really happy to be with you!
AH... YOU SAID IT.
ME TOO.
You're annoying!
I'M HAPPIEST WHEN I'M WITH YOU TOO, EMI.

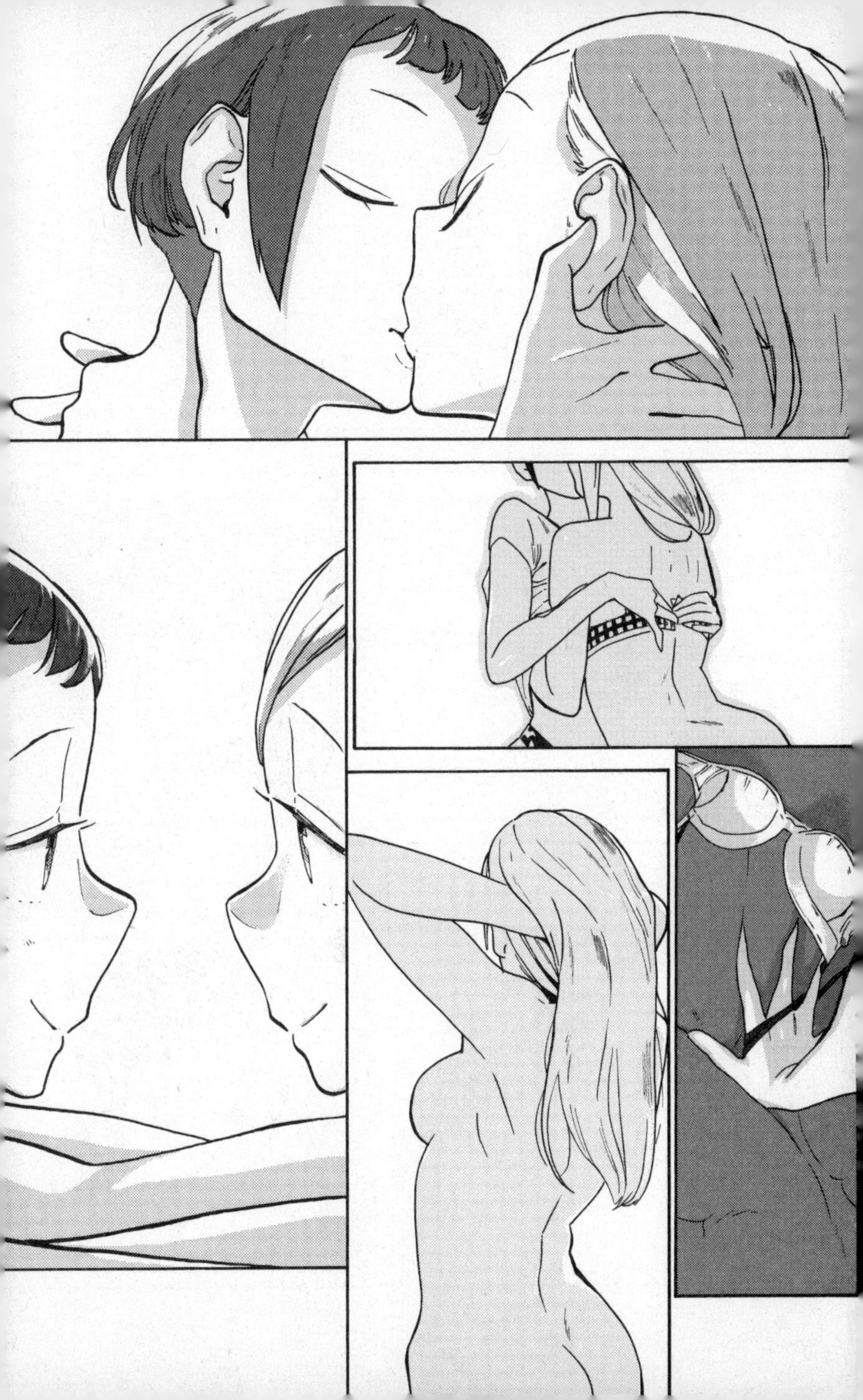

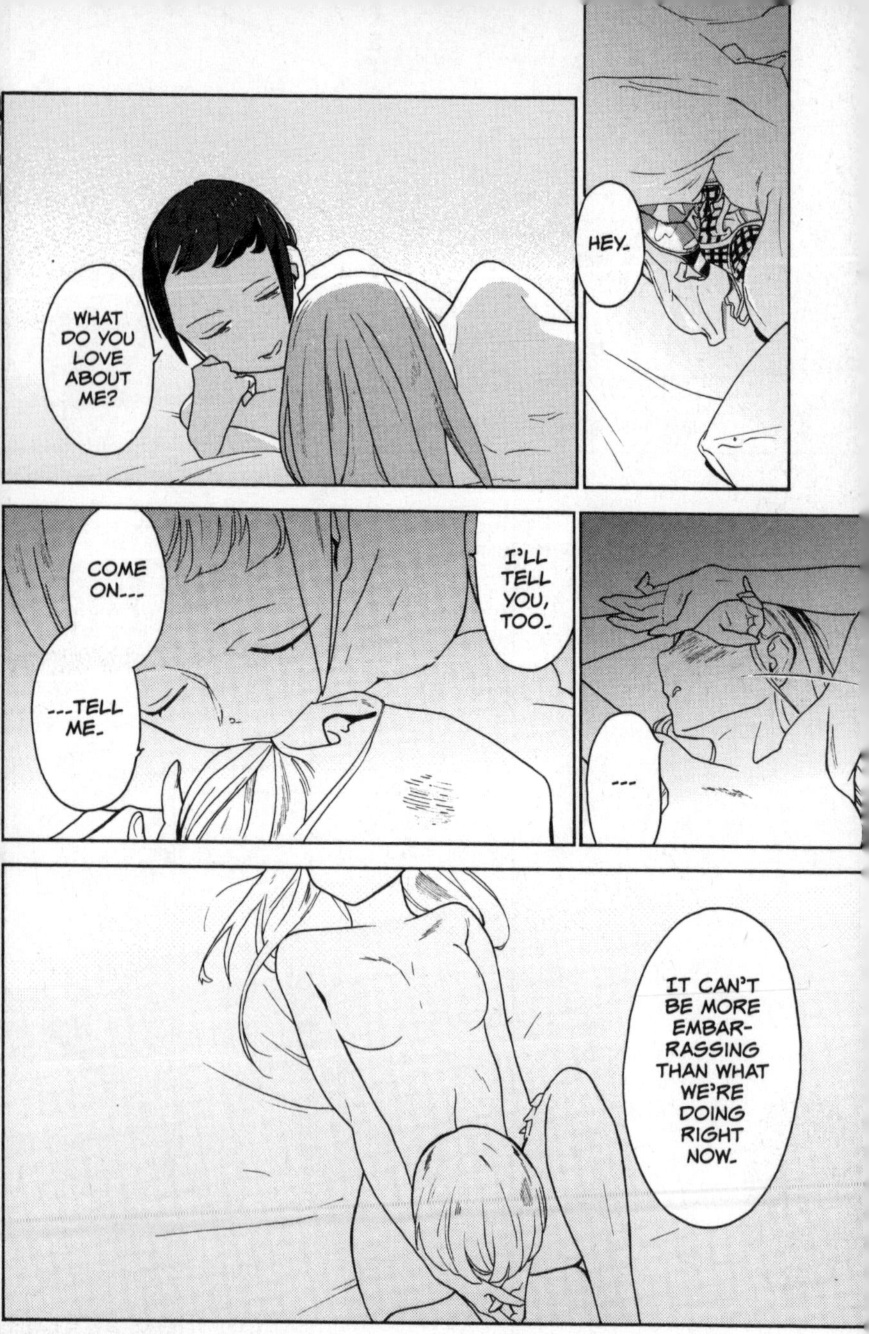
HEY.
WHAT DO YOU LOVE ABOUT ME?
...
I'LL TELL YOU, TOO.
COME ON...
...TELL ME.
IT CAN'T BE MORE EMBARRASSING THAN WHAT WE'RE DOING RIGHT NOW.

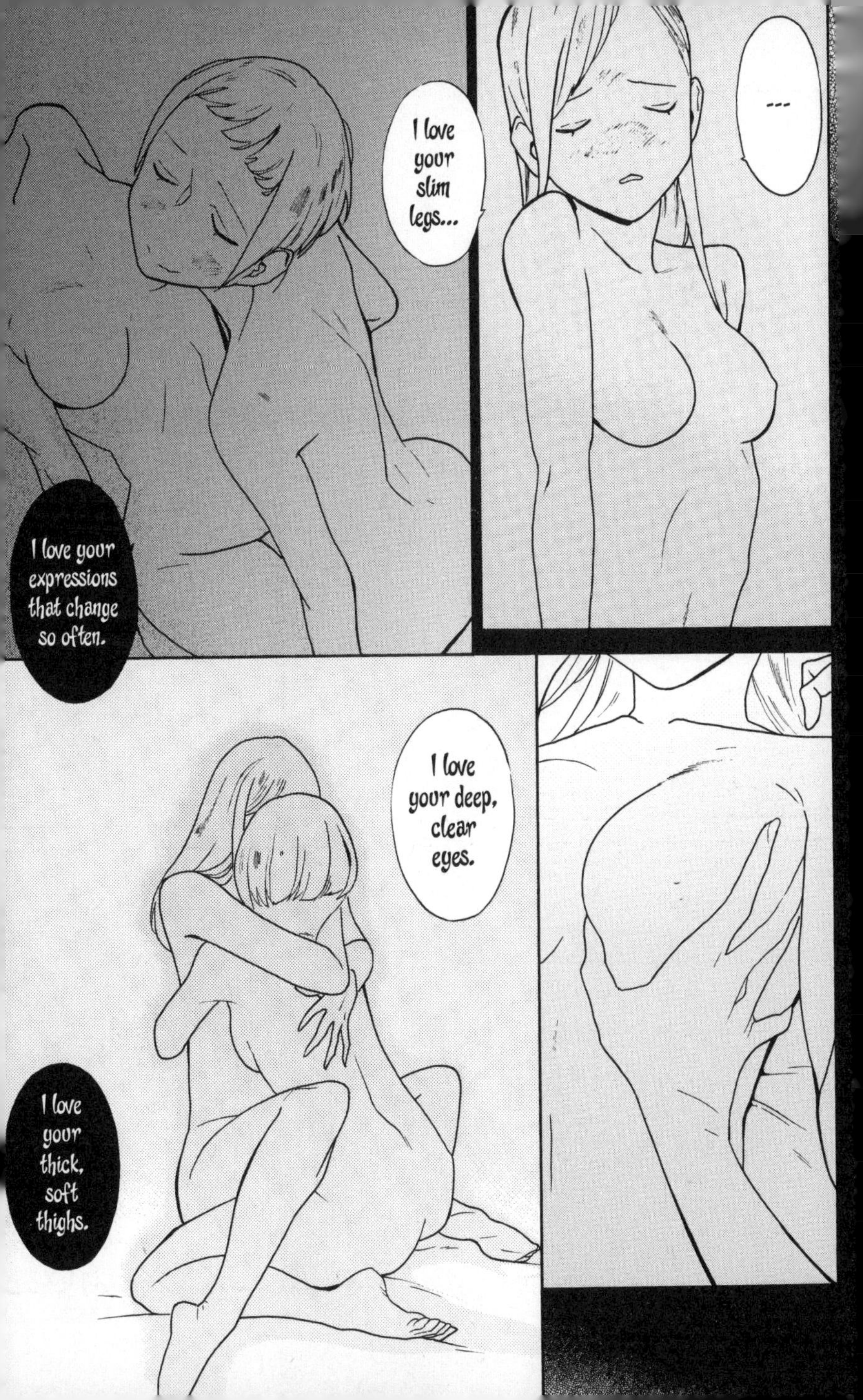
...
I love your slim legs...
I love your expressions that change so often.
I love your deep, clear eyes.
I love your thick, soft thighs.

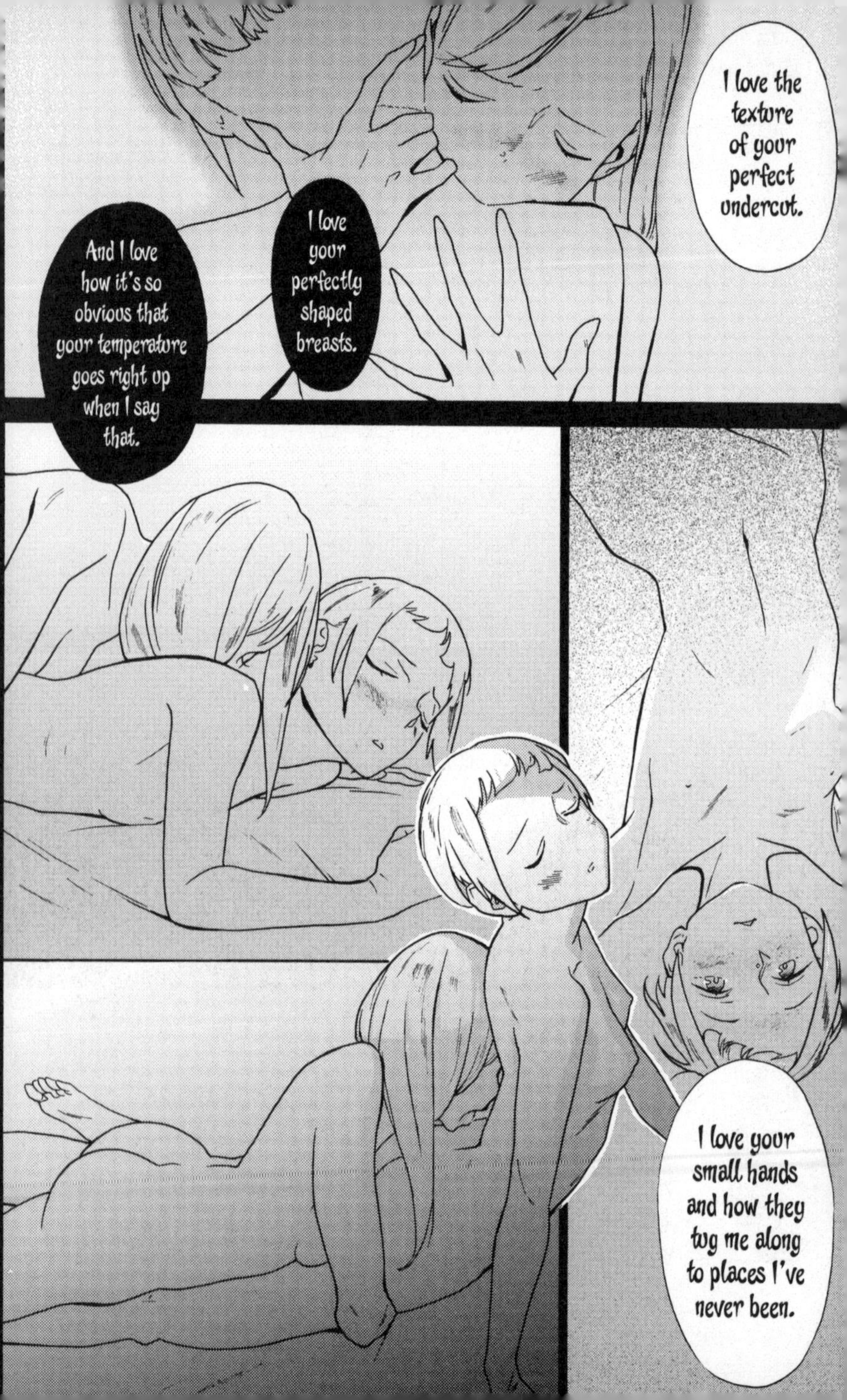
I love the texture of your perfect undercut.
I love your perfectly shaped breasts.
And I love how it's so obvious that your temperature goes right up when I say that.
I love your small hands and how they tug me along to places I've never been.

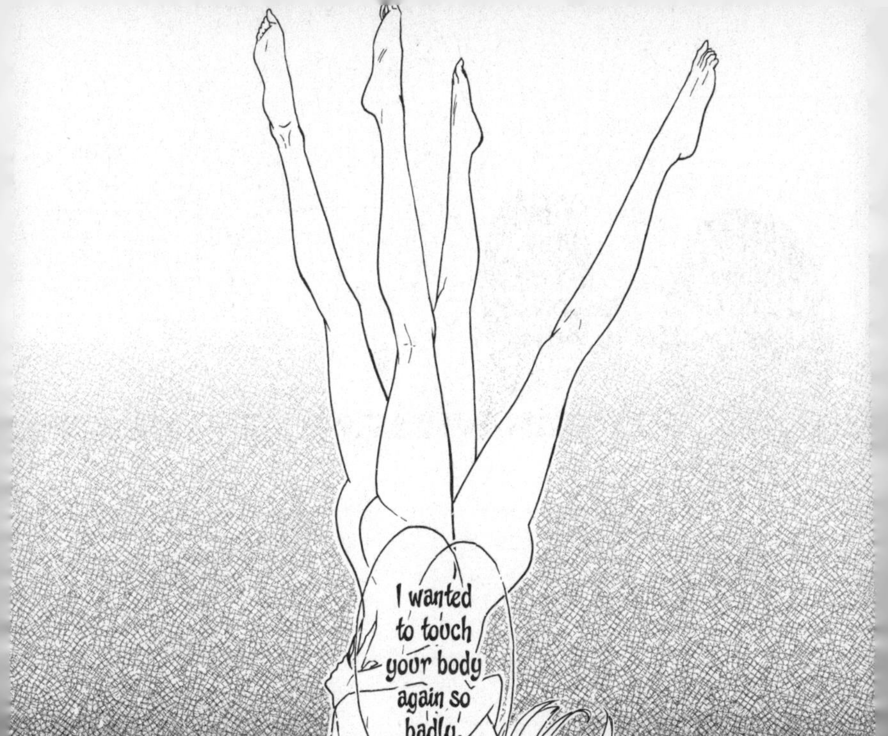
I wanted to touch your body again so badly.
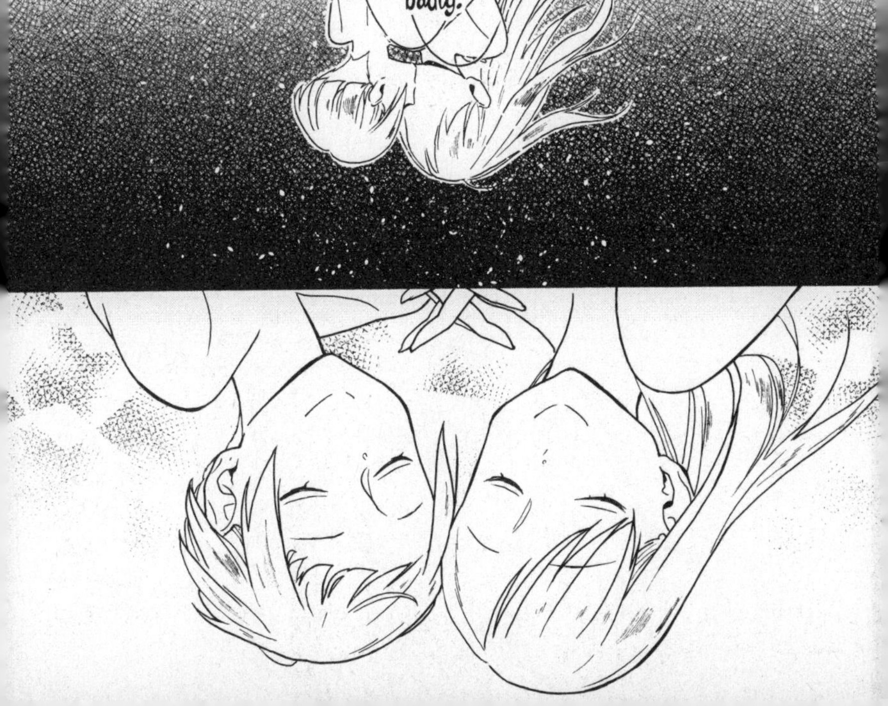

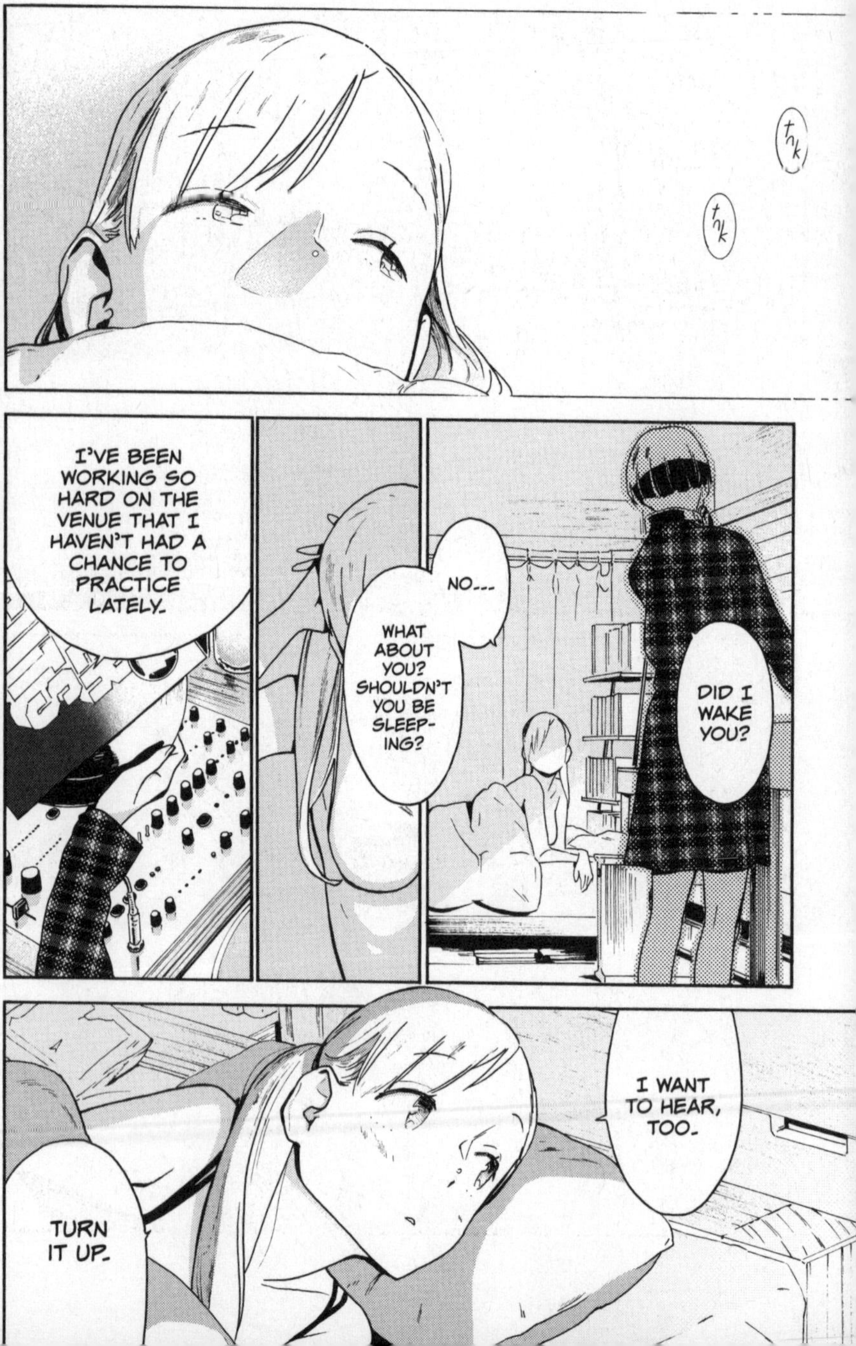
thk
thk
DID I WAKE YOU?
NO...
WHAT ABOUT YOU? SHOULDN'T YOU BE SLEEPING?
I'VE BEEN WORKING SO HARD ON THE VENUE THAT I HAVEN'T HAD A CHANCE TO PRACTICE LATELY.
I WANT TO HEAR, TOO.
TURN IT UP.

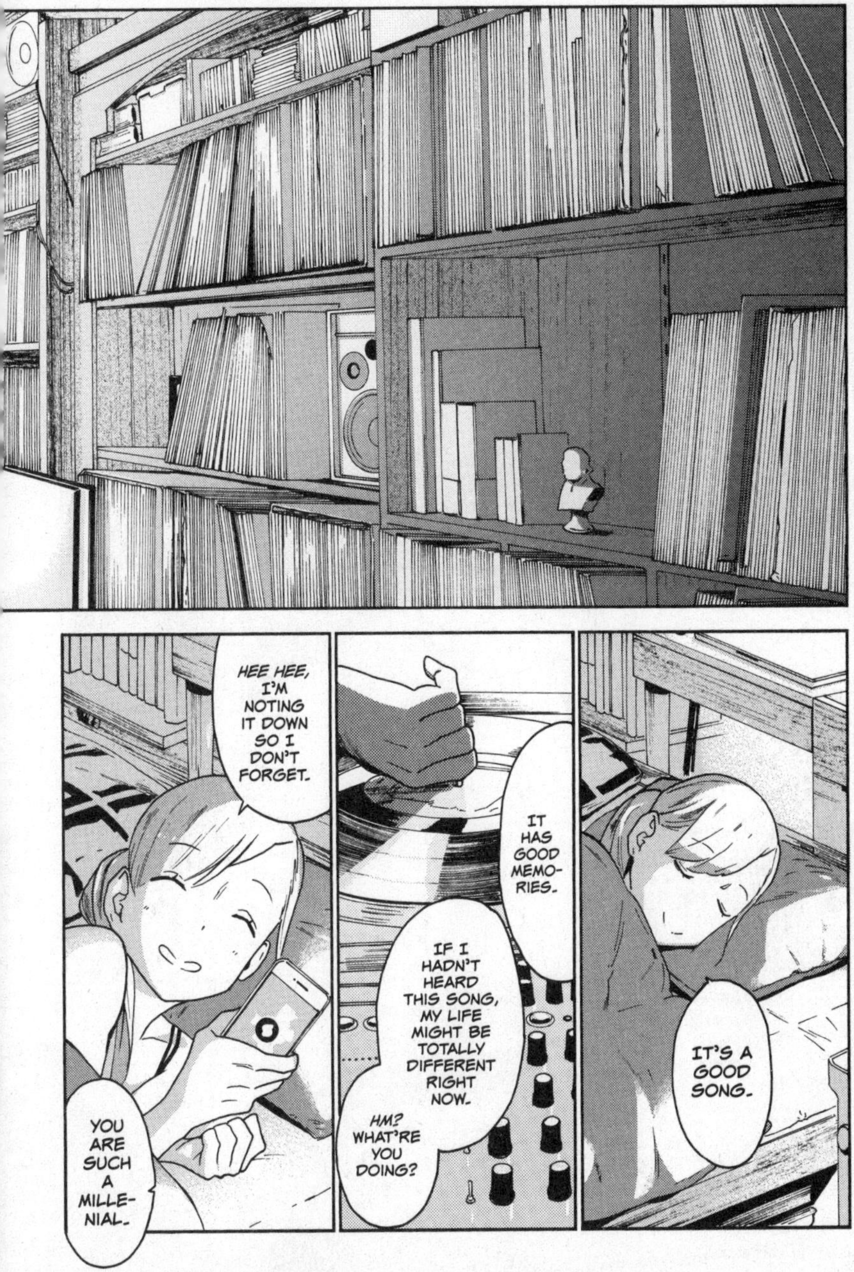
IT'S A GOOD SONG.
IT HAS GOOD MEMORIES.
IF I HADN'T HEARD THIS SONG, MY LIFE MIGHT BE TOTALLY DIFFERENT RIGHT NOW.
HM? WHAT'RE YOU DOING?
HEE HEE, I'M NOTING IT DOWN SO I DON'T FORGET.
YOU ARE SUCH A MILLE-NIAL.

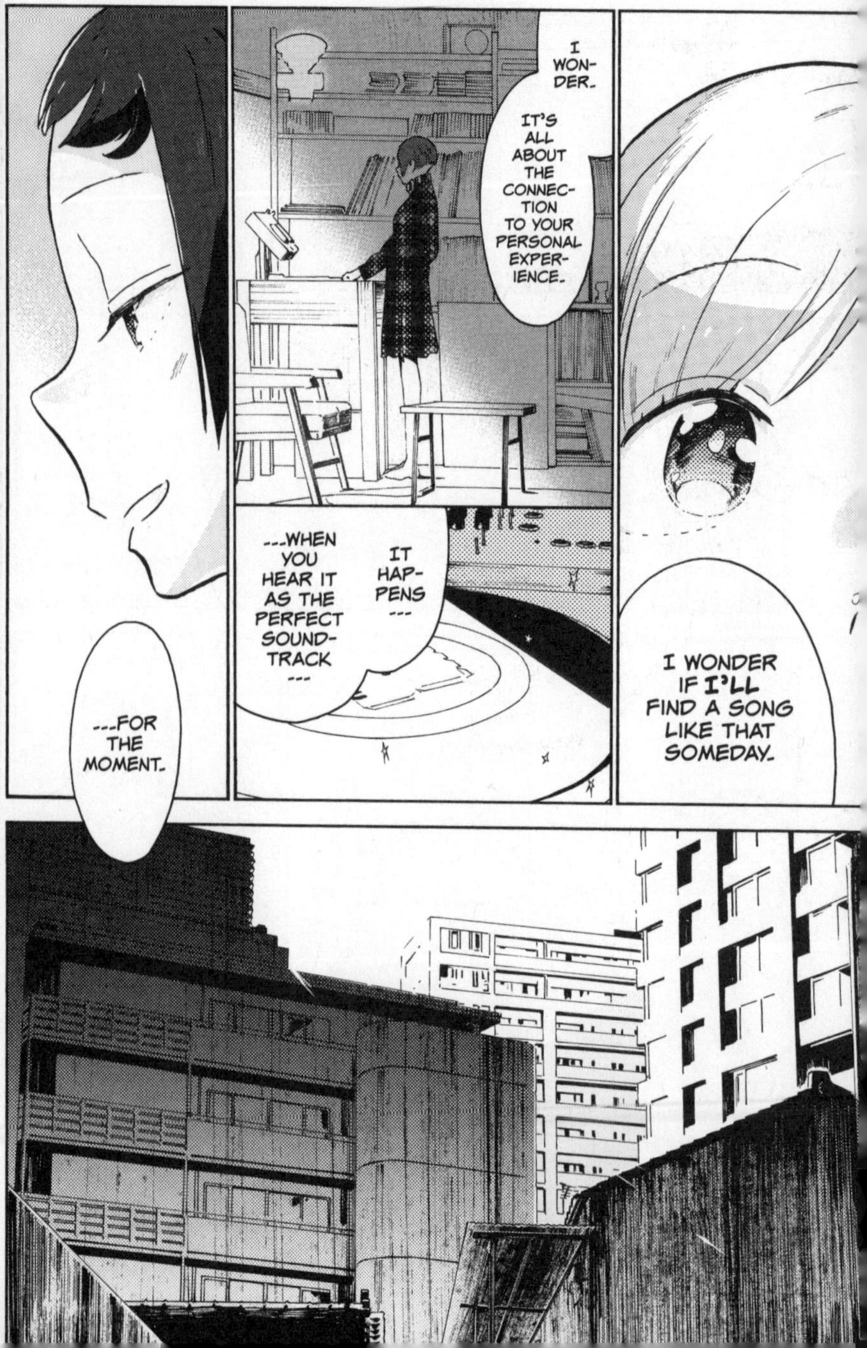
I WONDER IF I'LL FIND A SONG LIKE THAT SOMEDAY.
I WONDER.
IT'S ALL ABOUT THE CONNECTION TO YOUR PERSONAL EXPERIENCE.
IT HAPPENS ---
---WHEN YOU HEAR IT AS THE PERFECT SOUNDTRACK ---
---FOR THE MOMENT.

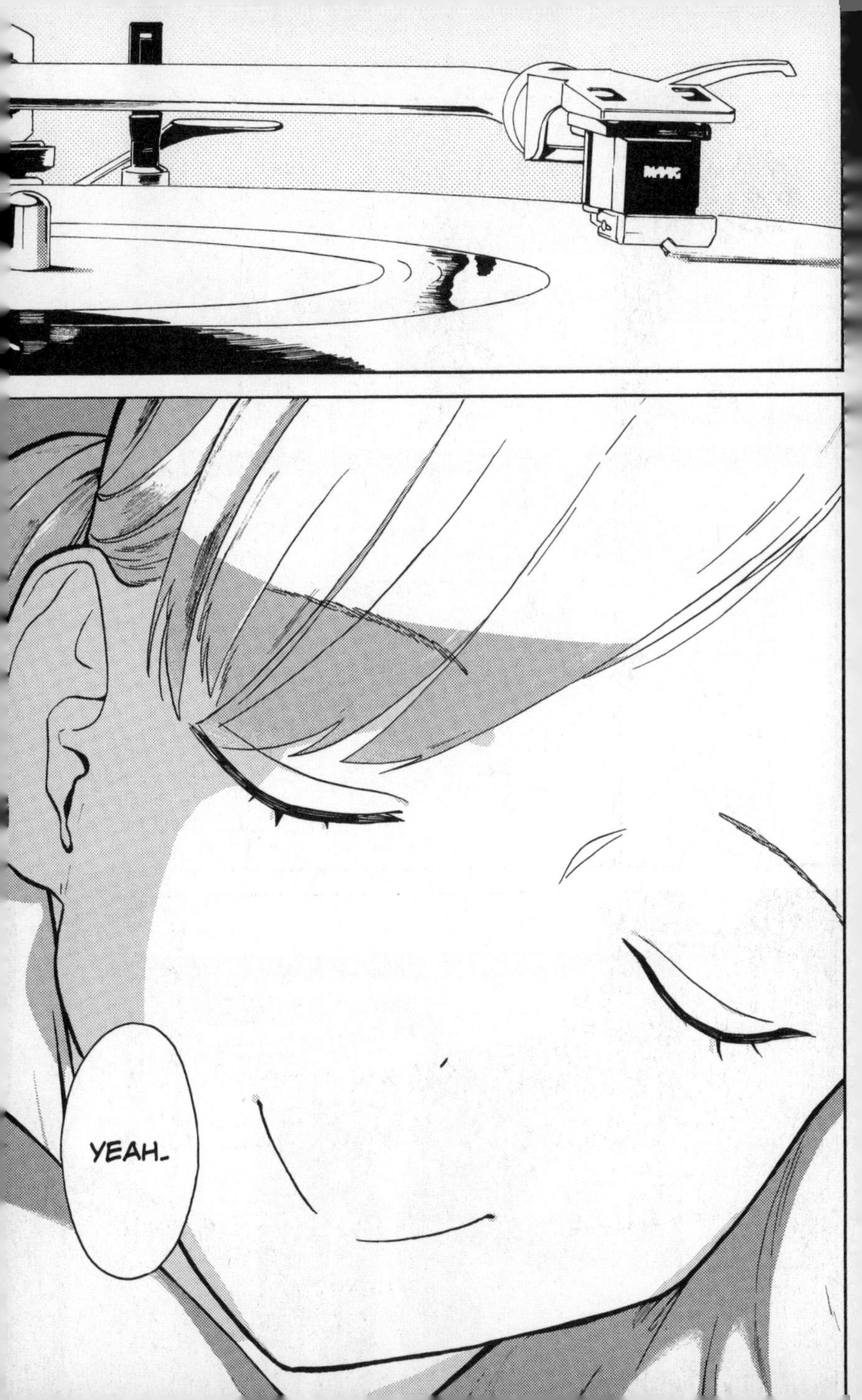
YEAH_

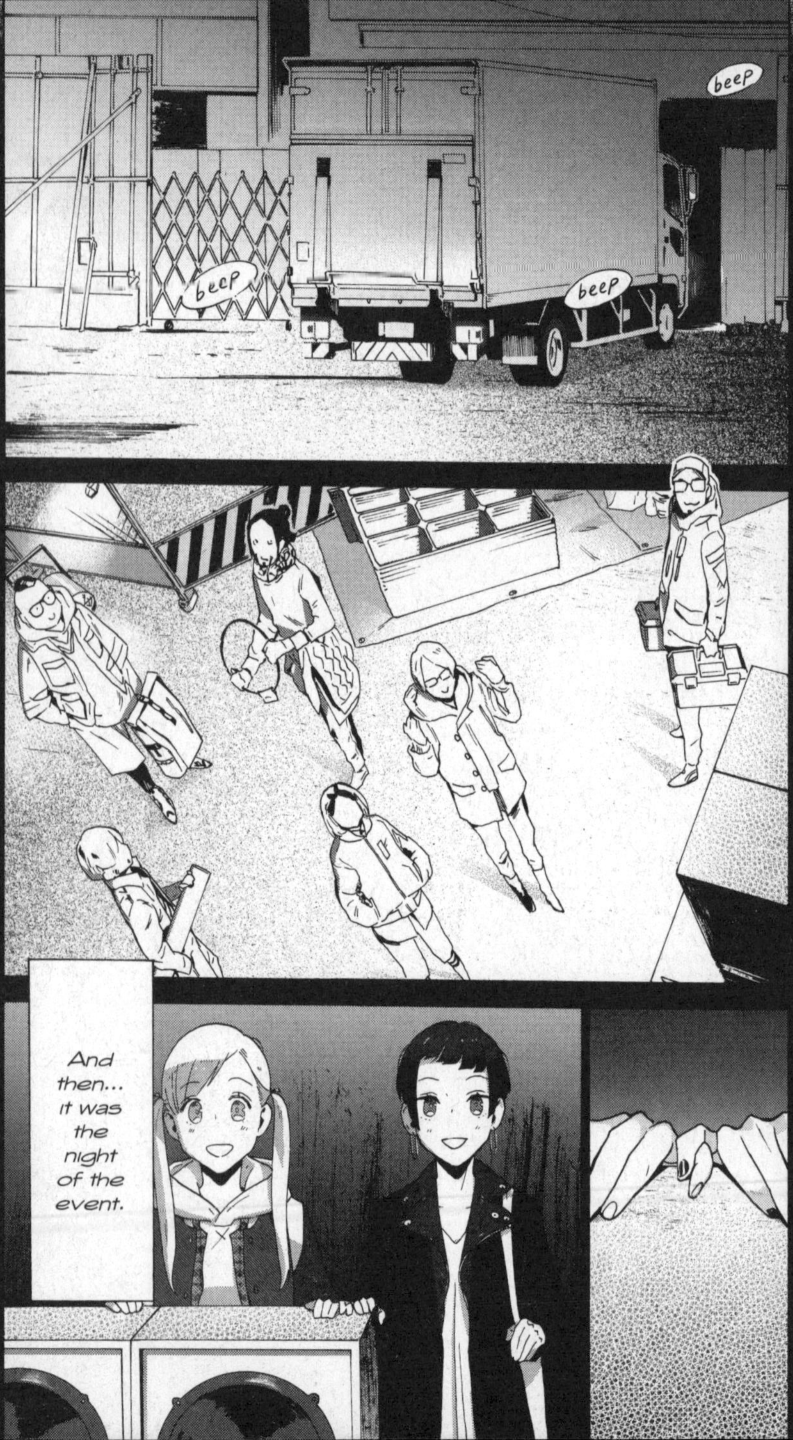
beep
beep
beep
And then... it was the night of the event.

Yuhta Nishio is a manga creator,
illustrator and sometime painter.
He has also been a bookseller and
has joined Takashi Murakami in a
group exhibit as an artist. His debut
manga, *Irigachi*, started serialization
in *IKKI* magazine in 2014.

AFTER HOURS
VOLUME 2 • VIZ Media Edition

STORY AND ART BY YUHTA NISHIO

English Translation + Adaptation **Abby Lehrke**
Touch-Up Art + Lettering **Sabrina Heep**
Design **Shawn Carrico**
Editor **Pancha Diaz**

AFTER HOURS Vol. 2
by Yuhta NISHIO
© 2015 Yuhta NISHIO
All rights reserved.
Original Japanese edition published by SHOGAKUKAN.
English translation rights in the United States of America,
Canada, the United Kingdom, Ireland, Australia and
New Zealand arranged with SHOGAKUKAN.

Original Design **Keita MORI** (Sekine Shinichi Seisaku Shitsu)

Printed in Canada

Published by VIZ Media, LLC
P.O. Box 77010
San Francisco, CA 94107

10 9 8 7 6 5 4 3 2 1
First printing, June 2018

viz.com

Written by the creator of **High School Debut!**

MY love STORY!!

KAZUNE KAWAHARA *Story*

ARUKO *Art*

Takeo Goda is a GIANT guy with a GIANT *heart*

Too bad the girls don't want him!
(They want his good-looking best friend, Sunakawa.)

Used to being on the sidelines, Takeo simply stands tall and accepts his fate. But one day when he saves a girl named Yamato from a harasser on the train, his (love!) life suddenly takes an incredible turn!